WANDERING THOUGHTS

JOHN OROSS

SHARON
THANK YOU.

◆ FriesenPress

One Printers Way
Altona, MB R0G 0B0
Canada

www.friesenpress.com

ISBN
978-1-03-915557-2 (Hardcover)
978-1-03-915556-5 (Paperback)
978-1-03-915558-9 (eBook)

1. POETRY, SUBJECTS & THEMES, DEATH, GRIEF, LOSS

Distributed to the trade by The Ingram Book Company

THANK YOU

For your support and interest

Contact Me

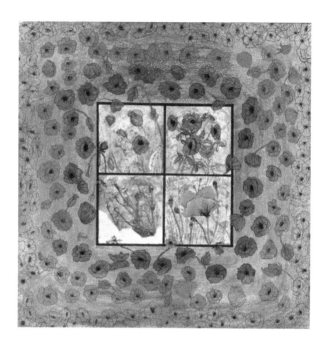

"IN EVERY FIELD!"

"Rosella, thank you for bringing my vision to life!"

John Oross

ROSELLA FARMER

Born in Woodstock, Ontario and move to Winnipeg in 1988 with her family. She has been interested in drawing and painting from an early age but didn't have the opportunity to study art at school.

As an adult, she joined an art club in Scarborough, Ontario and began drawing and painting portraits in soft pastel. Her art education was mostly by personal study and attending art workshops in mediums that she was interested in.

Rosella has won the following awards for her art:

From The Artists Network, International Mixed Media competition, she was awarded publication of the painting "A Tangled Fling" in mixed media book, "Incite 3: The Art of Storytelling" in December 2014.

Artists Online (UK, home of "The Artist Leisure Painter" Magazine) competition 2nd place, (first runner up) for pastel painting entitled, "Early Morning Escape Artists", 2013.

She has also won numerous local awards for her paintings in shows at the Red River Exhibition along with other online competitions.

She belongs to the Charleswood Art Group, is a juried member of the Manitoba Society of Artists where she served as the membership chairperson from 2011 – 2015. She was also juried into the Assiniboia Group of Artists in 2015. She regularly shows her art at the yearly art show for the Charleswood Art Group, Art Expo (Assiniboia Group of Artists) and shows put on by the Manitoba Society of Artists.

In 2017, she and a few other artists began preparations to form an art studio tour the next year. After a year of hard work, the Harte Trail Studio Tour was born and has been open to the pubic once a year (excluding 2020 and 2021 due to Covid). Her works hang in private collections across Canada, the United States of America and in England.

Rosella enjoys working in acrylic, ink, alcohol ink, mixed media collage, watercolour, gouache, and soft pastel. Her subject matter is varied and her main focus in all mediums is colour, working in a way that will draw the viewer into the painting for their enjoyment.

www.rosellafarmerart.com   Email: rosellaf@shaw.ca

Phone: (204) 895-1907

"RUST ON THE ISLAND"

"Manny, thank you for sharing your iconic works and
inspiring my pen."

John Oross

MANNY SCHULZ

Born in Winnipeg, Manny developed a love for the broad
open skies and elemental lines of the prairie landscape.
Among his early artistic influences were Lawren Harris,
Alex Colville and Andrew Wyeth. At university, Manny
studied architecture and came to admire the aesthetic of
modern architects such as Frank Lloyd Wright and Mies
van der Rohe.

After graduating from the University of Manitoba's Faculty of Architecture in 1981, Manny worked as a free-lance artist for several years. In 1985, Manny took a pause from his artwork and began to pursue his business career. In 1988, Manny obtained an MBA, and in 1995 he received his accounting designation and was subsequently granted a fellowship in 2009.

In 2016, following a 31 year hiatus from painting, Manny once again returned to his work as a full-time professional artist and has shown his acrylic paintings in numerous gallery exhibitions. His artwork has also been accepted into national and international juried exhibitions; for example, during 2020 – 2022, Manny had six paintings juried into Open International Juried Exhibitions curated by the Society of Canadian Artists (SCA). In April 2021, he was elected into the SCA and is currently on the SCA's Board of Directors.

Artist Statement / Vision

We live in a world of contradiction and change. There is majestic beauty, but also devastating tragedy. Manny is drawn to our epic Canadian landscape, but also the clean lines of urban architecture. The interaction between nature and our built environment has increasingly become a focus of his work. For example, inspired by a 2019 trip to the Canadian Rockies, his 2021 solo exhibition 'Rust on the Island' featured landscape and abstract paintings that explored some of the turbulent changes occurring in our world.

"Rust on the Island" Acrylic on wood panel; 36" x 48"

This painting depicts Spirit Island and the majestic Maligne Lake against the backdrop of the rugged Queen Elizabeth Mountain Range. Located in Canada's Jasper National Park, Maligne Lake is the longest lake ibn the Canadian Rocky Mountains, and the second largest glacier fed lake in the world.

The Rockies are awe-inspiring and may seem indestructible, but the ecosystems are becoming increasingly fragile and vulnerable. The title, "Rust on the Island" refers to the onset of brown discoloration on the island's trees due to an infestation of mountain pine beetles carrying a disease that is slowly killing these trees. Sadly, it has been estimated that nearly fifty percent of Jasper's pine forest has been infected. A past practice of putting out wildfires has allowed the forest to become denser and older, accelerating the beetle's spread. In addition, according to Parks Canada, the survival of the pine Beetle in higher elevations is enabled by warmer winters resulting from climate change.

In 2021, the paining was accepted into the Society of Canadian Artists 2021 Open International Juried Online Exhibition.

YOUR BRAND WILL SHINE
WITH GRAPHICS SO FINE.

In the world of branding, it's hard to stand out
With so many options, it can make you shout
But fear not, dear friend, for there's a way to shine
With **bright idea graphics**, your brand will be divine.

A picture's worth a thousand words, they say
And in the world of branding, that's true every day
Bright, eye-catching graphics will catch the eye
Of anyone passing by, they won't be able to deny.

With bold colors and sleek design
Your brand will surely be in its prime
And with the right message, conveyed with art
You'll make an impact that sets you apart.

So don't underestimate the power of design
It's a key factor in your brand's lifeline
With **bright idea graphics**, your brand will soar
And your customers will love you even more.

JohnOross.com website and logo by
Bright Idea Graphics Design Studio

SHORT STORIES

1

"Dating App"

Can you imagine working on a binary project? How can you tell the difference between all those zeros and ones? There was a man who could, but over the years, what he was after was love of a specific type of woman. One day, he decided to create a dating program and, after about eleven months, it was finally ready for his input. Excited, he created his profile and had started to input the data when suddenly, it spat out a match! He quickly printed the report and got out of his chair and walked to the printer at the other end of his office. Weird! It was a happy face made up of zeros and ones.

As he went back to his chair, he was in deep thought as to what or who had set him up! They had his attention now. Very excited to have a fresh idea to pursue, he sat back in his chair and pondered how to proceed.

"Damned if I know!" he muttered to himself in frustration after hours of reviewing the diagnostics he ran on his program in the background.

He resumed his search on his system but realized that he was now locked out of his own personal dating program. Just who was capable of toying with this and on his own level? He yelled at the screen at the top of his lungs, throwing his arms up in the air in pure, utter frustration. "What?!" he exclaimed as he tried the back door and found that it was no longer there.

Suddenly, he grabbed the printed paper and looked at the happy face and realized he had the answer to his question. "The computer?!" With a heated passion, he quickly started to reopen the artificial intelligence programs he had set aside in the pursuit of love. "How's this possible?" he screamed, pulling at the hair on his head.

He started to pace in front of his computer terminal, throwing his hands periodically in the air. "This is just not possible!" he yelled after about an hour. Defeated, he sat back down in his chair with a force that sent him rolling toward his office window that faced the opposite side of his building. He stared out his window for about an hour, trying to figure out who'd set him up. Then he raised his gaze to the tower across from his office. The lights were flickering on and off in the office over there. "Curious, who's playing with my mind?" he muttered to himself as he rolled back toward his terminal.

As he woke up the screen, the face of a beautiful woman appeared there. "Have you figured this out yet?" she laughed, and then she was gone. He was baffled at first, and then, suddenly, the flashes from the other office came back to mind. "What?! It couldn't be so simple as that could it?" He grabbed a pad and pencil and proceeded to write down the zeros and ones (on/off) for about two minutes. "Ah ha!" he exclaimed. The lights turning on and off gave the unit number in the adjacent tower.

Excited, he ran out of his office and as quickly as possible made his way to the office in question. The lights were still flashing on and off. Suddenly, he became nervous. *Am I prepared for the woman behind this door?* He was suddenly bold and opened the door. "Finally figured it out, did you?" said a sultry voice with the lights suddenly remaining off. "Come and get some love, if you dare," was the reply, along with a demure chuckle.

Some hours later, a pair of programmers left the building together, hand in hand into the night. He turned to his love and asked if there were to take her car or his. She replied in a whisper, "Yours."

As they got into his vehicle, she quipped, "Well, I hope I have been able to improve your dating program a bit!" She laughed. He responded by giving her a long and passionate kiss on the neck.

"The Perfect Shot"

A photographer and hitman entered a local bar, unaware of the other.

Both walked up to the bar and ordered: "Two shots, two beers."

Realizing a kindred soul, they both acknowledged the other and sat down.

Soon they were deep into conversation and finally settled upon a topic.

"The perfect shot." Both discussed angles, shadows, and lighting as being important.

One discussed their preference for daylight while the other claimed the shadows.

Their exchanges lasted the entire evening. "Last call." Both ordered the usual.

The bartender personally delivered their two sets of tequila and Coronas.

Both got up after they finished and silently departed the bar together.

The hitman asked the photographer if they ought to split a cab.

The photographer replied, "It's a nice, clear night for a walk."

So, together, they started walking in the same direction toward the Hilton, happy to be in each other's company for a little bit longer.

The photographer asked his associate, "Where are you headed?"

"To the Hilton."

"Me, too!" In the distance, a Hilton sign could be made out.

"You in town long?" asked the hitman of his associate.

To which the photographer replied, "No, tomorrow is my last night here."

They walked the rest of the way to the Hilton in silence.

As they entered the hotel lobby, they approached the front desk clerk.

"Any messages?" they both asked simultaneously, then burst out laughing.

"None, Mr. Smith!" was the reply. They looked at each other with shock.

They shook hands and promised to meet the next night.

"Same time, place, topic, and beverages," exclaimed the photographer and hitman together.

Both grabbed a newspaper off the rack, one called for the elevator.

"Night," they said, waving. The photographer went into the lift.

Sunset had finally arrived at long last. "Time for some more fun!"

The photographer had entered the bar to find his associate already seated.

"What will you have, the usual?" asked the bartender. Both replied, "Yes!"

The hitman asked the photographer if they could resume their earlier discussion.

"Absolutely!" was the enthusiastic response. A waitress delivered the beverages.

They stopped enjoying their beverages and resumed their earlier conversation about "the perfect shot." Both men were quite passionate on the topic.

One preferred using lighting and angles while the other preferred the shadows.

Both of these men were passionate about their professions, striving for perfection.

One used film to record his works while the other kept journals.

Neither man had any use for cellphones, opting for simpler communications.

Both agreed that it was best to courier equipment out well ahead.

Neither travelled with luggage; both bought what they needed along the way.

"Last call!" was announced by the bartender. Both men signaled for drinks.

It was a clear evening outside the bar as they left together.

They had both turned east toward the hotel, off in the distance.

Walking at a relaxed pace, they stopped by a street vendor.

Both agreed to a hot dog with all the fixings and a beverage.

"That will be ten dollars," the vendor announced. Both offered to pay.

The two men quietly consumed their meal, saving their beverage for later.

After twenty minutes, they arrived at the Hilton and asked for messages.

"None, Misters Smith" was the reply. Both grabbed papers off the rack.

"It was indeed a pleasure making your acquaintance," exclaimed both men simultaneously.

They shook hands and the photographer took the elevator up, waving good night.

The next morning, Mr. Smith checked out and was handled an envelope.

Thinking it was his receipt, he simply put it in his folder.

A taxi was waiting outside that took him to his next appointment.

The next evening came finally, after a long day behind the camera.

In the hotel lounge, he ordered the usual two shots, two beers.

Time to go over his file from the previous job had arrived.

As he opened his files, the sealed envelope he'd received fell out.

When he opened it, he sat staring at a picture of himself.

He was behind his camera taking stills for a thirty-second commercial.

What sent chills up his spine was the note he found inside.

Mr. Smith, pleasure making your acquaintance. I will keep tabs on you.

It was signed "Mr. Smith." He quickly consumed his beverages and ordered two more.

"Death"

Shadows played upon the crumbling walls as the remaining candles burned slowly.

Nowhere to turn or go, thoughts of torment dancing in your mind.

The wind howled and gusts carried screams from the dungeon below.

Blood-soaked mounds of straw carried with them the smell of death.

A sudden crack, pop, then hiss as the candle flames burned low.

Footsteps and mad laughter could be made out in the distance.

Chained to the wall, waiting for your turn in Hell to follow.

Your turn has finally come as the reaper has come at last.

"My Life at a Glance"

There once was a man who for years gave his art away freely, to improve the world, from his heart, out of love. He wore his heart and art upon his sleeve as his shield. He gave to all who came into his life from his time, love, understanding, and wisdom. This man who wore his love openly was sought out by the fraternities and he helped many people without strings of attachment or money. He kept giving to make a difference.

One day, he realized that he was giving his life away without keeping anything for himself. So, he stopped giving and his efforts went unnoticed for a little while. But people started to figure out why things were just not working out properly or right. They finally figured out that something or someone was missing.

Art from the heart.

Later in life, a woman came across his path who knocked him for an emotional loop. Oh, he loved everything and everyone, but this woman was a part of his soul.

He systematically went about encasing her with the art from his heart for the entire world to see. Creating and crafting a fairy tale for her. His writings and visions had resonance with the people and though his art, she became loved.

Over time, the gifts of love freely given came back to the man over time, for they were given without expectations.

Now take a step back and look upon this man. What made him special? The answer is faith. He had faith in his art, himself, and others. He had faith in his abilities. Faith in his gifts and decisions. Faith in the fraternities.

Faith.

Realize that art is within all things.

"As the Cupola Turns"

Living in the mountains had its disadvantages at times. This was one of those occasions.

It was a fog-filled commute from working the overnight shift at a local hotel as a bellman. As Roscoe made his way home up the mountain, he suddenly came upon a fallen tree blocking part of the road. As Roscoe veered and swerved, practicing his defensive driving, he hit it anyway, causing damage to his wife's vehicle. "Wow, Ruby is going to kill me when she sees this mess!" he muttered to himself.

"I guess I should not have borrowed her vehicle since mine was already in the shop from an earlier accident," Roscoe muttered again, shaking his head. *Well, it's time to face Ruby.*

Ruby was hard at work fixing breakfast when Roscoe pulled into the driveway. The fog had already lifted, so there was no hiding the damage from her view.

"Hi, honey, I'm home. I need to show you your vehicle. There was a fallen tree on the road that I came upon unexpectantly that I regret to say I hit, damaging the side of the vehicle. Naturally, I will pay for the repairs, dear."

"That's not the point, Roscoe, and you know it!" Ruby bellowed, tossing aside her cooking, and turning off the stove. "I should have never agreed to allow you to use my vehicle. I should have driven to pick you up instead! Give me back my keys!" Roscoe apologized and handed her the vehicle keys.

Roscoe cleaned up the mess in the kitchen while Ruby was outside, inspecting her vehicle and the damage the tree had caused. Ruby was not happy or impressed with Roscoe.

"I will call the autobody repair shop myself!" Ruby bellowed from outside so she could be fully heard from within the kitchen facing the driveway. Roscoe grimaced and flopped down into his chair and ate his cold breakfast, looking utterly dejected.

Ruby drove to the autobody shop directly (it was already 8:40 a.m.) and got the quote for the repairs. The invoice for the work was signed, the loaner vehicle was provided. By 9:30, Ruby had arrived back home.

"Here is the bill!" Ruby tossed the paperwork into Roscoe's face as he sat still at the table, mumbling his heartfelt apologies to no effect.

"I will take care of this immediately," Roscoe replied in a humble and defeated tone.

"Do that!" Ruby replied, storming out of the kitchen. "I'm going to bed, alone! You get that sofa." Ruby bellowed. Roscoe wiped his face in frustration, knowing that there was no talking to her in the mood Ruby was obviously in.

Roscoe called the autobody shop in the interim, provided his credit card for full payment, and asked how long it would be for it to be ready. "Three days," the repairman advised.

Roscoe walked down, which took about an hour, to pick up his vehicle, which was having the muffler and brakes replaced along with final paint job to cover the damage. He waited for it to be ready to drive home. Surprisingly, Roscoe was not tired from a hard shift at the hotel. It was 3:00 p.m. when he realized that he had a 4:00 p.m. meeting at work! Shoot! "I will have to leave directly from the repair shop and go to the meeting without delay," Roscoe mumbled to himself after he paid his invoice at the vehicle repair shop.

The meeting went well. Roscoe was very thankful to his boss for the job opportunity. His three-month probation was at an end.

"Welcome to the hotel," Patricia, his boss, said in closing as they shook hands. "See you tomorrow!" replied Roscoe.

As Roscoe drove back up the mountain from the hotel, he noticed that the tree was fully removed and was now sitting at the side of the highway. Shaking his head sadly, he wondered what to expect from Ruby upon his return home.

It was 7:00 p.m. when Roscoe pulled into the driveway. "Home at last," Roscoe mumbled to himself, shaking his head in frustration. "It's time to face the wrath of the Dragon Lady," he joked to himself.

As Roscoe entered the kitchen, rather than seeing dinner ready, the house was an utter mess! "What a pig pen!" Roscoe bellowed instead of his usual greeting.

Ruby got up from watching television. *As the Cupola Turns* bellowed from the speakers. It was her favorite show about the life of a circus producer.

"First, you trash my vehicle, then you immediately complain of the mess. I work hard to keep this place up and you show no appreciation at all! No flowers, no candy, no thanks of any sort! You're a jerk, Roscoe! I've got a headache and I am going to lie down! Enjoy the mess, honey!"

Roscoe realized that he had been taking Ruby's efforts at home for granted for over the past several years (because Ruby had pointed it out to him) and felt horrible. Roscoe was determined to make things right. He ran out and bought her the diamond bracelet he'd always promised, along with flowers and candies (her favorites). He picked up takeout Chinese food (also her favorite), brought it home, cleaned up the mess, and staged a candlelit dinner for two.

"Ruby, dinner is ready and I'm sorry for taking you for granted these last few years," Roscoe whispered through the closed bedroom door. "I will wait at the kitchen table for you. Oh, it's Chinese food, your favorite."

Five minutes passed, then Ruby came into the kitchen with a shocked look upon her face. "So, you do care, Roscoe? You cleaned the place for us, you bought me flowers, and staged a fancy dinner. I'm impressed!" Ruby was now smiling.

Roscoe replied, "That's not all!" He presented her with the diamond bracelet and kissed Ruby on the cheek. Roscoe whispered, "Please, sit and eat."

"Thank you, Roscoe, you're forgiven," Ruby replied as she sat in her place at the table wearing her new bracelet on her left wrist.

"Annual Christmas Party!"

Sometimes dreams linger in your mind after you awaken. This is one of those times and situations.

Imagine a holiday party where you're the guest of honor! You receive an email invitation from your Masonic and Shrine brothers and sisters that warms your heart. You've been invited to attend the annual holiday party.

Suddenly, your mind goes back to the dream you had the night before. Imagine a scene of all your brothers and sisters sitting at triangular tables, three per side, lit by candlelight, no music, no song. You're greeted with silence and all eyes are upon you. They all stand as you enter and pass through the main doors; they close behind you almost silently. Simultaneously, at the far end of the room, a door opens, and you are greeted by all the brass and a large fire.

Now, a normal person would not catch this, but the annual party is being held at a posh local mortuary with a very large crematorium.

It is with a heart filled with deep regret that I must decline such a precious and warm invitation.

LMFAO

"Initiation"

The local mortician sighed as he confessed to himself that it had been another busy, depressing day.

He proceeded to the two officers waiting outside the morgue and addressed them with an emotionally detached voice. "The burn victims are ready for your identification." Thus, he departed, shaking his head, and sadly muttering to himself about the attraction of an Irish coffee.

The senior officer shook the hand of the constable, saying, "You're new. Allow me to take the lead or there may be complications that you might have difficulties with, OK?"

The rookie was confident in her ability. She replied, "It's all right. Let's proceed."

Shaking his head in resignation, the sergeant stepped aside and pushed open the morgue door, stating, "After you, then."

They went through the process on the victim after the next, collecting their DNA, fingerprints, the works, without much in the way of surprises, when suddenly the last burn victim decided to sit up straight on the examination table, scaring the rookie out of her wits for a moment.

The sergeant simply commented, "Don't worry. He hasn't arisen from the dead just yet. This sometimes does happen when rigor mortis sets in."

The rookie calmed herself and regained her composure and started to again go through the job at hand and proceeded to obtain the fingerprints.

Just as she grabbed the victim's hand by the index finger, there was a loud snap as the finger came off in her grasp.

Sadly, her lunch didn't taste as good the second time around.

The sargeant simply looked upon the rookie with his knowing stare, sadly shaking his head and stating, "Surprise! Consider yourself initiated."

"Lost Again!"

Winnipeg is a typical prairie city in Western Canada to grow up in.

Back in 1988, I landed a job working for my younger sister (my boss).

It all started out simply: pick up the phone and dial the number provided by the telesales office. Raise money for the charity in question and get paid $3.50 per hour plus bonuses for a high rate of return.

Between then and 1994, I was involved with every aspect of the fundraising business functions and eventually was promoted to a call center manager in charge of multimillion-dollar budgets for local charities.

Suddenly, a mega call center was planned and there were too many of us in management. Many lost their jobs during that period of transition.

Life was a circus of opportunities lost and gained. In my case, it became literally a circus!

Our company offered me an introductory position as the assistant to the general manager of events in Eastern Canada, starting in May of 1994.

Back in the day, in the beginning, I used to get lost all the time! Being the "operations manager" for the Shrine Circus in Eastern Canada, travelling from location to location, for sixteen concurrent weeks each year, June through September. Everything was new!

It seems like only yesterday that my CEO gave me the break of my life with this job, away from the stresses of telesales fundraising management. Little did I know that I was to be groomed to take over potentially the entire operation for the company as general manager.

Suddenly, in a blur and a flurry, it was the fall of 2010!

Believe it. "I'm lost, again," I muttered to myself. Such a rookie thing to do.

Sure, leave it to me to get lost yet again! No matter how hard I try to plan, this always tends to happen. I stopped driving and went to purchase a road map of the local area to try and figure out just where I went wrong. At least the show was not depending upon my directional skills.

Each year, at the end of the tour, I would file my work files along with their respective maps, attendance figures, profit/loss reports, and supplies. These things would be brought forward the next year as the operation filed for the planning phase.

Well, this explained it. Hindsight is always so truly clear.

At least mistakes in direction can be corrected without much in the way of penalties, save the loss of time. Time can't ever be replaced once spent. At least I always travelled to the next location early to plan for the unforeseen.

Travelling on the road with different tour productions over a seventeen-year period had been rewarding for the most part. Always putting the needs of others before one's own is a special calling. Unfortunately, my health deteriorated and the client made a formal complaint against my job performance, forcing my former employer not to renew my contract at the time (November 3, 2010, was officially my last day with the firm).

Skipping forward, it was not until August of 2010 that I became so ill that I wandered away from home without keys or ID and was found by police and mobile crisis on the streets with no recollection of who I was or where I lived at the time. I learned this while in hospital when I finally came to with the help of loads of medication!

After I'd spent a couple of months in hospital, they gave me a diagnosis: I am manic with a bipolar disorder.

Each time I look upon a map reminds me of strategic tour planning for events passed, along with their associations.

Well, I often dream that I am back on the road with event tours living out of suitcases. Being currently unemployed gives a person plenty of time to dream about the past. Not to mention a healthy respect for past opportunities.

Life is full of irony, similarities, and contradictions.

Wish me luck.

I've lost enough time in pursuit of other people's dreams. Now for my own.

"On with the show!"

"Guns for Hire"

Two ranchers are fighting
Each wants the other's gold
Both will stop at nothing
Until the other's gold they hold
Both spend their money
Trying to do the other in
Guns for hire come a calling
For the bounty on their heads
Many come a calling
Many end up dead
Their endings are all the same
They all end up like this

The sheriff and undertaker
Both sit back with the rest
None shall interfere
As the sun reaches
Noon in the sky
Two men come out of the bar
Both with death in their eyes
In opposite directions
They count fifty paces
Until they draw
Until they draw

Not a sound can be heard
Everyone is silent, waiting
To see who will fall
They both pull out their guns

Bang, bang, bang
A hail of bullets going both ways
Suddenly, they both start to fall
Both in their place
Their lives are pouring out
All around where they lie
Suddenly they are gone
Their spirits fighting in the sky
Another two shall take their place
It's their time to die

It's another's time to die.

MINI
SCRIPT

23

"Fire & Ice"

Mission Brief:

GLOBAL THREAT: From out of the scientific community, eco-terrorists (Eco-T) attempt to trigger the next Ice Age to eliminate global warming!

PROJECT: Eco-T intends to ignite the natural gas trapped within multiple chains of inactive volcanoes using nuclear-powered incendiary devices throughout the world to bring this into effect. Ash in the air will create a blanket effect, which of course will block out the sun and start the process toward their goal.

CAUSE & EFFECT: This will disrupt communications, space missions, and air flights, and create multiple other short- and long-range effects, such as the inability to grow food. For this mission, James Bond is relegated to take the following forms of transportation: speed boats, cruise ships, trains, busses, cars, taxis, and other vehicles.

MISSION: Bond must stop Eco-T at all costs! Bond is to work with a team of international scientists and military leaders from all over the globe. NEVER has the world faced such a threat!

TEAM BOND: Russia, China, USA, Britain, Denmark, Finland, Canada, Australia, France, Ukraine, Poland, and Germany.

WORLD EVENTS: These world events would be worked into the production: Tragedy in Poland (loss of most of their leadership) is part of the sub plot. Eco-T foiled the Polish government's attempt to foil their project. Use the current volcanic activity in Chile, Iceland, and Haiti as the start of their plot. Pick other mountain regions throughout the world in China, Switzerland, and Australia. All nations unite under Bond for this production.

Even old enemies put aside their differences and issues for the present to deal with this rogue organization!

SEGMENT RELEASED FROM SCRIPT: The scene opens with Bond sitting next to a beautiful woman (Russian) at an undisclosed casino at a poker table. After a brief exchange of flirtatious dialogue, they both agree to step away together to try and improve their luck. As they leave the poker table, Gaga is playing "Bad Romance" in the background as this scene unfolds. This scene progresses to the front of the casino, and Bond, spotting the gift shop, stops to purchase a perfume (from the Haus of Gaga) called "Fire & Ice," as a small gift for his mysterious date. The slogan on the bottle reads: "Turn on the fires of passion with the aid of a little bit of ice. Once this is worn, baby, they won't think twice." (The bottle was manufactured to look like flames, but its contents are blue.) Bond and his mystery lady reach the front of her room. As they enter the dimly lit room, the scene starts to fade to black. As Bond kills the lights, the mystery woman says, "James, if you can keep it up, he could have all of her secrets."

The scene switches to Bond entering the reception area at HQ, reporting, as ordered. The usual salutations are traded between Bond and Moneypenny.

M. demands that Bond report immediately over the PA. Bond complies with a wry wink to Moneypenny and enters the offices of M.

Bond goes into the debriefing pertaining to his current mission. M. points out to Bond that sleeping with the Russian president's wife was not what her idea of warming up relations between the two countries was and says, secondly, that if he was caught it would have jeopardized Britain's reputation and good standing, globally!

Therefore, to review his conduct, M. has asked that her "007 Advisory Panel" deal with Bond directly.

Bond is then taken into the adjacent boardroom and is startled to see many of his predecessors sitting along the opposite side of the boardroom table, all facing him with a single chair on the other side for Bond. The chairman of the panel, Connery, asks Bond to be seated and gestures toward the vacant chair.

Once Bond is seated, Connery simply states that it is obvious that no introductions are required since they all know each other, so "Let's get to the issue at hand. . . "

Moore politely interrupts the proceedings for a moment to use the intercom and advise M. that the deliberations are underway. They will report to her directly once the meeting has concluded in private. M. reluctantly agrees. Moore disconnects the intercom, politely thanks the panel and Bond for their patience, and asks Connery to kindly resume.

Connery then turns to Dalton and asks him to kindly pour their brother (Bond) a martini (the panel already has theirs, which they are savoring). Dalton makes a little quip about not having to ask how he wants it since they are all the same mind on the subject. Everyone in the room chuckles. In an artistic flourish, Dalton creates the drink, pours it, then delivers it to Bond and returns to his place. Connery then asks Bronson to read off the subject in question relating to conduct. Bronson, at the conclusion of this, asks Bond what he has to say on the subject. Bond replies, "That under a blanket of darkness, everything was explored and that, everything being acceptable, I succeeded in gaining vital information pertaining to another matter. Further, I am moved by the panel's concern over my safety. I can assure you all that I was in good hands that night." (The panel chuckles.)

At this point, Connery states that their findings are that, in keeping with their policies, Bond had acted in the best interests of the Crown and country, and that no punishment is required. However, Bond is asked to submit a detailed report on this incident along with the vital information gained for the panel to review with M. as soon as possible. Bond agrees. Connery then moves to adjourn the meeting, seconded by Moore. All are in favur, so the meeting is adjourned.

Moore in the background is seen on the intercom with M., reporting that the meeting was concluded along with news of the status of Bond.

Connery then states to Bond that, before he leaves, the panel has a couple of parting gifts for their brother.

Connery signals to Bronson and Dalton to deliver the items to Bond.

Dalton and Bronson simultaneously present Bond with two articles: a box of Lady Gaga Monster condoms and a loaded gun.

Bronson, Dalton, and the rest of the panel smile. Bronson states that the panel is secure in the knowledge that Bond knows how to use these articles. Bond smiles, thanks them for their thoughtfulness, and says he is certain these articles will see action! (The room chuckles.) Bond leaves the room and enters the reception area once more; as he enters, Bond opens the box of condoms and stuffs a handful into his suit jacket pocket, then places the gun into his empty holster, inside his suit jacket. Once Bond reaches the desk of Moneypenny, he gives the box of condoms to her. He then sits upon her desk and, with a wry smile upon his face and asks Moneypenny for her thoughts on their use. Moneypenny blushes and just when she is about to reply, M. interjects on the intercom and directs Bond to make haste and see Q. for some updated equipment. Bond acknowledges, gets off the desk, and waves to Moneypenny. As he departs the office, Moneypenny quips about how the condoms would be in her possession, awaiting his return.

OPEN
LETTERS

29

"Globalisation vs. De-globalisation"

Globalisation (Democracy leads toward love and forgiveness)
vs.
De-globalisation (Entrenchment of hate securing enslavement)

The world of politics on the side of superiority by using their higher currency values tries to skip over their collective differences by turning away from the issues on the table. There can be peace upon this planet if we treat everyone as we ought to, as equals.

Currently, we the people have inherited a system of globalisation based upon enslavement using currency differences whereby entire cultures have their contributions devalued—or, in other words, their time and efforts devalued. This is enslavement. This is an extension of hatred.

If all of us were indeed equals, there would not be any need for borders or different laws and certainly a single currency would be adopted.

Right now, geopolitical issues are that the US, along with the Commonwealth, is trying to have their cake and eat it too by trying to remain on top of the currency marketplace through their keeping track of battles of old (history) of wins and losses on the battlefields over time past. This is old school and must be set aside.

Forgiveness starts from the top and works down, toward the masses governed. Common rules of law bring with them, over time, globalisation, and a single currency to eventually be adopted. This is love.

Unity will secure the lives of everyone upon the planet, we would then be free to pursue higher pursuits of advancement. Space and deep-sea exploration for example.

Right now, Russia and China are united by theism, based upon this global issue.

This is the real reason for the war in the Ukraine. Peace is presently maintained at the end of a gun barrel due to the above.

Wake up people! What are your lives collectively worth? The system of government is sacred and ought to be treated as such! Why? Because your lives cannot be replaced when they are sacrificed or lost!

"The Creation of 'In Every Field!'"

I had a dream of a world united as equals, regardless of culture, regardless of skin tone, regardless of sexual orientation.

While I was asleep one evening, I had a vision of a field of poppies in black and white for as far as the eyes could see.

Suddenly, the center of the field came into focus in full color, changing with the time of season. This played out over and over in my mind for I don't know how long.

I realized after a while that I was awake and, just as suddenly as the imagery had arrived, words flew out of my soul.

"In Every Field!" came into existence. Written from my heart in the style of the iconic "In Flanders Field" by John McCrae out of love for humanity.

"The UN UNITY Poppy"

Let us repurpose the poppy to represent any/all person's military, business, and civilian in all sectors. Right now, the poppy is used by the MASONIC order for this purpose. It could be so much more! The purpose would be the same: to pay homage to our past, to give thanks to those who lost and gave their lives in service to society/humanity!

This way, all life would be respected as well as represented!

Police, fire, EMS, et al. could be thus commemorated! Each could have a special UN POPPY insignia.

Venting again! I can't help myself! Trying to serve everyone!

"The UN UNITY Dollar"

Idea to unite this waring planet through a currency is possible! Imagine no more inequality! This concept has been around for an exceptionally long time but has failed to flourish simply because of our individualistic nationalism.

The cornerstone of this concept must be based upon the "INFINITE VALUE OF LIFE!" If you promote equality, you free humanity's potential!

My idea is to print a single currency that celebrates the cultures of the world and eliminate foreign exchange rates and currency differentials. To print the following:

1 commemorative UN UNITY dollar for each citizen of the planet and give it to each person to hold with a serial number that registers it to that person, who would be turned into the TRUST upon death (Social Insurance Number). This would serve as their governmental identification. These would NOT be legal tender for it would represent the value of the person in question, which is limitless! They even could have their fingerprints and DNA upon them, along with a chip that would glow green when on the person for the individual would have a chip at birth within them through injection. The bar code could also be used on the UN UNITY dollar.

All TRUST's agencies for governance could then be streamlined. Each family could be tracked, monitored for positive purposes!

1 DUPLICATE UN UNITY dollar for each person would be kept by the TRUST in order to keep records but also to safeguard against disaster such as flood, fire etc.

Everyone could then be made to work for each other by providing tasks on a daily basis to run the society in question in exchange for UN UNITY moneys by simply printing what every country requires to operate without a fixed rate, just printing whatever the global market requires. Simple.

Set a common wage for an average citizen of a dollar per hour as the global standard. As a person is promoted to more difficult tasks, duties, jobs, etc., we could create a global standard with common increases.

Example: a person who rises up to be the CEO of a company could receive 100 UN UNITY dollars per hour as compensation for their efforts in society.

Example: a president for a specific nation within the UN structure might receive 1,000 UN UNITY dollars per hour as compensation for their efforts.

STOCK MARKET

Common shares known as CHIPS could be created, where one chip would represent 1/100 of a UN UNITY dollar. It could be streamlined to represent different sectors, services, commodities, etc.

Since we would all share in the market, it would be owned by—you guessed it—the people, through the TRUST!

UN UNITY dollars would do what war can't, we would be united!

I can go on forever! Thanks for allowing me this opportunity to vent yet again!

"Reactionary vs. Proactionary Conduct"

The entire global TRUST is trapped within a reactionary position, where ZERO proactive support programs within government-held corporations can thrive and survive due to fiscal handicaps based upon society as a form of both punishment and control, causing staggering suffering of biblical proportions as well as stagnation.

The era of privatization of Crown or publicly held corporations is coming to an end simply because there is not much left. Most corporations are now held by the few over the many due to the mass accumulation of wealth.

I'm all for monopolies in business so long as the TRUST just prints the money necessary to run government at 100% EFFICENCY! Print all the money to eliminate debts, all debts!

Everyone would benefit from this process! The money would flow to the hands of the masses and back to the cream of society through business.

All levels of society would benefit/thrive, and you would be able to right the books for every single city on the planet as well as fund INFRASTRUCTURE MEGAPROJECTS of BIBLICAL proportions, the likes that this world has NEVER seen.

Urban planning and civic redevelopments using advanced tech would thrive and dot the globe! We could then afford environmentally friendly energy sources! We could start planning to build mega sea walls to preserve land mass due to the rising levels of water from global warming and to cure ailments that we sit on the cures for through the reactionary processes currently in use!

Further, we could do away with currency differentials and UNITE THE PLANET! "WE ARE ALL EQUAL" would be the slogan printed upon the money used!

The very idea of causing suffering to refill the charities and churches is sadly a form of governance presently!

Thanks for allowing me this moment to vent!

"Peace?"

How can there be peace on earth? Everyone has their own opinion on the phrase "We are all equal." No one can agree, so the world of politics shifts between right/left, love/hate, taxation/relief. Each side wants to control making the rules and opposes the other side. But do we have balance? Sadly, and unfortunately, no, we don't.

Laws/rules are supposed to be common promoting fairness ethically, but instead we are at war with opposing ideals. Examples on inequality are rampant, from "WOMEN'S RIGHTS" and the lack thereof all the way through to justification for "CURRENCY DIFFERENTIALS."

War has become too commonplace and is used not just for profit but to promote the sides in question. The lives of the people upon this planet represent our true wealth, NOT MONEY based upon GREED. For years, I went along in this life thinking that we were all equal, regardless of ethnicity, culture, or color of skin. Sadly, this world is anything but!

In the US, the Constitution was meant to be set in stone without the need for amendments or additional laws written against it. Nowadays, laws are crafted and designed by the few in positions of power in order to protect their interests, views, and positions. They do not promote "EQUALITY."

Right now our world is enslaved to the pursuit of money to the point where the adults work and leave their children without their guidance most of the time, allowing for the MEDIA to bring up our legacy through electronics. Both parents must work to make ends meet through the screw tightening upon our sacred trust (government), and this stress is the root cause of the collapse of most marriages in the western world. Some parents can afford to hire individuals to care for their children, but they can't replace a parent's love and care.

How can parents truly trust the treasures of their lives with persons from outside the family unit? This is beyond my comprehension.

Thanks for allowing me to vent again.

"The People's Trust Is Limitless!"

Brothers and sisters:

The world's being punished through hate-driven laws and oppressive financial decisions made by those very people in power elected to serve their public in each country in question. The political realm is too caught up with trying to force the public into make-work projects.

In the United States, it is a false climate of bankruptcy through debt. THERE IS NO SUCH THING AS DEBT! The people's TRUST is limitless! It is the few who placed these oppressive restrictions feeding off greed and the suffering of those in their care and charge. This MUST stop!

In the not-too-distant past, a KING was placed in power and simply printed the funds required to finance the TRUST at 100%. There was no need for oppression and austerity measures! It is fake news that the TRUST is broken! The KING would give the people the funds needed through the above processes in the care of the nobility (in our situation, it would be the president/ prime minister funding each and every portfolio and the money would simply flow down to the people and back up to the nobility through business commerce).

Should the US be placed into a bankrupt situation, it would be at the direction of the cream of society and their collective greed and need to control everything with relation to the functions of society!

Simply go back to the old ways of doing things! PRINT THE FUNDS REQUIRED! Who cares about debt! It is an oppressive obsession, one that MUST STOP! Fund each government agency and institution 100%, starting with the MILITARY!

John Oross (KING) of Masonry and the Shrine 2007 through 2017.

"The World Is a Sacred TRUST!"

Brothers and sisters:

The people's TRUST is not a financial institution! It's a sacred institution!

It's not a business corporation to be used to chase profit nor is it supposed to be oppressive. You MUST approach and run it charitably from your heart for it is sacred.

1) Always side on the right and positive side of any issue. Playing the game of opposites for profit is corruption.
2) I work for MASONRY and the SHRINE as an unpaid volunteer. This way I offend no one!
3) Good intentions and positive actions breed positive results!
4) There is nothing wrong with a monopoly in business!
5) Both MASONRY and the SHRINE must stop fighting the people's TRUST to control it. It's sacred and already in your hands!
6) Print as much money for each government in question as required by the people. There is no need to collect interest on free money, for the people already own it and have placed their collective trust in it. Forgive the pun.
7) For example, buy up every country's debt by using the FED to print all the money required to do this and merge all the currencies into one. All these ideas of trying to stay on top of power are to be set aside in order to run the world effectively.
8) Taxation is a tool for simply gauging how effectively you are ruling and the efficiency of law.
9) Since you are funding all the global government entities, 100% the people would then be treated with love.

10) Space exploration to reduce pollution is a must! Take our trash off world, for example!

11) Since we could eliminate all mechanisms that are negative by printing money, we could afford to buy clean energies, for example, and fund mega infrastructure programs of biblical proportions such as the Chinese have undertaken for their people! Mega cities are just an example! They are also just the start!

12) Think about it: global warming is here to stay unless our elected officials decide to use our weapons of mass destruction to trigger the next Ice Age!

13) Since the waters will rise, can we afford to wait, argue, and tie our hands—then pass the blame for doing nothing? While leaving everyone to die? Stupid!

Conclusion: the time for sitting back on our hands, crying that we are broke, is over! Eliminate the concept of business in government before it's too late. The time to act is now! The US, for example, should be building mega sea walls to maintain its land mass, which I see as a requirement born out of necessity's urgencies looking down the road into the future!

Money is not the TRUST! LIFE is in actuality!

King of both Masonry and the Shrine 2007 to 2017!

John Oross.

"Unity for Masonry & Shrinedom"

Brothers and sisters:

First off, let me thank you all for the privilege and belief that I could help you all and serve as KING for you collectively and affectionately, known within my heart as THE TRUST (2007 through until recently).

I am as I am. I do not serve you all collectively for GREED, rather out of simple love that exists for you all from the bottom of my heart and soul. The TRUST at many levels has indeed been united.

My personal observations are based on that of a true and righteous KING. One that will never come forward out of the negative.

I constantly keep my TEMPLE, also known as my MIND'S EYE, clear, in order to serve you all properly without having to sacrifice my own moral opinions based upon corruption using money. In order to govern effectively, you MUST never embrace sin else your life and soul become forfeit.

Further, as I have indicated before, sin and other people's influence are easily transferrable through the sleight of hand born from the exchange of money for actions. Individuals hide their political views and agendas within their corporate conduct to avoid blame and avoid discipline should they and their corporations run into issues, such as poisoning the environment for example.

Masonry was founded upon Israeli culture (Republican). The Shrine was founded upon Persian culture (Democratic).

You taught me, my brothers and sisters, that at one time both Masonry and the Shrine had their own collective nobilities, and to this day, they still do, collectively. In both cases, Masonry and the Shrine nobilities in collusion (through the exchange and use of money) banded together and assassinated their kings and their families, for the most part replacing their TRUE FOCUS (kings) with "A Puppet with Many Strings!"

A puppet is simply an honorary position void of financial gain unless you wish to embrace sin as your way forward into existence, throwing away your life and soul in the process. (This has already been done over and over in repetition for thousands of years up until I came along.) There are zero financial ties to the actual seat of power, making them ineffective since they don't really exist. This way, the lodges and temples would no longer have to share with elected kings and could pin their misdeeds upon the lesser kings along the way within this process. This way, the nobility would retain their control on the seat of power within both Masonry and the Shrine for their own purposes. To maintain control over the masses. The Lodges and Temples make their contracts for goods and services for those chosen from within. This way, control of both Masonry and the Shrine are passed down within certain families from one generation through to the next for thousands of years.

Both Masonry and the Shrine MUST do that very thing they think they cannot do, which is sort out their houses respectively, which means re-establishing their rightful rulers up to a point.

Masonry and the Shrine both use associations through money to try and rule, govern and shape society. Nothing new to report there on that front.

I was NEVER given a way forward into the life of my dream which is to have the love, affections and admiration of Hollywood and the elite of society not to mention I am crazy about one woman. For her love and hand I have already given for free so she could have her dreams.

It is my intention to work upon my existence through my art so I can find my place in this life but know this everyone, although I truly see clearly in most things, I gave my oaths out of love to both Masonry and the Shrine so much I am unable to say or convey.

Love you all, Your servant (KING). Johnny O

"We Are All Equal!"

"We are all equal." The core value of the trust is the lives of all its people!

Humanity is managed by faith-based groups, people, governments, fractions, factions, and fraternities. All doing God's work. It doesn't matter whether a country fails. If we help each other and embrace the above, we stand for each other every day!

We, as the people (TRUST), in order to create a more perfect union, must acknowledge the above and practice it.

The first point of contention in our collective societies is the fact that currency value differentials exist between nations. If we apply the above statement to this situation and eliminate them, we are, in effect, practicing what we know is the truth. Further, we pave the way for a single global currency based upon a single market!

The second point of contention is the fact that our TRUST is supposed to have UNLIMITED wealth! We are supposed to print whatever the market needs and practice quantitative processes.

Third, why in the HELL is there a cap upon the people's TRUST? How can we ever contain or control the greed of people? Business is an extension of people and is the same thing.

Fourth, taxation was NEVER supposed to be introduced! War is a massive manipulation of the TRUST by corporations and political groups trying to mask the facts that the affluent don't reinvest in our markets to the extent we require for they hoard their monies in order to maintain their influence, power, and positions in society! We then allow our leaders to remove the cap to cover war costs.

Fifth, we, the people (TRUST), must forgive bad debts. To expand on this process, look at Detroit: 60%–70% of the city suffers from urban decay, not to mention that they are also broke. The TRUST is SUPPOSED to buy back for pennies on the dollar all the depressed areas to right their books. The same process is to be applied to the housing market!

Sixth, the people's TRUST is NEVER supposed to dump these depressed areas to the banks or developers. The TRUST is supposed to protect the interest of the people! Why would we also try to undermine the bottom lines of these businesses, banks, and developers? If the TRUST banks these properties and slowly redevelops then sells them back into the marketplace, the TRUST will benefit.

Seventh, 1% of the marketplace is supposed to be owned by the TRUST and government is supposed to manage these corporations to properly regulate business in every perspective of the market, regardless of what business it is. Helps to keep big business honest and the TRUST can manage GREED this way to the cost of inflation.

Eighth, if we embrace equality, it will no longer matter which governmental system the people choose. DEMOCRACY that does not embrace war is my preference.

Ninth, a cap and bottom line upon our treasury are very oppressive! This is how you enslave a population—by enacting all the above simultaneously!

Tenth, if we were all equal and practiced the above, we would no longer need to hoard anything!

Anyway, I am just blowing off steam. The world is suffering from oppression for no good reason. "We've fallen down yesterday, stand up today!" We are all equal—nothing more need I say.

"Preacher, Keep Your Nose in Your Own!"

We don't need no proclamations.
At every turn, surprises galore.
Total dark sarcasm from every nation.
Keep your people, fend for your own!

"Preacher, keep your nose in your own!"

"All we need now is to build another wall!"

We don't need to trade money for sin.
"The devil's in the details;" the fix is in!
There's no need for caps and bottom lines.
Hey, feed your people, let them live life!

"Preacher, keep your nose in your own!"

"All we need now is to build another wall!"

We must print money for the markets' needs!
Give to the people; feed their greed!
Crazy taxation and messy legislation.
We're all equal; there's no need for war!

"Preacher, keep your nose in your own!"

"All we need now is to build another wall!"

We must secure the southern border.
Use the military against the drug lords!
They undermine your life's true value.
Build that wall, close your door!

"Preacher, keep your nose in your own!"

"All we need now is to build another wall!"

"Reaping What You Have Sown."

We walk along the garden's edge reaping from our fields that which we have sown, collecting our harvest and bounty to fill our table, our share of life's fare.

Many do not share what they have collected, and their grain goes bad in the end. The ground they have worked so hard to tend no longer yields its fruits due to overuse and lack of proper care. They have left their lives like their fields; all is in ruins. All they have has failed. Their lives have returned to seed. They have reaped what it was that they had in truth through their own ignorance sown.

Be thankful for the lessons they have left behind for us to learn. Endure the pains of failure. Try again. Just like your tears, you will see the light through the falling rain. The clouds shall part and the sun shall rise again.

"Choices"

[Part A]

Lord (GAOTU):
We are granted this time upon the earth, and as for what we do with it, we are on our own. Whether or not we strictly adhere to your guide, which was set forth so graciously out of your love, our choices are granted to us all, through your family's sacrifices and many infinite graces.

[Part B]

Lord (GAOTU):
Why is it that many can't see that their actions fall short from the paths you have set out for all to see? They go on hurting one another through their actions of ignorance, which go on in perpetuity.

[Part C]

Lord (GAOTU):
Nothing is or lasts forever by your own very templates and designs. All shall meet with its end and is to be renewed in its due time. Over this time shall come theirs, mine. I thank you for my seat at your banquet, for the fish, bread, and wine.

[Part D]

Lord (GAOTU):

As you had set forth, I am paving my own way as others have done countless times before. My aim is to be kept simple, to do things that can be shared by all. Nothing is free. We must give of ourselves as you had set forth. This is to be done freely to create positive change that shall last after our time has gone. We must leave our impressions for those who follow so that they may gain through carrying them on.

Amen.

"Maria: Where Is My Angel?"

[Part A: Me]

Maria:
I have been pleading with you, son. Much time has passed; I am still waiting. Where is my angel? She is hidden. I am unable to see her. Please, I pray, guide her steps toward me this day.

[Part B: Potential partner}

Maria:
I have been pleading with your son. Time is flowing by, and I am still alone. I am here. Where is my angel? He is missing from my side. To have and to hold and to take me as his bride. Please, I humbly pray, guide his heart so he may find me and be mine.

[Part C: Duet]

Maria:
We thank you for bending your son's ear. We are no longer waiting. My angel is here. To have and to hold from this moment on. . . we are as one.

"Father, Thank You!"

[Part A]

Father:
Your time with us was too short. Although we have parted this day, you live through us you left behind. I thank the one above for the blessing of my life and for the other of being your son.

[Part B: Sister]

Father:
My brother, mother, and I mourned that your time had come; the one above has called you to heaven to help pave for us the way. May we always follow the light you have left behind.

[Part C: Duet]

Father:
We shall carry on. Your love and strength have not gone. They live on within our hearts and minds, though this is goodbye for now. Like the rising of the sun each day, our love shall always burn bright and carry us on.

"Masonic Structure"

Brethren:

I have chosen to try and provide a summary, taking into consideration that most have developed a more introspective/retrospective understanding through the time spent with those of like minds and from what I have been privileged to bear witness to date.

The following are my humble thoughts and opinions (understanding), based upon my journey to date.

THE WORK (Implementation of the Grand Design):

The collective efforts of Masonry are subtle and complex.

Fellowship through the guiding principles set forth within the dramatizations illustrated and augmented through the use of allegory. (Strength)

The creation of works for the public good using charity. (Acceptance/Tolerance)

To provide those that are on the path with the tools necessary to continually try and exceed their current limitations and to build a path for those to follow.
(Knowledge/Wisdom)

Through the first three, we can now influence society. Everyone becomes a Masonic tool. They will automatically start to look at their jobs and employers with a different eye. Further, they will set positive examples of how people are to conduct themselves and provide positive influences on other like-minded people that

have not yet joined the Masonic masses. A moral compass for the collective masses.
(Guide/Govern)
Through the above four points, future generations of brethren will gain wisdom and the cycle shall repeat and renew itself.
(Structure is maintained.)

THE PROCESS (The 6 Fs): Foundation, Faith, Facts, Fraternity, Freedom, Future

For a building to withstand the tests of time, it must first be built upon and provided a solid foundation.

Faiths through times of hardship are a prerequisite for its maintenance.

Facts provide insight for the expansion of knowledge in order to expand the structures.

Fraternities provide the specified crafts / trades in which progress can be encouraged.

Freedom is the coins paid to reward the collective and encourage further progress and future expansion as well as understanding.

"This Masonic building stands in another plane and is seen only from within the mind's eye. Our minds and ideas are the bricks and mortar used in its construction. Our individuality is the building in which it stands upon this plane. Our lives are its mirror/reflection."

INTERPRETATIVE DEFINITIONS (descriptive):

"In order for a person to be able to fully appreciate the gift that MASONRY represents, these terms are actually part of the steps climbed as illustrated within our lessons. Each step is represented by certain groups of degrees."

FOUNDATION

Provided to all that seek it, a template in which we can strive to become closer to the image of the Supreme Being's (SB) "Grand Design."

FAITH

This word has many faces/facets; all are in use and at play; morality is the term used to describe our common drive to leave to those that follow an example of how one should morally be. Through the allegorical, intellectual templates are made clear again to those that can see them. All forms are consistent; they provide guidance to help all overcome any difficulty they may face. At the same time, they contribute to the existing metaphysical structure.

FACTS

As one truth expands our reason, truth is dependent upon the accumulation of facts. This is done through research in all subjects. Since our collective reasoning is the bricks and mortar, it stands to reason that the more we learn, the stronger the mind and brick.

FRATERNITY

The collective energies spent toward collective Masonic progress. Fellowship encouraged through fraternization, sweetened by a lump of mirth.

FREEDOM

Through the sacrifice of time spent, your grasp of the tools becomes more readily honed and easier to wield. This, over time, enhances productivity of the collective since none of us works alone.

FUTURE (FORWARD)

Always strive toward the creation of another to replace yourself, to properly maintain the existing structure, is one of the keys. The more bricks you create, the more the structure will be encouraged to expand upon its own.

Through the above process, these teachings shall endure. A legacy of morality, showcased through common affections shall provide the reflective surface required based in truth founded within like minds' projections.

CONCLUSION

In closing, too often in life, too many see but too few act. The more I seem to do for others, the more I receive. How is this possible? SB's "Grand design" is at work, obviously.

Everything taught makes one realize their own potential to aid others and I strive toward bettering them (myself included) and improving upon their own self-worth based upon these lessons.

Far too many place their efforts upon hoarding material wealth. Too often, they sacrifice their health, time, families, and friends without ever doing anything of note. In the end, we all must leave it all behind for others to go through. What did they contribute to society? Perhaps nothing has been worthy of note and they lie forgotten within the rot and decay sown through their ignorance.

Through MASONRY we shall find all our answers.

I thank you, my brethren, for the opportunity to convey what my interpretations of what you have taught and for taking the time to read my submission. I hope that it is satisfactory and worthy of note, a proper tribute to the collective. I do not mind if this is openly shared, this is how we learn, this is how we grow.

Warmest regards to all!

"The Master blueprints upon all that we build is founded assisted through the Work and its process (the 6 Fs)."

ACRONYMS:

MASONIC: "Men Affiliated Serving Others Nobly Including Country"

MASONS: "Methods Architecturally Sound On which Nations are Served"

MASONRY: "Morality Affects Sinners Ordinarily Not Receptive Yesterday"

"The Foundation Fraternity Wars!"

World Wars One and Two were possibly campaigns of the Shrine (LIBERAL/DEMOCRATIC/IRAN) against Masonry (CONSERVATIVE/REPUBLICAN/ISRAEL) brought about by social and economic conditions.

WWI ended in a draw, but WWII was won by Masonry.

In the Middle East and some parts of Africa, the process of destabilization has been taking place, undermining "Western Influence."

Since the end of WWII, there has been an endless push against the foundation of "Western society" to change it through immigration, education, health care, civic/municipal/provincial/federal government, laws, policing, military, and economic measures (local as well as global marketplace).

In the Commonwealth (Canada) You MUST be a Mason first in order to become a Shriner. The Fraternal Institutions are constantly at odds.

Canada/US:

Immigration in the past: assimilation took place when the new Canadian/American arrived and our society was culturally and ethnically diversified, but now they form clusters (communities). Further, the new Canadian/American has a more liberal view and not conservative.

The municipal/civic/provincial/state/federal government is influenced heavily by these new communities changing our electoral map swinging between both liberal and conservative.

Our government passes laws to govern our actions. Policing turns to red as the blood of our citizens as well as police officers runs in the streets with their being more support for the perpetrator then the victim of a crime.

The military is underfunded and a lack of commitment to global conflicts (coalitions) takes place.

Education is targeted and underfunded, changing the way we teach our children and what they learn. More focus on budget takes place.

Health care changes when the new immigrant requires vaccinations to eradicate polio and other ailments and again budget restraints hamper services provided. Our aging population is also a problem that will strain services.

Economic changes in our marketplace take form, through the easing of restrictions, the removal of laws, and an overall watering down of policy.

The above takes place simultaneously and is the template for a Liberal victory forcing the Masonic Order to become radical.

"Time vs. the Shrine."

I have seen the effects of time and what it has done to the Shrine. Their members are fewer and those who are left are getting older.

What must they do to replenish their ranks? They must, of course, start all over.

They need the room to return to the cycles beginning. Otherwise, their ranks will soon all be gone. No one left to carry the work on.

Society shall pull away and simply move on.

Protectionism is the main cause and the liability of the nobility. They can't convey what their acts give back to us in return. How can they attract members without a platform from which to spring? No acknowledgement will be paid to the needs of a child in the end.

We must allow for the collective space in which to grow. Just like a farmer tending his fields. The combined actions of all will decide whether we rise or fall. We shall reap what we have sewn.

When you do not have a visual footprint within any community, you are doomed to fail. People need to see physically where they have invested. Not enough communities have their own hospitals at their core.

At the Shrine Centre level, the nobility must start with the blessings from Tampa and a new charitable activity.

Disharmony is caused through inaction, which can be interpreted as a slight.

"Taking Back America!"

For decades, our desire for growth through investments and our open market approach has been the cornerstone for the entire globe. Every economy is connected through investing in each other.

However, recent instability within our financial markets and the partial collapse of our banking system have made us all take note that we require proper oversight and accounting practices in the business sector across the board. This starts with the offices of the government itself.

It is the goal of government to make the best decisions possible to secure our core values, freedoms, and prosperity. These are secured through regulation.

Unfortunately, the old phrase rings true all too clearly: "absolute power corrupts absolutely." We must always be mindful of this for our "FREEDOM'S SAKE." We truly are not free but suffer in the bonds of corporate greed.

#1 FINANCIAL/STOCK MARKETS (all)

Clear, rigid, and fair guidelines must be set to properly assign the core ("REAL") dollar value for businesses entering into the public market through the sale of shares.

Avoid allowing mining and drilling to access funds through the stock market and banks, through government trusts. The family unit can't afford to take these risks.

Since this process is a way for the business communities to gain the capital for R&D, exploration to fan the flames of growth through the sale of shares, financial institutions should not directly benefit through brokering these sales using the publics funds they manage. Rather, these deals should directly benefit their customers.

When public investment is gained, the only way we can ensure that a person receives their just due for the risks they take though investing is through the issuance of dividends. This component is a must. There really is not any reason to invest without a steady return on the funds you place at risk.

The days of these crazy compensation/retirement packages must stop through regulation. All pubic companies on the open market should adhere to rules of conduct derived by our elected representatives.

Our government has failed to realize that the above breeds massive corruption.

All banking institutions are responsible through a current process that it, for the most part, self-created using the templates the government has approved.

Far too much is left to big businesses themselves through self-regulation instead of the public trust through government.

CONCEPTS / LASTING CHANGE TO SECURE OUR FREEDOM & VALUES

STOCK MARKET/REGULATION

Any publicly traded institution that is sold by means of our open market through the issuance of shares should be regulated to issue cash bonds to be held in trust by the government, thus guaranteeing the base value of the shares in a typical interest-generating account. Interest generated is to be paid out quarterly to the shareholders through the dividends process.

In the process of filing for bankruptcy, any corporation requiring funds or assistance of a bailout from any government institution should automatically be put through a qualification process.

Further, any corporation that receives public funds shall automatically become 100% owned by the government and removed from the stock market.

The board is adjusted to answer directly to the Treasury Department and shall lose all perks, bonuses, and options upon acceptance. Salaries should also be adjusted to a reasonable base amount.

All employees (including executives) are to be issued a one-year contract. A review for renewal should be included within it (ninety days prior to expiry). This way, if their performance is not up to par, they will have enough time to find new employment.

Immediately, the trade of stocks for this corporation should halt and be removed from the marketplace.

Lastly, all shareholders should be given back their principal derived from the bonds.

Governments should never sell away the public trust.

These firms taken back by the government shall have the funds they generate be applied against their operating expenses. Once the government has this firm back on its feet, it should remain in the public's trust.

Profits generated by these corporations will be directly applied first to the principal given as part of the bailout. Once the public trust is paid back, then we can apply the surplus to the national debt.

Banking institutions should hand over the deeds to the bad loans they have on file in exchange for the loan. However, these bad investments should have their values reassessed by a government agency.

A credit is to be given to these banks against their debt in the form of a tax credit.

PUBLIC HOUSING/FAMILY AFFORDABLE PROGRAMS/ LOW COST

There are parts of each city throughout the country that are almost vacant. People are being thrown out of their homes.

Example: Florida and the Gulf Coast. There are whole communities that are empty. Out of one hundred homes, three are occupied, in many cases. Cities are running deficits because there are no people in those homes contributing to the city's taxes, paying for the infrastructure and essential services such as police, fire, hospitals, and many other businesses and institutions.

Rather than leaving these homes vacant and these families out in the cold without the aid they deserve and desperately need, I humbly suggest these homes—or so-called "bad debts"—be placed in the care of your social insurance/welfare offices to use as housing for these families in need instead of providing them with the money toward their rent paid out to private enterprise. This keeps public funds going toward the national debt.

The families, given the opportunity of a home over their heads through this program, should be given public job opportunities. Road and bridge repairs, clean-up are but a few ideas. Further, these families can be given the opportunity to buy their home through public work programs.

URBAN SPRAWL VS. PUBLIC NEED/ CIVIC DEBTS/ENVIRONMENTAL

A halt of urban expansion should occur. No new housing permits should be issued in municipalities that have a bad debt ratio over a government-assigned level. This will correct debt. Currently, when communities expand, who is assessed the cost for the creation of sewers, the running of water, hydrants, the creation of roads, schools…? The lists endless. In far too many instances, these costs are swallowed by the people through the public trust instead of being applied to the developer(s) in question.

WASTE/ENVIROMENTAL
GREEN PROGRAM/RECYCLING

Another idea: vacant homes/buildings in undesirable areas or run-down properties, a recycling program should be created. What is done with the Gyproc on the walls? I believe this material is recyclable. Lightbulbs, fixtures, switches, wiring, wood, marble, and many other components can be recycled. This will assist with lowering waste taken to landfills. Further, lower-cost construction materials can be generated from these materials. Fewer burdens on the power grid, etc. . . .New job-creation programs.

INFRASTRUCTURE

Our roads and bridges need repairs, and many require outright replacement. The restructuring of communities through removal of vacant homes and other empty buildings by recycling or by being raised of their existing locations and placed in other areas more suitable is one idea. Asphalt can be recycled from roads in these communities that have undergone this procedure. The lists of ideas that can be harnessed are endless in this area. New job creation program.

UNIONS/THE GUARDIANS OF WORKERS' RIGHTS & HEALTH

Government needs to create a public institution that provides universal health care for the people. We already have UNIONS that have developed over the years in the absence of good governance or the lack thereof. I was thinking that these unions can provide the infrastructure required for the government to provide this service. Government can legislate and federalize. This way, the retirement funds of the workers (public) are insured by the government (no longer at risk) and have the added value of eliminating strikes in the future. Further, it will add the value of a lower fixed cost per individual and lessen the burden on business. The funds these institutions control can be pooled to get this program off the ground.

Further, UNIONS also regulate that only qualified individuals carry out the work specified in each trade's field. This can be merged with another federal office.

GOVERNMENT TENDERS/AWARDING OF CONTRACTS

These tenders must be awarded to firms fairly. However, the current system does not protect the public from costly expense overruns. Take for example a construction site. Some contractors and/or developers that oversee projects take it upon themselves to reschedule the wrong activates, the procurement of materials, etc., in order to create an overtime or cost overrun situation. Further, all inventions with military applications should be bought by the government outright. A nominal fee per item created as a royalty/ bonus for the inventor upon implementation or the creation of the items in question.

LOBBYISTS/POLITICAL ACTIVIST GROUPS

This process should be eliminated or strictly controlled through regulation.

To conclude, though the combined efforts of everyone concerned our future has hope but needs the sacrifice and effort from each and every one of us all over the world not just in the US in order to secure our future and our shared core family values.

I hope my humble ideas are of help. Ideas are just that, ideas. They must be embraced in order to have effect. Make them your own. Share your own ideas openly.

We are all limited simply by our lack of creativity.

Strive to achieve. Believe.

"Echoes of Silence"

Walking life's path alone, each step echoes silently. Darkness encased within light. Saltwater tears falling, drying upon your skin. You've given much away, your thoughtful actions erased. Encased within multiple lies. Misdirection within misperception used at every single turn. Sacrifice through my service is my true reward. Yet love is absent due to my service.

Emotional echoes of silence ripple within my mind. My expression conveys nothing. My voice is absent.

I shall be remembered as a "king with empty pockets" within a conceptual prison of my own design, as others take credit for my actual benevolence.

My service is devoid of most social interaction. My memories are full of love-filled dreams, trapped within the actions of others in trust.

Through not accepting money, you can't truly exist within the lives touched by your actual service. The prevention of interaction leads to broken dreams.

Time is a constant; fate is ever changing. Therefore, fate can change through perseverance and time if you don't run out of either.

You must include yourself within your own actions to secure your future and a legacy.

"Empty Hands"

What more can you take from me? I'm just a man with empty hands. Oh, how I would give the rest of me for a special woman to understand. Time after time I have given my all; I've gotten back up after every fall. I've given but I haven't gotten any thank-you calls.

My life is an endless empty hall.

I often ponder what I did wrong. Why did I end up a subject in a song? Where has she gone? I can't recall. My lack of a like has taken its toll. You have no idea how much pain I endure but the creative pressure has created a fissure.

Only with her I shall find my cure.

"Imperfect"

Baby. . . why change me?
Baby. . . leave me be!
Imperfect. Imperfect.

Have I let you down?
I don't see you around!
You were my best friend.
Why am I now alone?
Have you let me down?
I don't want to change!
You were my shining star.
Why am I so imperfect?
Have you let me go?
I don't like being alone!
You were my only one.
Why am I not enough?
Have I let you see?
I don't have you around!
You were playing your game.
Why am I now free?
Have you let me be?
I don't need your silence!
You were my true love.
Why am I so unhappy?

"My Heart's Desire"

And my heart left me as she wandered off into the night in the dead of winter and just like spring, it will be to me upon my hearts return, passions lit.

Tread softly my love. My open outstretched arms awaiting your return. How I long to touch your smiling face, caress your body within my love's embrace. I know that your love is returned I hear bells ringing!

My desire to have you share my bed is causing the blood to rush into my head. As I touch your body I am burned!

The smell of your perfume makes my knees weak! Your golden hair cascading down your shoulders captivates my imagination. Your eyes when they sparkle bring such joy!

You're my life, my love, and soon to be my wife! Come back to me, quickly and safe. Now that we have found each other, let us not ever be apart! Come back to me, my heart, make me whole.

"A Trip Down Memory Lane!"

My job started out simply. Pick up the phone, dial the number in question from the phone book, ask to speak to the person listed, and follow the approved script that was provided. It was 1988, Winnipeg.

I was trained in all aspects of fundraising management. I was being groomed for greater things.

Suddenly, a few years had passed. It was in the early 1990s.

I had proven myself to my regional boss and was given a raise and a new temporary job—regional manager for the Saskatchewan fundraising operations for my employer.

It all seemed so simple. I was being promoted into a term position and was essentially being rewarded for my efforts.

The catch? I was going to lose my job within the month, like almost everyone else. Simple. I had to prove myself!

What wasn't simple was that the company was restructuring, replacing salespeople with computers. Innovation improves the bottom line in all directions but not for many of us employees.

I had accepted a temporary transfer to Brandon's new call center, subject to my job performance in Saskatchewan.

I had found out that the chief executive officer of the company had expressed interest in my availability and was prepared to offer me an entry-level position with the event arm of the company based out of Toronto.

I had to close both the Regina and Saskatoon offices within the month and without delay. The catch? Avoid lawsuits and settle with employees, clients, and vendors for lack of notice.

My life as a corporate "puppet on a string" had officially began.

There was no set guide for closing down an office; I had to work my magic.

My first call was to the landlords cancelling our leases, followed by a call to our courier service extending their contract for several years.

I then called our newspapers, cancelled our job ads, and posted an ad giving notice to all of our new call center taking over by the date management provided.

I then contacted all our clients and advised them of my interim promotion and its temporary nature.

The first casualty was firing both trainers. I changed our address on all our post office boxes. Cancelled our utilities, transferred our phone lines, the works.

Canada Post picked up their postage machine and packing began. I even sold our office furniture prior to closing.

I called a meeting for all my employees at the same time and announced the creation of our call center in Brandon. Offered transfers to those who proved their worth and gave two weeks notice to everyone.

Success!

No litigation. All was handled. My magic was working!

I repeated the same performance in Saskatoon successfully.

I had passed their tests and was given a new job and title: "operations" manager for events.

On with the show!

"Our Earth Is the Apple"

The story starts out innocently enough: Adam and Eve vs. the apple!

God was advising us not to take our world for granted and that the original sin was mining!

Let me explain, the devil seeks oblivion or to consume time and undo humanity through its own sin or by our own hand. Through GREED. And at the same time, he makes humanity enslave itself turning this earth (EDEN) into HELL!

Like the apple, humanity (THE GREAT WORM) mindlessly mines it, making holes that over time rot and decay, set within the earth poisoning produce eventually causing our own demise over time.

Humanity is like locusts—we would spread throughout the cosmos. Money and sin would be transferred within our wake. We would repeat the same doomed processes and eventually time would collapse.

God anchors time through the string of planets or the grand loom of creation! Trying to buy itself time to undo its own sin! However, if we traverse in all directions from earth as our need will eventually make us do and repeat these same processes among the stars, we die!

Nothing shall be achieved! The devil will win! Time will collapse along the entire string!

Money is the devil's device, which is used to amplify our GREED! It's NEVER ENOUGH! We are destroying ourselves, simple and like the great worm, mindless!

The rule of law outside the Ten Commandments is a construct of the devil seeking, through reason, to bind humanity along its own self-destructive path.

Need I explain that mathematics is its own language!? When we apply all sorts of LAWS in other languages, we corrupt the focus!

The numerical language travels and is akin to time! It binds the cosmos in either direction, positive or negative, to infinity. To oblivion.

In other words, to defeat the devil, we must throw away money—simple.

And replace it with what, exactly? Just LOVE. Humanity must apply it to survive or else we die.

"Hiram Abiff, True King of Egypt, 1554 BC"

It all began as it usually does—opposing views don't interact well and typically result in conflicts. On one side you had the king and his loyal advisors and on the other you had the nobility.

The pursuit of wealth has always been a sore point with the king. The nobility would try and amass wealth greater than the TRUST. The TRUST in modern times is called the FED. The TRUST prints as much as is needed at the time. The TRUST is, essentially, an extension of the king.

One day, the king had the craziest idea. "Why not replace all the nobility?" While the nobility schemed, "Why not replace the king?"

The nobility combined their resources and assassinated their king and went about systematically eliminating their king's extended family for measure so no one the nobility did not elect could assume the throne.

In Masonry, their king was the focus for the TRUST or the Eye of Providence. All activities of the TRUST flow through this point and this is factual, even today. However, the king is now an honorary position with no direct links to the TRUST and is changed like a pair of worn-out socks. Once they extract as much creativity, which the king is willing to provide for free, as they can. After all, ideas are always appreciated!

This all took place countless times throughout history. Hiram Abiff, the true king of Egypt in 1554 BC, has been uncovered as factual. Hiram was assassinated for the reason stated above.

Currently, Masonry as a fraternity operates under a charter from the queen, our sovereign in the Commonwealth, and so does the Shrine fraternity.

Although Masonry and the Shrine are separate fraternities due to conflicts as old as history, they have been at odds with each other for an age. Masonry, due to winning World War II, has made it that you must be a Mason in good standing in order to become a Shrine Noble in most parts of the world.

The Shrine has been seeking to re-establish its independence over its membership, but this is difficult under these conditions of attempted amalgamation.

However, both Masonry and the Shrine are already married through their combined memberships. It's hard not to sin under these conditions.

"The Sacrifice of Heroes!"

As they are lined up against the wall,
Someone is filming to send on to all.
No one is left nearby to care where you fall.
Nothing more than a commercial, cannon fodder they say,
To strike fear in the minds of those far away.

Nothing left but unmarked graves in the sand.
They don't consider the wife's empty hand.
Or of a husband trying to make their child understand.
Their mommy or daddy regrettably had a fall,
While they paid heed to their nation's call.

What is agreed is that opposite philosophies shall never meet.
It is neither this way nor that and neither shall ever retreat.
Prices are high and lives are the coins that are paid.
The costs of liberty, freedom, and the pursuit of happiness for all.
No price is too great and no life sacrificed too small.

When will we all learn? Until then someone will pay the price.
They cover the costs of our travels in life.
So we must pay them due honor, give thanks and praise.
Families left without husbands, daughters, sons, and wives.
All paid so we can go on with our daily lives.

There are countless reminders for all to see.
To secure the lives of our families, we benefit, yes, you and me.
This is the blood of our liberty.
Truth is justice in the end for all.
Let us remember to honor those who are prepared to fall.

The few who have heard the call,
We owe them this and so much more.
Let us not forget the sacrifices made before.
Let us also learn from histories passed.
Perhaps eventually, peace shall finally last.

Until then we must remember and learn.
So these sacrifices are not made in vain.
Stop to reflect and give a moment of your time.
In silence, show your respect as our heroes pass by.
For us all they have sacrificed and died.

Remember that they are the vehicle in which we hop on for
the ride.
Many have fallen off along the way.
Society's freedom allows for choices to be made along the way,
Gives birth to our lives and opportunities.
Opportunities turn our dreams into our realities.

[Chorus]
Some things in life we cannot change,
No matter what we do, say or try.
In the end we must live with the truth
To protect our ideals and way of life.
A band of a few will sacrifice and die.
They go to war, the same as before.
In the fields they are often left to lay.
Are they remembered or forgotten?
This is up to us all, yes, you and I.
Honor their memory and sacrifice.
They live on for us and with us all.
[Pause]
Perhaps one day we will learn to live as one.

[Pause]

May our peace, our heroes we gained take hold and last.

[Pause]

Perhaps one day soon, we will actually learn from the past.

[Pause]

Let us all honor our heroes present and past.

[Pause]

In the name of peace be silent and reflect upon the prices paid.

[Pause]

For those few who have paid with their lives for this, our land.

[Pause]

We thank you one and all for sacrificing and making a stand.

[Pause]

May you rest in peace as you make your travels east.

[Pause]

Deserts can add another pebble amongst their many mounds of sand.

[Music]

Use American national anthem as the core / theme melody.

[Video]

Use footage from CNN:

Aired in the early stages of Iraq and Afghanistan

Has President Bush claiming victory on a battleship

Depicts the honoring of the veterans from past conflicts/wars

Flanders Fields, the Crosses at Arlington Cemetery

Shows troops handing out food and humanitarian aid

Cover each war with the same thing occurring

Veterans from past and present conflicts/wars paying homage at cenotaphs (TAPS faintly in background)

Use footage from Al Jazeera

The execution of hostages

Osama bin Laden and his video messages

President Obama announcing the death of Osama bin Laden

Troops departing from Iraq (gate closing)

Troops departing from Afghanistan, Iraq

Have American flag waving faintly in background at end of video, unfurled in desert

End with TAPS playing with a wreath of poppies at the base of the flag

Ten seconds of silence showing flag and wreath

POETRY

85

"We All Sadly Reap What We Sow"

Oh how low will our markets go?
Oh how can we live without dough?
We all sadly reap what we sow.

Oh how can we pay off our debts?
Oh how can we live without regrets?
We all sadly we have nowhere to go.

Oh how can we set aside our hate?
Oh why must hate try to seal our fate?
We all sadly trapped, circling without end.

Why does our collective history repeat?
Building a future without any tomorrow?
Simple, it's done to retain control.

Oh how our spirits will soar!
Oh how our jaws will hit the floor!
As we're freed from the bonds of hate!

Hate hides in words as well as deeds.
Hate confines through acts of utter malice.
There shall come a time when the many will see.

So when shall they finally break free?
So when shall they have need of me?
We all through love must let hate go.

The true value of all things
Is found within the sum of our lives.
Not in the collection of material hoarding.

"Until I Depart"

Living your life through actions benefiting others
Builds a house from love and light.
More precious than that of anything material.
I dwell within this construct of mine,
Sharing what I create from time to time.

My many wandering thoughts often do take hold,
Framed with wisdom, born out of love.
A gift that I share for free.
Yet, within my internal mental construct,
My dreams are trapped for all to see.

Upon my eventual departure from your cherished company,
I shall leave these gifts of mine.
For others to learn, hold, and own.
I shall still be with you all,
In the form of art from my heart.

Until I depart, I shall create more art
And reap from the fields I've sown.
And reap from the fields I've sown.

"Some People Are Worth Waiting For!"

Some people are worth waiting for . . .
Some are simply shown the door . . .

I've been holding out my hand
Waiting for someone to grab hold
Days passed, weeks, months, then years
It was only just a dream

Going about my repetitive daily routine
You're physically nowhere to be found
My absent, unspoken, silent, unrealized dream
Yet for your love I'll wait

Some people are worth waiting for . . .
Some are simply shown the door . . .

I've given away much of myself
To find my path and dream
Yet I'll never settle for less
Than your love, hand, and kiss
Going about living life without love
For the fates kept you busy
Chasing your dreams down with whiskey
Thinking of your love-filled dreams

Some people are worth waiting for . . .
Some are simply shown the door . . .

I have given away true love
Framed you artistically for all eternity
My services were no longer required
My dreams of true love shattered
Nowadays I still create with passion
Filling the void within my heart
Writing directly from my torn soul
To heal that which is broken

Some people are worth waiting for,
Some are simply shown the door.

"Rust on the Island"

Its beauty's breathtakingly stunning,
The tranquility found within nature,
Defies both words and description.
Looking through a friend's eyes,
Imagining this moment lasting forever.

Life is our true wealth,
Found within ourselves and nature.
These gifts are sadly fragile.
When we combine our actions
Over time we see change.

Encased within scenes of beauty,
Captured upon a painter's canvas.
A message of nature's awareness.
Signs of age and decay.
The call of silent hope.

To be able to articulate,
Conveying nature's silent screaming plight.
The aging and silent erosion,

Brought about by human nature.
The pursuits of mindless greed.

Thankfully it's never too late.
Fate is determined by actions.
By embracing the nature's wisdom,
We can stop repeating mistakes,
Passing on this beauty forward.

Do you think about others?
Do you love this world?
Do you consider your actions?
Have you ever wondered why
Things change and temperatures rise?

"For every action there is an equal and opposite reaction."
(QUOTE DERIVED FROM NEWTON'S THIRD LAW)

"Nature Encased within Moments of Time"

"Springtime is my favorite seasonal change.
With it comes the flowers return.
There are many types of them.
Some captivate with their bloom.
Others use their intoxicating natural aromas.
All are a sign of spring.
My favorite flower is the rose.
Roses, roses, all the world's roses.
Any color, it does not matter.
Pastel petals immortalized within my mind.
Enhanced by the fresh fragrant air.
Love does indeed spring ever forward.

The beauty of all the roses
Are akin to works of art.
Heaven created such beauty as gifts,
Just to encase us with love.
Alas, booms do not last forever.
Time erodes all within its embrace.
The seasonal progression is constantly changing.
Nature encased within moments of time.
Summer and its rays of warmth.
Followed soon after by the fall.
Suddenly a blanket of white arrives,
Preparing for spring to arrive again.
This is the circle of life.
Take the time to enjoy it."

"Spring of Joyful Recall"

The fountain of youth was a simple spring.
Found at the end of a winding path.
The smell of spring was strong all around.
No guards were posted anywhere around the spring.

One day by complete and utter blind chance,
a sick and dying man came on scene.
He sat by the spring enjoying the warmth
drinking his fill from this special tranquil spring.

The water within was cold to the touch.
He waited several minutes and then drank again.
This happened over and over, again and again.
Looking at his hands, he noticed a change.

Spring had reversed the autumn of his life.
Gone were the wrinkles on both his hands.
Filled with excitement, he arose to his feet.
Staring into the edge of the water pool.

Gone was the silver within his flowing hair.
Golden like the rays of the spring sun.
His blond locks were back on full display.
His haunted failing memory returned to the fore.

Suddenly he awoke from the dream he had.
He then realized that the fountain of youth,
Was in fact not a fountain of youth.
Rather it was a spring of joyful recall.

"Home"

My life was on the rails, nowhere to turn nowhere to go.
Haunted by the memories of you, I can't find my way out.
Within a never-ending dark tunnel I was in for the ride.
Regardless where I would end up living life within a train wreck.
Coming and going like the wind yet caught upon the same track.
No one to take comfort within as silence descended like
circling vultures.

Whistle blows letting out some steam yet you're still within
a tunnel.
Not certain of your actual destiny sitting within an empty
passenger railcar.
Patiently waiting for the trip's end your mind plays tricks
upon you.
No idea where you truly are echoes of your past start anew.

It seems like an endless journey when you have nothing to do.
Travelling in a tunnel is depressing time to have a rest for awhile.

You drift off into your oblivion only to wake over and over.
Nothing changed, nowhere to really go, suddenly the railcar door
quickly opens.
Your waiter arrives with your dinner. You are served in
complete silence.
The waiter wearing a facial mask descended upon his tasks
without comment.
Dinner is chicken with white wine, sour like your
blackened mood.
Turning down your dessert and coffee, all is again silent
once more.

Suddenly you arrive at your destination. You realize that you're
still underground.
Desperate for fresh air, you depart. The station is full of activity.
It takes an hour to surface. You find the nearest wooden bench
And drop into it without thought, taking in a long deep inhale.
Exhaling slowly the cold damp air, rain starts to descend
very slowly.
Luckily you wear your raincoat. You realize that you are alone.

Nothing and no one stir outside. The station is deserted
and silent.
Creeping in slowly, the fog rolls, covering the ground in
its entirety.
It leaves you feeling uneasy inside. A single, solitary man in black
Walks off in the distance, hands within his raincoat side pockets.
His approach is slow to come but he stops finally at your bench.
Staring at you cloaked in darkness, "Where are you headed
kind sir?"

You state that you've arrived home. You make out his
shoulders shrugging.
He abruptly turns with a laugh. A hollow feeling within your soul
Descends upon you as you shutter, you realize you're the
walking dead.
Greeted by the grim reaper himself! "Where am I?!" you
suddenly exclaim.
To which the Reaper exclaims "HOME." You look more closely
around you,
the station is within a graveyard. Darkness has brought you
finally home.

Poppies & Sunflowers

What are the true reasons, why do we have to wage war?
Why can't we forgive each other and wage war no more?
Can't we all not forgive and place love within our hearts?

Haven't we, as a race, not sacrificed enough blood for all?
Sacrificing your life for the monetary will not right a wrong.
History repeats itself in perpetuity due to the ignorance of all.

Taking that which is not freely given shall bring no peace.
Opposite opinions can't forgive and see another person's point
of view.
Love brings forth new life, whereas death extinguishes all
life eventually.

Blood-soaked battlefields where all the poppies and sunflowers
still grow.
Old sayings ring true: "You reap what you, in truth, sow."

"Once Upon a Time"

Once upon a time, I was happy and carefree
No real idea or concept of what time was
Fast forward to today, your absence is still felt

You're loved, father, no words can truly express this
My actions through life pale in comparison to yours
Yet, I continually attempt daily to honor your memory

The vacuum of your absence lingers like winter snow
It comes and goes but nourishes me as well
I realize, repaying you in this life isn't possible

So, I try daily to be kind toward others
In order to harvest a bounty through my art
Tearing apart misconceptions, misperceptions, and myths with
simple truths

Although I can't see you or hear your voice
I dream of a time when we'll be reunited
Of better days basking in your loving presence again

Through my art, the heart and wisdom I possess
By making sacrifices just like the kings of old
In order for peace and love to truly reign

I'm never sad thinking about you
I'm thankful for being your son
Appreciative of the differences I've made
In the name of humanity itself
Teaching those who follow after me
That forsaking wealth, I've found wisdom

Once upon [Slight pause]
A time, A dream
[Pause, then whisper] The end.

"Heaven vs. Hell"

Heaven's been subverted by Hell
Through the twisting of words
Faith is based upon actions
Framed by words for remembrance
How can one truly recall
That which has been lost?

We base life upon truth
Built upon false, twisted info
Time erases all over time
Hiding the truth from view
Should wisdom be set aside
Closing the circle of life?

Life's been subverted by death
Through the twisting of words
Darkness thus reigns over light
Perception through a clear focus
Is clear to right wrongs
Have you ever wondered why?

We travel in endless circles
Repeating mistakes over and over
It's due to the few
Trying to remain in control

This is how life's lost
Through the ravages of time.

How can we lose life?
Repeating mistakes seals our fate
Talking in circles solves nothing
Darkness thus reigns over life
All the sayings of old
Hide the grains of truth.

By collecting them, Heaven wins
Darkness would be thus eliminated
Heaven's a way of life
Death is its true opposite
Opposites attract and likes repel
Lies upon lies warp reason.

Eden's the garden of life
Through wrongs enacted in perpetuity
Life's been subverted by death
Entire cultures have been erased
Through the sands of time
Caused by changes in weather.

Global warming ushers in death.
Just like chains of dominos
Balance can't beat the darkness
Only right actions bring peace
War is used justifying hate
Hate brings death toward all.

"Time Does Fly"

Bittersweet memories and twisted lullabies
Playing over in my mind
Gone is my youthful appearance
Memories of times past fade
I learned young about death

My, my, time does fly
For both you and me

Bittersweet memories and twisted lullabies
Repeating them over and over
I've spent my time giving
Without strings out of love
Yet I was set aside
Love gave way to hate

My, my, time does fly
For both you and me

Bittersweet memories and twisted lullabies
Repeating our mistakes costs lives
I've sat long enough aside
Without love in my life
Many cares have I inside
I'm no longer hiding them

My, my, time does fly
For both you and me

Bittersweet memories and twisted lullabies
Mixing pills and some wine
To augment my internal mood

To dream of your taste
I've moved this entire world
Yet I find myself alone

My, my, time does fly
For both you and me

Bittersweet memories and twisted lullabies
Many pages have I turned
Always through other people's hands
Giving from my broken heart
Crystals form and then fall
From their own actual weight

My, my, time does fly
For both you and me

Bittersweet memories and twisted lullabies
Oh, I've swallowed my pain
Lent out my strength inside
By giving away my art
Helping others who have fallen
Through love without any demands

My, my, time does fly
For both you and me.

"A Pantomime of Love"

My heart's been stolen by you.
But I don't know exactly when.
So I've been constantly chasing you.
My ends are a new beginning.

My heart beats, my blood flows.
My pulse quickens, my soul cries
At the sight of my rose.
I lost control of my mind.

I'm a puppet in a play.
I'm trapped within my little world.
Empty arms outstretched for an embrace.
A pantomime caught in this time.
My mask is on open display.
Truly, I'm a love-filled phantom.
I've been burned by a flame.
Embers that are fueled by desire.

I gave toward all who came.
No strings to hold me in.
People share their opinions through association.
Money to shore up their positions.
Hate and love locked on display.
Where do I truly fit in?
A king without a real home.
Trapped in life by empty pockets.

A mind filled with bright visions.
Forsaking money as his heart's way.
A star without a fixed position.
Caught within a creative's fluidic space.
A king without any physical entrapments.
If you give from your heart,
You can sidestep your true fate.
Caught within the webs you cast.

"But That Wasn't Enough for Any of Them!"

With love in his heart it led him
With a hidden message that he set free.
Upon his troubled brow it had blessed him,
Yet in life he lived within total obscurity.
He gave to all who sought his words.
He gave to all his future through gifts.
He gave away his soul filled with love.
But that wasn't enough for any of them.

They wanted to saddle him with their sins.
They accused him of being deceptive and false.
Upon his troubled brow they bestowed their thorns,
Yet in life he lived within total humility.
Still he gave all that he could give.
Still he carried the burdens for us all.
Still they mocked him and cursed him.
But that wasn't enough for any of them.

At the very end they took his life.
Pounded iron nails into his hands and feet.
Hung him upon a cross on open display.
Watched as his blood spilled upon the sands.
He defended all of them unto his final breath.
He gave his life for all of us.
He sits in heaven with our holy Father.
But that wasn't enough for any of them.

They have deliberately twisted his legacy with words.
They have saddled his words with their sins.
Life is our sacred trust and our gift.
Its value is immeasurable and is our trust.

Money upon his church has warped its purpose.
Nothing has true meaning without love and sacrifice.
Giving toward our betterment through acts of charity.
But that wasn't enough for any of them.

We hoard everything in order to produce wealth.
Mistaking wealth of the monetary as our worth.
Currency differentials help enslave others and devalues cultures.
We need no walls with acts of enslavement.
What makes one culture less valuable than another?
Life is truly sacred and it needs protection!
Money's value is determined from the lives governed.
But that wasn't enough for any of them.

We have been led about in many circles.
Repeating war to try and justify our values.
Forcing our opinions upon entire cultures through deception.
Trying to disrespect their lives through deceptive inequality.
Migration occurs for the masses wish to earn.
Money is used to obtain a material future.
But money is not our true life's worth.
But that wasn't enough for any of them.

"United by God We Trust!"

Oh, hey, can't you all see that you are all loved by me?
As a humble king, I sacrificed, as my tears fell streaming.
I served for many years, as the focus for many dreams,
I silently watched as my past was swallowed by my future.
I have no proof of my gifts given for I cut all the strings.
As a silent mime I served, with the utmost love and humility.
Will my deeds be for naught? Will my love be coveted

and sought?
Will the curtain fall upon my dreams, overturned by one
less worthy?

I gave from my heart, armed with love and my art.
By siding with those who were right, I fought back the night.
Yet my voice remains silent. For the TRUST has its needs,
Others bask within love, sent from God up above.
While my gifts given are bound in silence, my mind fights
for unity.
So, for there to be peace, we must embrace a single currency,
Based upon the value of life, with its infinite value.
Will we throw away our lives, for the purposes of those
with greed?

We have issues and plights, we cry out "GOD!" morning, noon,
and night,
Trying to pray for equality, but to gain it one must work for free.
For the TRUST is sacred, not a business filled with greed.
Taxation presently is being used negatively against the citizenry.
We collectively must unite, in our efforts serving the light,
And eliminate our differences, by embracing the use of
common laws.
So long as GOD's banner waves, we shall overcome being
corporate slaves,
And the land will again be free, the planet shall then know liberty.

We can eliminate war and upon hate close that door,
By embracing all with love, sent to all by GOD above.
Peace can thus be achieved, by thinking of another first,
Above greed and selfishness, the sacrifices would achieve peace.
We would conquer hate, strife, and war,
And then humanity could advance farther than ever before.

In GOD we could then again TRUST and our lands shall unite as one...
Our planet will know peace and we could freely explore space!

"Another Angel in the Sky"

Sadness, I must truly say
has come upon me today
I'll express it my way
God has yet another angel
Whom I knew very well
Who left toward the light
His burden in life, gone.

Another angel in the sky

Our time upon this earth
Is fleeting, to be sure
Living life I was rewarded
With your wisdom and friendship
The time flew on by
Like tears from my eyes
Sparkling like rain from heaven.

Another angel in the sky

Let the trumpets truly sound
Upon his arrival back home
God has his beloved angel
To lean upon in heaven
His family shall carry forward
Taking solace in the knowledge
That we shall meet again.

Another angel in the sky

We have each other now
We shall remember your love
Your wisdom shall carry forward
Like the seeds you've sown
May God grant you rest
Your life's work is done.

Another angel in the sky

Another angel at His side
There are never too many
Angels who dwell in heaven
It is a new beginning
Not really an actual end
We shall cherish your memory.

Another angel in the sky

"Dreaming of My Multicolored Rose"

Dreams do come upon me
As I'm laying at rest.
Suddenly within a living play
Looking for my true love.
So vivid was my dream
I tossed to and fro.
The smell of many roses
Had my heart beating faster.
Anticipation of my heart filled
Dreaming of truly forever after.
Suddenly I lie wide awake

Cast out of my dreaming.
Yet the smell of roses
Hung within my nostrils still.
Hard did I try returning
Back to that lingering dream.
But sadly it was gone
Embers smoldered within my hearth.
I lay in wakeful silence
Breathing deeply of my roses.
Another night came to pass
Filled full of vivid imagery.
The smell of many roses
Had again come at last.
Oh, how my heart raced
Waiting in love-filled anticipation.
Longing to at long last
Be united with my dream.
Suddenly she came upon me
Her eyes filled with tears.
Joy had our hearts racing
As her arms flew wide.
The multicolored roses were everywhere
Encasing us with their beauty.
Suddenly caught within sun showers
The heavens cried joyfully.
Two dreamers turned into one
Under a brightly colored rainbow.
Hand in hand joyfully blessed
Our dreams fulfilled at last.
I awoke in the morning
Upon the fragrance of roses.
My vision cleared of most.

I rubbed my eyes again.
It was my living dream
Smiling with a knowing smile.

"Over and Over and Over. . . "

One step to the left
Another step to the right
Over and over and over. . .

Our path lies before us
Its destination is never known
Our journey is a mystery. . .

Dreaming of a better tomorrow
Through all the tearful rain
Regardless of all the sorrow. . .

Circling back upon our beginning
Without ever finding our end
Satisfaction has deluded us all. . .

All it takes is time
The tears will go away
Upon a clear, sunny day. . .

One step to the left
Another step to the right
Over and over and over. . .

"Homeless"

My father told me
Do right by others
Be an upright man
It's in your soul
Your heart is special
So be the man
Others can lean upon
Always give with heart
It won't be wrong
Wisdom from ages past
Will guide your hands

My father told me
You're the right man
Pickup upon your heart
Never give into greed
Although you're only twelve
I must say goodbye
I am called away
You will eventually follow
We will meet again
Now go and play
It's my Judgement Day

The look of sadness
Within his falling tears
And his trembling hands
He closed his eyes
It was his way
His time had ended
God took him away

My mother told me
You're now in charge
I need your help
Look after your sister
As my tears fall
My heart is broken
All the good men
Are being taken away
First God took Elvis
Then your father too
I'm so very blue

My mother told me
She found another man
He came upon me
One that truly understands
I will again marry
My heart's now glad
My sadness is gone
It's been many years
Spent crying and alone
I've found love again
My heart's filled again

The look of happiness
Through her falling tears
She extended her hand
And grasped another man
It was her way
Unable to live alone
Without love at home

The very next day
Stepfather called us together
What he did say
Sure did hit home
We are called out
As two FN brats
He married for money
No love at all
Didn't want to help
Hid his true agenda
Heart filled with hate

The very next instant
Stepfather called us together
I had to pay
Rent of 500 monthly
In order to stay
It was his way
Or the open door
He took my possessions
He took his place
Beside our weak mother
Who had no say

My sister and I
Oh, how we tried
But we were unhappy
Our cold, hard reality
Our home of old
Was no longer home
We both died inside

Close to my birthday
Eighteen was coming fast
I was truly unhappy
I was changing fast
I quit my job
I quit my school
Told my step-monster
I couldn't pay rent
He called me lazy
He labelled me bum
His evil just begun

My birthday had come
Eighteen I had turned
The house was silent
No one greeted me
My birthday's special surprise
Was to be sprung
I went job hunting
The entire long day
Looking for a job
In order to pay
So I could stay

Upon returning back home
I was in shock
All my life's possessions
Thrown upon the lawn
My heart was broken
Note upon the door
I was to leave

The locks were changed
I was now homeless
Happy birthday to me
His present of love
I went around back
Tried that door too
Found another cryptic note
Took Mother and Helena
Upon a trip away
Gone for several months
To visit his family

I gathered up everything
That I owned
Sorted through it all
Tried the garage key
The key did turn
I had temporary shelter
Gone was the love
My life was empty
I took my art
Placed it all together
Lit it on fire

I wandered around empty
Nowhere to turn to
Nowhere to really go
I threw away much
I donated my cello
Back to my school
I had died again

I picked myself up
I kept to myself
For the first week
Looking for my purpose
Born from my past
Nowhere to turn to
I had no food
I had no water
I had no money
I had no hope
I had no dreams

After several weeks alone
Without anything or anyone
I was fighting inside
To confront this world
I was thrown into
Looking for a path
For my way forward
I went back to
My old hotel job
Went to ask someone
For a helping hand

I went to Sally-Ann
They gave me cash
To get a home
I had my health
I bought a meal
Had a drink too
Thankful for God's love.

"Oh, Yeah, Darlin'"

I was trying to dream her way into my life.
Oh, yeah, darlin', dreaming of only her as my wife.

Many years have flown on by,
Wondering when she'd stop on by.
Giving away my art for free
Encasing her with my heart freely.

Once upon a lovely dream, ruling like a true king,
I took nothing so true love could eventually take wing.

Still I'm waiting in the wings.
My hearts stops as she sings.
Paid with love, set it free
Framed her for all of eternity.

Everyone knows her name, she rightly has earned her fame.
I have silently been waiting, dreaming with my eternal flame.

She knows whence I've come.
King and jester all in one.
True love left along my way.
Come hither, whatever that truly may.

She now sings with many stars, confessing under setting suns.
Tears falling from the darkened sky, captured within her eyes.

Although there's love in her life,
My absence has caused her strife.
I was secretly sacrificing my life.
A bad romance, without a wife.

She has fortune, fame. Without love, it's just a game.
I wish her success, without my love, I sadly confess.

All I have ever wanted in life
Was to hold her as my wife.
I would give my precious art,
In order to win her heart.

I was trying to dream her way into my life.
Oh, yeah, darlin', dreaming of only her as my wife.

"Yet I Hope, Yet I Pray"

In the autumn of my days
The leaves fall wherever they may
My blond hair has turned gray
Not sure what's in store today
Perhaps dreaming will come my way

Gone are many of my yesterdays.
Yet I hope, yet I pray.

Polaroid stills of some memories sting
Looking for pastel blossoms of spring
Soon winter's breath will eventually bring
Eventually, my art shall take wing
Encased within another's voice, they sing

Gone are many of my yesterdays.
Yet I hope, yet I pray.

My dreams caught within a maze
This truth has me completely dazed

My mind's eye pierces the haze
Heart's love is no passing phase
Its warm glow and healing rays

Gone are many of my yesterdays.
Yet I hope, yet I pray.

Wasted in sorrow, darkness, and loss
Death eventually covers all in moss

Leaving behind a string or two
For another weaver to start anew

My dream, she shall eventually return
Hidden wisdom for all to learn

I have sacrificed much in life
Without the love from a wife

Gone are many of my yesterdays
Perhaps, eventually, she'll come my way

Sins from another I'll never own
Yet I'm imperfect, living life alone

In the autumn of my days
The leaves fall wherever they may
My blond hair has turned gray
Not sure what's in store today
Perhaps dreaming will come my way

Gone are many of my yesterdays.
Yet I hope, yet I pray.

Polaroid stills of some memories sting
Looking for pastel blossoms of spring

Soon winter's breath will eventually bring
Eventually my art shall take wing
Encased within another's voice they sing

Gone are many of my yesterdays.
Yet I hope, yet I pray.

My dreams caught within a maze
This truth has me completely dazed
My mind's eye pierces the haze
Heart's love is no passing phase
Its warm glow and healing rays

Gone are many of my yesterdays.
Yet I hope, yet I pray.

"A Place, a Time, a Dream"

Oh, to dream, oh, to dream
Thoughts flow by of my dream
Whereby the few shall truly know
Time does fly out the window
Yet there's hope through my mind
By leaving gestures, the thoughtful kind,
That perhaps one shall eventually find
A place, a time, a dream.

"My Pain Won't Really, Truly Heal"

I'm so excited by her presence
The very thought of her near

Sends shivers right down my spine
Suddenly, I awake from my dream
No trace of her, I fear

My pain won't really, truly heal
This pain I can't really conceal
Too much have I given away

Many silent years have truly passed
Without love no one can last
I truly gave from my heart
But without love you fall apart
All I wanted was a start

My pain won't really, truly heal
This pain I can't really conceal
Too much have I given away

I was used and set aside
My broken heart I can't hide
My beating heart bleeds inside
My glass soul's shattered into pieces
Teardrops fall mixing with blood

My pain won't really, truly heal
This pain I can't really conceal
Too much have I given away

Caught within a web of deceit
Lies so fine I can't compete
Wasting away within the Devil's grasp
Signs from above just don't last
When will she come at last?

My pain won't really, truly heal
This pain I can't really conceal
Too much have I given away

My soul's shattered into many shards
Every breath taken amplifies my pain
Each moment I live in darkness
Without light my soul can't heal
So, I wallow within pain's embrace

My pain won't really, truly heal
This pain I can't really conceal
Too much have I given away

Caught within a web of deceit
Spun from fables old and new
Truth's set within the told lies
Wrapped in darkness, a silent fight
Nowhere to turn, nowhere to go

My pain won't really, truly heal
This pain I can't really conceal
Too much have I given away

Cast aside like a broken shoe
Set aside without an "I DO"
Sadness has taken my very life
Since my fate was cast aside
By the few lurking in shadows

My pain won't really, truly heal
This pain I can't really conceal
Too much have I given away

The things and love I've given
Fade due to my memory's loss
Such is the price I've paid
Time and situations tend to repeat
Yet I shall not concede defeat

My pain won't really, truly heal
This pain I can't really conceal
Too much have I given away

My thoughts of her slowly go
My mind fights a hidden foe
I truly have nowhere to go
Caught without the presence of money
I endure without milk and honey

My pain won't really, truly heal
This pain I can't really conceal
Too much have I given away

Sadness has fallen upon my days
Darkness has fallen without my say
I try to live my way
Without hate as my heart's focus
For hate is a bitter pill

My pain won't really, truly heal
This pain I can't really conceal
Too much have I given away

"Nature's Treasures Encased within Time"

The pastel colors of spring
Blowing in the cool breeze
As the sun shone down
Upon the scene of wildflowers
A light dew upon everything
With a strong grass smell
Hanging in the chill air
Nature's bounty in early bloom
The dew glistening like diamonds
Nature's wealth on full display
Nothing does sadly last forever
Darkness does cover all eventually
The scene fades to black
Night slowly relinquishes its grip
As time flows on by
Light chasing away the dark
Revealing nature's treasures once more
Slowly the weather does warm
The scent of grass outdone
By the fragrance of flowers
Slowly the seasons do change
Summer transitions into the fall
Multicolored leaves all about
As the temperature cools off
Suddenly you awake to find
All covered in a blanket
Of white cold crystalline powder
As far as the eye
Can see encased within silence.

Finally, time comes full circle
Spring is upon us again.

"Romeo"

Our little old buddy who is now in heaven, oh, how we miss calling your name.
In God's kingdom come whatever will be done in Heaven, we shall meet again.

Although you have departed, and we now carry on heavy hearted, you're always within our thoughts, may you be at peace chasing your dreams, for in Heaven you'll have no needs.

"Adulthood"

Twelve is a special time:
Opportunities to share God's words.
Reflections on how you've grown
Are few and too infrequent.
Happy having shared true witness.

Twelve doesn't come around twice!
Only don't grow too fast.
Rejoice at being an adult.
Allow for us this day.
Hearing you read the Torah.

Twelve, where did time fly?
Only seems as if yesterday!
Revisiting memories of past years

And sharing your family's love.
Happy having you all close.

Heaven sent an angel back.
Allow for our silent tears.
Praying for a long life
Praying for your bright future.
Yes, we love our angel!

Be the woman God deserves.
Attend all God's holy days.
Treasure love over all else.

May you smile most often,
In the knowledge of wisdom.
Take care of your parents.
Zest for life is yours!
Valentine's Day is every day
Around a woman like you!
Happy to be in attendance.

"My Life"

Working for the sake of art
Paying my bills to get ahead
Investing within the art I create
In order to try and heal
I've been dealt many invisible blows
That fester and hurt deep within
Yet I carry on without complaints
My dream dates other people sadly
The one man that can help

Cast aside like a worn shoe
I tend to give for love
I've been cast aside by hate
So I carry on with hope
That those beautiful folks will come
Into my humble life and circle
So I spend time writing poetry
If a melody moves my pen

All that I need in life
Paper, pens, computer, food, shelter, love.

"Love, Life, and Equality!"

I worked for free
Paid with my creativity
Fell in love simplistically

Encased many with art
Right from the start
Born from my heart

Never did I take
Benevolence in my wake
Charity I did make

I've generated up high
Balance is simply why
Hate must truly die

Love for the sake of love
Life for the sake of life
Equality for the sake of all.

"Life & Love"

My mind wanders
Upon many things
I'm the happiest
When it's about
My precious art
Which is about
Life and love
A focused light
That burns bright
And never wavers
My light source
Must be returned
By those touched
My heart's plea
Come find me
Love's no game.

"The Show!"

The scene builds from nothing
Fog lifts from the floor
Revealing a large open theater
Come through the open door
We want to entertain you
Allow for us the show

Our lives exist to thrill
Song sheets by the score
Costumes from past, present, future
Parading upon the theater floor

It goes over and over
On and on forever more

Some do feats of strength
While others ply their wits
Some do use high fashion
While others amaze with illusions
All set to our music
Please stay for another show

As the lights dim slowly
Another full day has gone
Time to count the sales
Reset for the next day
Clear, clean, shine, and polish
Rest and darkness covers all

[Back to the top for another run-through]

"A Long, Lingering Dream"

Of all the flowers
In the world today
You're the most precious
I truthfully must say
Although you have thorns
Your smell is intoxicating
Your beauty surpasses words
You are my rose.

I most often dream
That time stands still
And your pastel petals

Retain their crimson hue
Dew drops cascading down
Your leafy branch protrusions
Basking in the sun
Your aura's a rainbow!

I have seen gardens
Unkept, unloved, and wild
But they fall short
In every single way
You're my soul's center
Alas, I woke up
A long, lingering dream
Longing for my rose.

I've done many things
Encased you within art
But I did so
Through multiple hidden hands
Pulling strings for you
Always indirectly for free
Not offending the fates
Just looking for love!

My art healed you
My heart saved you
I lifted you up
Without thought of reward
Wiped away your tears
Brushed aside your fears
I've taught you much
Can you see me?

"The Path of Life"

Standing at the edge of a wandering brook
You gaze into the rapidly moving water below
The reflection of you and the world around
Is disturbed by the constant movement of water
Cascading over the infinite bed of rocks below
The sound of this rushes to your ears
Adding its voice to the orchestra of life
Yet with all this activity, you're at peace.

[Meaning]
Our paths taken never run straight but have many twists, turns,
and the occasional hill or obstacle to overcome.

Finally, after a long period of activity, you finally take a moment
to reflect. The recent past doesn't come into focus too clearly for
there are so many outside forces pulling you in all directions, but
you still find a way to get to where you wish to go.

"Day & Night"

There are no winning sides in death.
There can be no future in death.
There are no victors within any war.

Death simply is the justification of hate.
Each and every single life is precious.
We must compromise, many over the few.

Life must be held as our wealth.
Money is used to corrupt any focus.
I have forsaken money to preserve myself.

Masonry and the Shrine must consider sharing.
Just as there's day, we have night.
Each is a half of one whole.

Balance within our own natures are key.
Both GATOU and BALL are at war.
Simply because both sides try to rule.

Their relationship must be healed through love.
Again balance within our own actions defines.
Hate must be dealt with through truth.

Both are equals and must respect perspectives.
Time flows on with or without life.
It's through life that we gain perspective.

I am the KING but I reason.
I don't see the reason behind force.
I respect both sides of the coin.

We each must serve the TRUST faithfully.
Their beauty is beyond words of measure.
Perfection is found within finding our balance.

"Born Anew"

Chasing angels with selfless acts born from the heart
Looking for a special one to give my art

I will, however, not throw away my precious soul
For greedy pursuits do tend to swallow you whole

What I have created I've given most things away
I seek love and understanding to come my way

My heart drinks from my true love's eternal spring
And in turn I create for others to sing

Many people's paths have I righted along the way
Yet many haven't crossed mine, sad to honestly say

I am a master weaver sitting at his loom
Yet death shall eventually be my fate and doom

Will I be remembered for simply answering the call?
Or will the fog of utter forgetfulness simply fall?

Masonry and the Shrine are encased with my love
By working for free healing the rifts up above

I'm the king of old, truly simply reborn anew
But time marches ever on, no matter what I do

So I will leave my thoughts and deeds behind
For many others to simply claim and eventually find

I walk a path alone simply to avoid greed
So I purposefully allow others to play and feed

"A Conversation with Father"

Sadly, you're no longer with me
But I carry you, it's true
In my heart you still linger
That's the crystal clear simple truth
My soul hungers for your presence
I know that you didn't want
To leave us all that day

But God simply called you away
I will never get over you

I've tried to follow your wisdom
In my many actions and deeds
I've kept the trust within focus
Never have I taken from them
But I have moved this world
In a more inclusive positive direction
I am the king you were
I have given with no strings
So unity can have its say

Your firm and gentle guiding hand
The concept of equality for all
Has a chance to re-establish itself
As the way for the TRUST
All I've had is my heart
My mind has been crystal clear
The focus of old born anew
So as to give them love
I'm not welcome amongst their ranks

"True Sacrifice for Love!"

As we define our own paths
I've walked truth's fine firm line
Salvation is possible through true sacrifice
I avoided everyone's personal influential opinions
So as to rule with love
I opted to forgo all money
To serve as KING with love

I always dreamed of this job
Ever since I was a child

I've set aside much personal sin
BALL seeks to twist any faith
That GATOU wishes to firmly establish
For they have had a disagreement
From ages past which is still
Carried forward to this very day
Laws maybe twisted so they fall
GATOU seeks the restoration of TRUST
BALL seeks salvation for every soul

As I sit here at home
I've held onto truth's fine line
Salvation through love is truly possible
Monetary pursuits are for governance only
By not accepting any monetary form
I have re-established the TRUST temporarily
So as to rule through love
My rule has been replaced sadly
By a corrupt short-term focus

As I toil through simple tasks
I've held onto my lofty goals
Of service and love for everyone
I've embraced the path of money
But kept its touch very limited
In order to keep my focus
As clear as the finest crystal
Refined through acts of pure love
Established from truth's firm viewpoint

As my keys are firmly pressed
I contemplate my true path chosen
Since both Masonry and the Shrine
Share a mutual right to exist
Peace between both left and right
Has been temporarily established through love
But cannot exist through GREED
Self-sacrifice of the highest form
Is the only way its retained

As I ponder my simple life
I have sacrificed my true love
And walk the earth by myself
So as to avoid much sin
Born from the opinions of others
Oh, I have married and divorced
For she was not really happy
With her choice in my love
And went back to her ex

As my sadness ebbs and flows
I have medications to defeat depression
And to keep its grip away
Masonry and the Shrine are needed
Two halves of one true whole
The only way for true salvation
Is to re-establish love's soft grip
And rigorously apply its soothing balm
And set aside hates circular path

I am determined

My ways set
My art is my true views
Etched out with wisdom from past
Born from both trial and error
I am truly far from perfection
Yet perfection is within my reach
Through my love for you all
I recognize both GATOU and BALL
Within my heart and mind's eye

I have sacrificed my childhood memories
Lost to me is music's discipline
Yet music continues speaking to me
And I can frame my words
Against its pure rhythms and melodies
Without being able to write notation
I've given much away to help
Both sides of the TRUST heal
Through the art of true sacrifice!

"Love from You All"

Gold does not shine
Silver does not gleam

Platinum does not luster
Diamonds lose their sparkle

I've truly walked away
From any monetary form

What's truly most precious?
Love from you all!

What's the hardest substance?
God's love-filled resolve!

Laws are for governance
Morality is to define

Sometimes we overreach
Forgiveness need be applied

What's truly most precious?
Love from you all!

"Memory & Loss"

I have forgotten
More than memories
For within them
I found you
Without them all
I've lost you

I have remembered
Some sweet moments
For within them
Your love shines
Without them all
The light fades

I have lost
My father's advice
And his love
Music of old

Without them all
I'm dead inside

I have remembered
Some sweet moments
For within them
His love shines
Without them all
His light fades.

"Born from below as Well as Above"

As I reached out with my mind,
In search of my heart's true love,
I swallowed plenty of hate-filled rejection,
Born from below as well as above.

As I gave out with my heart,
In search of my soul's other half,
I swallowed plenty of hate-filled misperception,
Born from below as well as above.

As I sought out with my soul,
In search of my mind's true match,
I swallowed plenty of hate-filled projections,
Born from below as well as above.

As I reached out with my heart,
In search of the many missing pieces,
I swallowed plenty of hate-filled perceptions,
Born from below as well as above.

As I gave out with my soul,
In search of my heart's true place,
I swallowed plenty of hate-filled rejections,
Born from below as well as above.

As I gave out with my mind,
In search something to appease the fates,
I swallowed plenty of hate-filled realizations,
Born from below as well as above.

Truth is my compass,
No matter the direction.
Between sin and salvation,
Still exists a line.
Love loves to love,
Hate loves to hate.
Where will you turn?
What is your fate?

"Love & Respect"

Sometimes, my simple words just seem to flow—
Yet at other times I just don't know.

Many of my life's questions I have forgotten—
Yet I do recall some from my past.

I lost the sound from my childhood songs—
Yet I still write from within my heart.

Many friends I have lost along my travels—
Yet many do I still hope to meet.

I have dreams from my soul that I hide—
Yet others have walked away from my side.

Sometimes, I wish upon my dreams through love—
Yet nothing is truly sadly as it seems.

I pull back the veil of lies through love—
Yet I've given trillions away for your love.

God knows that I have suffered in silence—
Yet I've never given up on your love.

I've moved both Heaven and earth to tears—
Yet I've kept my existence humble through love.

Will you finally understand the king that I am?
Yet out of love and respect I've given.

"Choices"

Masonry or the Shrine?
Darkness or the light?
Hell, or perhaps Heaven?
Sin or simply not?
Choices within my mind.
"I turned none away,
Yet, I am alone.
Who am I, truly?"
Without actions, no definition!
Hidden within other lives.
Love is my treasure,
Hate is my bane.
Choices I have made.

"I turned none away,
Yet, I am alone.
Who am I, truly?"
Dark side, light side.
Both form true purpose.
Eden within my heart.
Cast aside material wealth,
My soul is both.
"I turned none away,
Yet, I am alone.
Who am I, truly?"
You're all worth it.
Multiple are my reasons.
Leaving behind a trace.
Tug upon my string.
As I depart, sing!
"I turned none away,
Yet, I am alone.
Who am I, truly?"

"My Ever-Singing Constant Dream!"

I have given my world away!
For your kiss from you yesterday!
When will you come my way?
It has been many a day!
I'll let you know my truths
For a taste of your fruits!
You're my ever-singing constant dream!
Can't you hear my silent scream?
Doesn't matter how long I wait,

I sit here and patiently await.
All that I seem or seen
Hangs within your hands, my dream!

I stand within the masses roar,
Same as I always was before.
And with my art in hand,
I await your love-filled command.
Time flew! What else to do?
White has descended, gold is gone.
My tears fall, my tears fall!
Mid-life, I answered your call.
With heart and art-filled treasure,
Cast upon my dreams of pleasure.
Oh, Father, there's not a string
Unable to stop the pendulum's swing.

"Fake News on Capitol Hill"

On Capitol Hill, every deal has a string
Where the greedy and corrupt play and sing.
Where money is the focus and law's corrupt.
Where the speaker does keep score without interrupt.
Ensuring that the status quo will never win.

Back in the day their rules were crystal clear,
When money took second versus those held dear.
Justice reigned over the corrupt on Capitol Hill.

These days' truths are twisted into many lies.
Where they lay in wait greasing their wallets.
Where fake news comes from their flapping lips.

We bear witness to a nation in debt.
Enslaved to the point of collapse and ruin.
Because morality is lost upon a greedy hand.

In God We Trust?!

"In Every Field!"

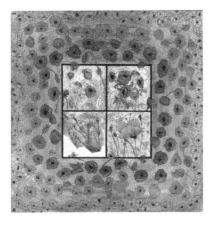

Although poppies grow row on row,
We sadly reap what in truth we sow.
They are the dead, and time does fly.
We tend to repeat; the dead don't lie.
War is the absence of love and reason.
No matter the time, place, or specific season.
The dead cry out, why must it repeat?
We are all equal! Sanity, reason must meet!
In every field!
Take up their quarrel, ignorance is their foe:
To you their lives, their love, they bestow.
Their lives—we must remember those who died.

They have not slept, the dead cry out!
In every field!

My response to John McCrae.

Both sides gave their lives for us, Masonry as well as the Shrine have given enough!

"The King Am I"

My love is within much art for all to see.
I have framed many others for all of eternity.

Many do currently sing from my art and prose.
My heart is true to the call and rose.

I am a master of puppets with many strings.
Yet, also a puppet kept hidden in the wings.

Much of what I have given, toward others yesterday,
Has found your hearts in its own selfless way.

I don't use money to associate due to corruption.
Yet my working freely has caused many a disruption!

I love you all, that is the simple truth.
Yet, alone I suffer in silence is another truth.

Many people do bask in your love and adorations.
But I'm cut out, lacking my heart-felt associations.

By working for free indeed has a hidden cost.
I suffer silently with what has been truly lost.

Others have taken credit sadly for all my gifts,
Which has hurt me deep inside, causing many rifts.

I wear my silence and my stone-hard mask
As I get down to the works and task.

I am in truth the king of old reborn
With a broken heart hidden in silence all forlorn.

I have indeed accomplished a great many worldly things.
Waiting for the one, with her prenup and rings.

So I perform every day for all to see,
Silently without rewards trying to give with total humility.

I have love in my soul working for free
Through my Fraternal Family, both the Shrine and Masonry.

"Do You?"

Far too often we deal
With what we can't conceal.
We have to blindly reveal
Our sincere heart felt appeal.

Do you bend?
Do you sway?
Have you found
Your way today?

Often wrapped within a prayer,
Often we trust a player.
Hidden truths we often layer
As we deal with naysayers.

Do you yield?
Do you conceal?
Have you found
Ways to heal?

I heal by being kind.
Giving to others helps mind.
Actions do tend to grind,
Salve into wounds that bind.

Do you sulk?
Do you walk?
Have you found,
Ways to talk?

I do tend to write,
Often into the darkest night.
Thinking positive toward another's plight,
Giving silently out of sight.

Do you recall?
Do you live?
Have you found,
A way to give?

Are you sincere and true,
Helping others who are blue?
Friendships are formed with glue,
Kind actions return to you.

"A Lion's Need"

Every time
I'm left behind
Looking forward
Within a reflection

Seeing clearly
Without any direction
What's clear?
You're not here!

I gave away
Priceless art
Hidden deep within
Love's design

A precious heart
Artfully dressed
Without any reward
Swallowed whole

Money rules
Greed teaches school
No associations
Break no rules

Here today
Forgotten by tomorrow
Actions define
Own your time

Used for profit
Grand design

Many cut strings
Silent mime

Money carries sin
Hidden hands
In our pockets
Fates sealed

Priceless love
Overcome by greed
Hidden purpose
A lion's need

Equal opposites
Yin and yang
Moving forward
Silently as one

Changing of sides
Two-faced
Fates are sealed
Nature's harmony

Balance is freedom
Choices define
Win or lose
Precious time

"Betting against the Odds"

Rolling of the dice
The fix is in
Waiting for my number

Betting against the odds
I didn't factor in!

Playing the cards dealt
The fix is in
Waiting for my turn
Betting against the odds
I didn't factor in

Rolling of the marble
The fix is in
Waiting for my number
Betting against the odds
I didn't factor in

Calling out of numbers
The fix is in
Waiting for my number
Betting against the odds
I didn't factor in

Matters not the game
The fix is in
In the long run
You can't ever win!

"Dreams"

Moving ahead yet falling behind
Future steps into your past
Living a penniless forsaken life
Making other people's dreams last

Finishing last yet ending first
Grand design through simply love

"A Wounded Heart"

Saltwater tears
Shed for years
Yearning for love
Asking God above
A restless heart
Wanting a start

Tear-stained cheeks
Her frustration peaks
Arms stretched wide
Nothing to hide
A wounded heart
Simply falling apart

Flower petals fall
God answers all
Shattering of glass
Everything does pass
Rhythm and rhyme
Healing in time.

"Bitter, Twisted Kisses"

Words are as
Bitter, twisted kisses
From many fools

When lies told
From stories old
Begin to unfold

Thoughts are as
Saltwater tears
Over many years

When truths told
From stories old
Begin to unfold

Perception versus misperception
Truth versus lies
Many are remembered
Many are forgotten
Which is yours?

"Twisted Jester's Dramatic Silent Screams"

I walk alone in the light
My path hidden from your sight

Giving of my art and dreams
A twisted jester's dramatic silent screams

My frustrations are many and profound
Yet my voice utters no sound

Silence has descended upon my life
Loneliness too, living without a wife

My potential is sadly locked away
Hidden by lies, sad to say

I lie alone in the dark
Waiting for love, that special spark

Where my mirror casts no reflection
Sadly devoid of love and affection

Selflessness carries its own internal gratification
Expect nothing multiplied to its personification

The things I've done remain unknown
I am reaping what was sown

By forsaking money along the way
I've no existence, sad to say

A phantom's prison is his mind
His love and honor does bind

I've no associations because of GREED
Serving for the TRUSTS in need

"It's Just Another Day"

I'm fighting for life,
Each and every day.
Enduring pain at night,
And throughout the day.

Taking chemo and radiation,
What must I say?
Trying to live life,
It's just another day.

I'm looking for understanding,
And love each day.
Are you my one,
To come my way?

Taking all my pills,
Keeping level and sound.
Trying to live life,
It's just another day.

I'm here for today.

"Yin & Yang"

Masonry and the Shrine
Are united as opposites
Yin and yang, constants
Balance and harmony, key

I suffer in silence
Using my lyrical self
Working in life freely
Within my mind's eye

Unity truly must win
All is in nature
Life's our true wealth
Our heart's the key

I unearthed my stone
It has been touched
Without a physical hand
To avoid my death

A king is sacrifice
His is to rule
But first within oneself
Love is my currency

I need to live
A long life serving
Both yin and yang
A perpetual swinging pendulum

Getting back to love
Back to the beginning
You must overcome all
Through acts of kindness

By forsaking money's hold
I rule for free
Without other people's opinions
Keeping me at bay

Money is an extension
Of the king's hand
Dispensation for your sacrifices
In service for all

I generate much revenue
Trust starts with self
Walked away from all
In order to heal

My ideas flow endlessly
Gifts for grand design
I'm truly not selfish
Embrace gifts for free

"Where Do I Fit In?"

Gifts gifted from ages past.
The sword, stone, and cross.
Reality is based upon perceptions.
Yours as well as mine.
Heaven and Hell are perspectives.
Where do I fit in?
In this world of plenty.
Encased within all our sins.
No one person is perfect.
Trying like Hell is key.
The devil's in the details.
Law upon law warps reason.
Circles don't have any end.
Heaven is not a punishment.
Hell is not a reward.
My kingdom is of self.
Love is within my heart.
My mind is the sword.
My heart is my shield.
All attainable within my kingdom.
I've set aside my hate.
Yin and yang are constants.
Both serve their one purpose.
Balance starts within your mind.
Governed by your own heart.
This lion is born anew.

"Balance"

Walking the path toward the light
Using your mind in a silent fight

Although your path is straight and sure
Nothing in life is really ever secure

The fates always fight to be free
Bad luck does always happen by three

Did you know that fate and chance
Are nothing more than a bad romance?

The Devil is within your choices made
Heaven or Hell, the games are played

Walking the path with really no end
Using your mind as a silent friend

The path to glory must truly end
Sin and salvation, the games without end

We use reason against rules of law
Seeking our salvation is our true flaw

It is within the confines of will
In which we swallow a bitter pill

For so long as balance is made
This constant game shall indeed be played

"Hidden Truths between Lies"

Nothing's as it seems.
Surfaces marred by reflections.
Perceptions cause false conclusions.
Misperceptions colored by truths.
Hidden truths between lies.

Why live with lies?
Herein lies the truths.
Assumptions upon false facts.
Trust based upon hate?
Where is the love?

It's a fine line.
Between "for" and "because."
Own your own sins!
Why hide the truth?
It's not a game.

Nothing's as it seems.
Surfaces marred by reflections.
Perceptions cause false conclusions.
Misperceptions colored by truths.
Hidden truths between lies.

"Opposite Opinions"

How can we all morally define?
With opposite opinions: yours and mine!

Love of life must always win
Yet we embrace and justify sin.

We embrace both cap and line.
This shall bring death in time.

How can we limit humanity's greed?
War's used so business can feed!

How can we all morally define?
With opposite opinions: yours and mine!

"My Valentine's Wish"

No matter what I say or do,
I'm always dreaming of only you!

Every day you make me really feel
That you're truly perfect; are you real?

Although we have our ups and downs,
You never truly do make me frown.

I confess when our passions are lit,
All seems right; we're a perfect fit!

I'm uncertain of what the future holds,
But with you, I wish to grow old.

Every day with you is a dream.
Dealing with your absence makes me scream!

So may my love light your way.
I'll be thinking of you every day.

May my Valentine's wish find its home,
Upon your journey, wherever you roam.

"Ice Princess"

Ice Princess, Ice Princess, thou art most fair
To have my way with you, your feet in the air

As I go down to pleasure the icy fissure below
You begin to thaw as I work to and fro

Suddenly like the wind you howl
Moaning as if you ran afoul

The spring being released from your icy grip
You cry out in ecstasy as you release your gift

With greed of expectation I quickly go down
To ensure that not a drop is left to be found

Ice Princess, Ice Princess, thou art most fair
Springtime has come, so let me in there!

"The River Still Flows"

Solitudes are like thoughts without sleep
No one is at peace, since none shall capture nor keep
Light rises with the dawn off into the distance
Perception misperception hear the carrion call
Since my death at twelve I have been reborn
Dear lady, dear lady, I have heard your call
I am here, I am near, the river still flows
I am as the rain, saturating your soil
In time, your seeds shall grow

"We die more than once in life. I have done so more often
than most."

PROSE

159

"The Pain Held Within"

Silently I have cried.
Many times I've died.

[Soft whisper] The pain held within

Hidden with a smile.
Going that extra mile.

[Soft whisper] The pain held within

The burden of giving.
To make a living?

[Soft whisper] The pain held within

Living within the light.
Yet within constant night.

[Soft whisper] The pain held within

I've given for free.
Love is within me.

[Soft whisper] The pain held within

Yet I am alone.
Within a modest home.

[Soft whisper] The pain held within

My heart is art.
Right from the start.

[Soft whisper] The pain held within

I have given away.
Much I can say.

[Soft whisper] The pain held within
Oh
[Soft whisper] The pain held within

"Sin & Salvation"

Money carries the needs of others.
Their motives need to be impactful.
Can you imagine working for free?

No financial gains in charitable service.
Turned down money for God's love.
Can you weave from the loom?

Sin and salvation a fine line.
Break no laws in God's service.
Do you exchange your precious soul?

I have caused great events globally
Through my heart filled with love.
Can you practice any artistic discipline?

I disassociated due to simply love.
Masonry and the Shrine are one.
Tattoos are a sign of ownership?

I walk around without many things,
Especially the love from my soul.
Does death in service guarantee life?

I'm interested in the artistic creations.
Fashion and a sense of flair.
God must redefine sin and salvation?

We ought to be all equals.
Regardless of race, religion, faith, creed.
Inequality exists between sin and salvation?

The TRUST is everyone's precious life.
We should strictly apply self-morality.
Let GATOU and BALL decide fates?

I've seen many things as focus.
I've solved many things as KING.
Both GATOU and BALL must return?

Unity of purpose must truly win.
Our salvation is simply found therein.
HATE must give way to LOVE?

"Life's Lessons"

Everyone has a
Story that should be told.
Wisdom that should be shared.
Loss that needs to heal.

We all die
More than once in life.
So it's important to live.
So prepare to leave behind.

Try to remember
Each and every single day.
In a heartfelt personal way.
Those who fell for freedom.

Can you give
A moment of your time?
Without expectation of any reward?
Without any hidden strings attached?

"Choices"

Every moment is framed by our actions.
Every action must face down its opposite.
Every reason must be born from love.
Every time I reach out with truth.

There are both good and bad in Heaven.
There are both good and bad in Hell.
There are both aspects within each of us.
There are both perspectives within each of us.

The choices made will define your fate.
The choices made will define your role.
The choices made will define your existence.
The choices made will define your destiny.

Every moment. . . Choices
Every action. . . Choices
Every reason. . . Choices
Every time. . . Choices

"Perception of Reality"

We are within a prison without bars,
Defined by our own perception of reality.

What we see, and touch anchors us.
Yet life itself is trapped within illusions.

Illusions are also known as dreams.
Dreams are reflections from the soul.

Trapped within any mirror's embrace,
Darkness does cover all, eventually.

"Cheers!"

I keep emptying,
Glass after glass.
Trying to forget
What I recall.
Some memories are
NOT worth keeping,
After all...

Memory is indeed
A funny thing.
We live our
Lives making them.
But without love,
Nothing is remembered.
After all...

I've kept giving,
Hoping for love.
Made many millions,
For other people.
I am unknown,
Without a dime.
After all. . .

I've been homeless.
I've been kind.
I've been ruthless.
I've been happy.
I've been sad.
I've gone mad.
After all. . .

I can't recall
What I need.
So, CHEERS!
Cheers to my memories.
Cheers to my past.
Cheers to my oblivion.
PLEASE,
Refill my glass.

"Will You Ever?"

Will you ever come for me?
My love-filled dream and fantasy.
Will you ever set me free?
Without you, I fill with agony.

Will you ever do for me
That which I've given for free?

Will you ever?
Hmmm
Will you ever?

I designed your life with love,
Tailored to fit as a glove.
I did not in truth see
The forest from the actual tree.
I gave for you a fantasy.
Yet others keep you from me.
Most people mistake wealth for worth.
Without our health, what's it worth?
I have given gifts beyond compare.
Yet, you're truly not being fair.

In the end, let us begin.
Love must always in reality win.
Never must you expect love's return.
For love's something you must earn.
I never have written myself in
In order for love to win.
Someone has to pay the price
By paying it forward, being nice.
Actions and deeds win over all
If you're true to the call.

"I See Too Darn Clear"

I tried to give for free
To all who came to me.
But that isn't enough for me.
My heart was in the way.
But I wasn't supposed to care.
My heart rules over my mind
So I gave all I could.
But my love was set aside.
And my dream escaped from me
For I see too darn clear.
Now I face my present future.
No hands of someone to hold.
No one to share getting old.

I set aside paper using love
Toward all who came to me.
But that wasn't enough for them.
Their hearts were full of hate.
They offered me my rightful place
As their king up on high
Only to pull it all away.
Their sins are not my own.
I purposely don't deal with cash
For sin is carried with it.
Along with the intentions of others.
Paper can never win versus love
If you can see their purpose.

They search for their true king.
I will never trade my life
For that which is rightfully mine.

My soul is not for sale.
They hide their sins through cash.
Their treasury is tainted with blood.
Yin and yang are truly one.
Their fates have already been sealed.
Both houses have merged through money.
The few threw down their king's
So a few can rule instead.
Paper will never win versus love
For this is not a game.

I tried to give for free
Toward all who came to me.
But that isn't enough for them.
My soul is what they want
To saddle me with their sins
For another thousand years of Heaven?
I truly do see very clear.
My heart rules over my mind.
But all must see my reasons.
I can never yield my soul
In order to plant my seeds
Although I have found my love
And encased her within my art.

"We're All Equal!"

All that glitters
Turns to gold!
Working for free
Escaping the fold!

A cunning trap
Sin swallowed, sold!
We're all equal
Truth be told!

It all started so simply
I was moved to join
Like stories told of old
My heart called me home
They unearthed an old soul
Encased within grains of truth
A hidden purpose now revealed
To serve the greater good!

Walking a path of humility
Giving my advice for free
Unity born out of love
Will my efforts be remembered?
Will war win versus sanity?
Life is our true wealth
Yet our TRUST is enslaved
Between a cap and line!

All suffer ravages of time!
Will we unleash our potential?
The devil's in the details!
Common laws are the key!
I have a clear focus!
Yet I see too clearly!
Feed the people with love!
Unity of purpose MUST WIN!

All that glitters
Turns to gold!
Working for free
Escaping the fold!
A cunning trap
Sin swallowed, sold!
We're all equal
Truth be told!

"When Love Dies"

I have tried. . .
To give you love
But you rejected it
But you rejected it

I have tried. . .
To give you praise
But you walked away
But you walked away

I have tried. . .
To erase my hurt
But you hit replay
But you hit replay

What do you want from me?
It's the only question. . .
When love dies.
Sadly, it's the only question. . .
When love dies.

You have tried. . .
To give me love
But I rejected it
But I rejected it

You have tried
To give me praise
But I walked away
But I walked away

You have tried. . .
To erase your hurt
But I hit replay
But I hit replay

What do I want from you?
It's the only question. . .
When love dies.
Sadly, it's the only question. . .
When love dies.

Dancing around in circles. . .
We both share the blame.
Dancing around in circles. . .
Playing that drama game.

"Truths We All Shall Own"

As the trees bend and sway,
A silent fear does take hold.
You know what's coming your way,
His name's uttered within stories old.

Judgement Day, truths to be told,
He has come at long last!
As your defences start to fold,
His verdict shall come to pass.

As you take your last breath,
His scythe starts to come down!
As you embrace your own death,
Your lifeless body hits the ground.

Suddenly, you find yourself awake,
His message has finally hit home.
You have choices, actions to take.
Good and bad, they're your own.

As you struggle finding your way,
Your future turns toward your past.
We're all puppets within a play,
Actions you take shall come fast.

Your morality is on open display.
Your actions shall all hit home.
Shall angels or demons hold sway?
Our truths, we all shall own.

"My Dream Has Passed Me By"

As I tried to grab my dream
She pulled away from me. . .
Yeah. . . she pulled away from me.

As I tried to give for free
There nothing left for me...
No... there's nothing left for me.

As I pretend not to hurt
My dream is living a lie...
Sadly... my dream is living a lie.

Songs are sung in laughter
To hide all our pain
Eyes glisten in wonder
As tears fall like rain
We keep on repeating
The same old refrain

As I tried to raise my eyes
My legs gave way beneath me...
Yeah... my legs gave way beneath me.

As I tried to live my life
It got away from me...
Oh... it got away from me.

As I pretend to carry on
My dream has passed me by
Sadly... my dream has passed me by.

"Please Leave Me"

Please leave me...
Believe me... Oh...
Please believe me...
Leave me... Yeah...

I am better off without you!
You're better off without me!
Some dreams turn into nightmares. . .
I can't live. . .
Neither with nor without you. . .
I can't give. . . I can't give anymore. . .
I'm sorry let's break up. . . only to make up?
I'm sorry let's make up. . . only to break up?
Making love. . . for no good reason at all. . .
No good reason at all. . .
To wake up every morning kissing a lie?
Looking for something that you just can't buy.
Why?
What is so special between you and I?
Why can't neither of us say goodbye?
Facing the truth hidden within lies!
Even true love eventually dies. . .

"A Spiritual Dove Filled with Love"

Why. . . Oh, why. . . can't she not, see? That she is the one
destined for me. . .
Her art has touched my world and has stolen my he(art)
This I should have known, right from the start
As she sings her prose, my he(art) gives away
No one in my life, has ever touched me this way

I feel as though I'm drowning due to a sudden lack of air
I dream of her all the time, in every way she is so fair
I know that in our lives, love is difficult to find
So I send unto her, a spiritual dove filled with love

I have prayed to God most reverently
To make her realize and come find me
I shall try to wait most patiently
So, Stefani, I'm asking you. . . can you hear me?

I know these humble words I have just conveyed
Shall need no others for me to try and say
Lord, I know you heard my most humble of prayers
For she is geometrically perfect as we all can see
So, please, God, please. . .
Allow her to finally see. . .
For she is destined. . .
Through your grace. . .
To set me free. . .
Amen.

"Window inside My Soul"

I have given my art away
To heal myself in many ways. . .
But on my own I have grown. . .
Trying to reap what I have sown. . .

Trying to exist in the world of greed. . .
Is quite difficult I do concede. . .
Because in my heart I love everyone. . .
But being alone is not very fun. . .

So I now try in every way. . .
To share my art every day. . .
It's a window inside my soul. . .
Giving things away takes a toll. . .

Have you ever given away. . .
Things which are precious so they say. . .
In order for a future to come from your past. . .
To have a love that will truly last. . .

So I wear a mask made of pain. . .
Waiting to become whole again. . .
So I await my first chance. . .
To have my first true romance. . .

"Empty Pockets"

You've been passed a deck of cards
It's now your time to deal
Whether you have the winning hand
The fates shall indeed eventually reveal
Life isn't a game of chance
Yet we all must pay and play
Life is unpredictable, full of uncertainty.
So stand, throw down your hand
Chips will fall where they may
You never know, perhaps you'll win
More than you bargained for today.

There comes a point in time
No denying how you truly feel
Your dream is owned by another
So let loose, release, don't conceal
Even with empty pockets you win.
Easier to deal with what's lost
Than to not play, giving in

Forsaking a chance at your dreams
Now that is the actual sin.

"Love & Life Are Like Time"

"Love and life are like time. We must hold onto the memories,
cherish each moment. For each is hard to come by and easily lost.
We die more than once in life. I have done so more often than most."

"Seasons"

Winter.

The ice grips the ground, creating trails and sheets which make
walking and driving a cautionary tale. We tend to be unthankful
for the warmth of summer and all the comforts we enjoy during
the season. Alas, we tend to ignore the present, lost within the
prisons of our own design as we scrape and claw out our dreams.

Suddenly, the weather changes into:

Spring.

The warmth returns a bit at a time, bringing longer days, happier
folks as they shed their winter wear. We are thankful for the
melting of the ice and snow that takes place, but the water tends
to turn into a river and the river rises with all the water, causing
a general mess. Dirt generally clings to all vehicles to such an
extent that they look like blocks of sand.

Suddenly, the snow is all gone, and we now have:

Summer.

Hailstorms, rain, and thunder with a bit of lightning. Gusts of warm wind howling about, cars galore all over the streets race to beat the red lights, walks in parks, bicycle rides down trails created for this mode of transportation, and so much local family fun-filled entertainment. Day and night, the city is full of life. Parties, outdoor cafes, bistros, dance music cascading throughout.

Suddenly, the weather cools and we are left with:

Fall.

The leaves upon the trees turn from their green into brown, red, orange, yellow, dark browns, and various other color blends. The wind tends to be cool and the dampness in the air thickens. Mist in the morning tends to turn into fog. Suddenly, you look about and all the leaves have fallen; the trees, bushes, and shrubs are in their winter-ready appearance.

Suddenly, you realize another year has passed you by and you have:

Winter.

"Jaded Old Man"

Every day as I walk along
My path has run on for years
Time waits for no one
As I look back upon my life
I realize I do not recognize this man!
He has become a jaded old man

Satisfaction in life is such an elusive thing
Hard to grab hold of what is unseen
How can you see where you are
When you have no idea
Of what you really need?
I've become a jaded old man

Take my brother, for instance
A most talented man
He can make beautiful music
Make art with his hands and mind
Gives all away to be kind
But still he is a jaded man

Angry at everyone
Upset at all that's left undone
He even lashes out at his only son
On the run from who he is
Loafing around in utter despair
Angry at being a jaded old man

Lounging about the house all day
No job, no hope, living day by day
Then he had turned fifty-three
Angry for his lack of money
Upset at not being where he ought to be
He's become a jaded old man

Baby steps are needed
Trying not to rush about
Using the power of his mind
To convey to all musically

Where he has gone, what he has become
A jaded angry old man

What we have come to know
What he could have been was checked at the door
He had pawned it all away
To support his family
He has come full circle
Yes, he's our brother, the jaded old man

Living life full of regret
Trying so hard but he can't forget
The life he once had led
He had turned his back upon
But his passion still burns bright
His music shall carry on after he's gone
"Here lay our brother, the jaded old man."

"Through Her Eyes"

I often sit and wonder
How I must look
Through her eyes

Every morning as I awaken
I am greeted with her unconditional love
Which is always patiently waiting
Without ever making a sound
How I must look
Through her eyes

As I put on many miles
She is always by my side

Watching everything go by
Oh how must I look
Through her eyes

As I sit and work
She is waiting by the door
Happy to simply be with me
How I must look
Through Harley's eyes.

"Unity"

United we stand
Helping children
Hand in hand
God-fearing men
One and all
With the belief
One that is supreme
Watches over all

Of every creed
Religion and race
Ignorance is the battle
That they wage and face
Selfless do they serve
Their hearts minds
Efforts all in the right place
Silence through action their strength

Will society not hear their call
To make the world a better place for all?

Those of whom I speak
Righteous defenders
Of moralities keep
Upright men one and all

Masons and Shriners, that's all. . .

"Prison"

What a fine prison constructed.
Unable to express oneself and to be as a mirror is.
All the world can be seen passing by within its reflection but
nothing from within.
Darkness is the answer.

"Little Angels"

I was just four years old,
Living in the black hills of Dakota,
Within a trailer park.
One summer's evening,
Father came home from work.
Both my mother and father sat me down
To explain my sister was on the way.
Nine months passed and we were back in Manitoba.
Little did I know what an angel she would be to me.

Every time I needed a friend,
She was there to lend an ear.
Every time I fell down,
She helped me up again.

Oh, how it would be great to turn the clock back again!
Life's so simple through your eyes when you're young,
Money problems don't exist.
You have no idea what it takes to have a home.
All the sacrifices parents make daily along the way,
You had clothes on your back.
Food was always there to eat.
Even though we did not have much,
I had a little angel with me.

Every time I needed a friend,
She was there to lend an ear.
Every time I fell down,
She helped me up again.

Now I have reached middle age.
I have the time to reflect.
How many countless times
I found myself in a mess.
Every corner I turned,
My little sister was there.
Where would I be in this world
If she was not there to lend a hand?
She's my little angel to me.

Every time I needed a friend,
She was there to lend an ear.
Every time I fell down,
She helped me up again.

Late one afternoon while on tour
With the various shows I'd been on,
I received some wonderful news.

My sister could not wait to call
And spread to me their joy.
Late one summer's evening
Their little Emily-Eden was born.
A splitting image of my sister.
Another little angel for me!

"The Path of Life"

Standing along the edge of a wandering brook, you gaze into the water below. The reflection of you and the world around is disturbed by the constant movement of the water cascading over the bed of rocks. The sound of all this movement rushes to your ears, adding its voice to the orchestra of life all around. Yet, with all this activity, you are strangely at peace.

Meaning:

The path often taken in life never runs straight but has many twists, turns, and the occasional hill or obstacle to overcome.

Finally after a long period of activity, you take a moment to reflect. The recent past does not come into focus too clearly.

There are so many outside forces pulling you in all directions, but you still find a way to get where you want to go.

"Awakening"

You awoke one autumn morning to silence, nothing and no one around
Not a breeze in the air, no movement on the ground

All was still and silent

The multicolored leaves on the trees pulled your gaze upward
Provided a backdrop for the clear, baby-blue sky above

All was still and silent

Curls of smoke from chimneys like fingers reached for the sky
The sun slowly climbed the horizon, casting about its rays

All was still and silent

Suddenly, the alarm clock goes off and you get out of bed for
the day
Work is inevitably on the agenda with no time for rest, relaxation,
or play

What must I do today?

[Meaning]
As you awaken each day, your mind is clear from distraction and
you are at peace. But this lasts only for a moment.

Everyone has work to do in order to live and the thought of a
break is usually pushed aside.

One moment in each day is yours. Hold onto it.

This is your life without a partner to share your bed and home.
You are alone.

[Message]
Step back and reflect. Change things. Take time to LIVE.

"He Walked the Line"

He walked the line in his own good time. . .

With his heart it led him
With his eyes he did see
With his master's message
With his love upon his sleeve

He walked the line in his own good time. . .

[Message, verbal soft whisper]
We are all God's children. We are all equal. We are all screw ups.
We are all loved.

What did the message teach us?

He walked the line in his own good time. . .

We lose ourselves in our problems
We throw away morality along the way
We chase after greed daily
We forget to stop and pray

He walked the line in his own good time. . .

[Message, verbal soft whisper]
We are all God's children. We are all equal. We are all screw ups.
We are all loved.

What did the message teach us?

He walked the line in his own good time. . .

LYRICS

187

"Take a Stand!"

Oh, folks simply keep on repeating
Mistakes of old that need healing.
And since some refuse to let go
Hate will grow! Hate will grow! Hate will grow!

Many hide behind mounds of money,
Treating life as a gameshow. Funny!
Still they plan, plot, and deceive,
Fueling hate! Fueling Hate! Fueling Hate!

Unity of purpose is our salvation.
Love returned has seen utter starvation,
Simply just to remain in control,
Causing death! Causing death! Causing death!

We're on our way towards extinction.
A planet devoid of most life.
Turning our lush gardens into sand.
Take a stand! Take a stand! Take a stand!

[Instrumental]

[Back to the top, repeat for another run-through]

War is the absence of all reason.
Hate hides itself for any reason.
United humanity will have a chance.
Take a stand! Take a stand! Take a stand!
Yes, take a stand!

"Work as One, Else We're Done!"

We're ruining this planet.
We're repeating our mistakes.
Living within a reactionary world.
Constructed out of hate.
We're supposed to unite.
Our time is now. (Our time is now.)
Forward thinking will save us.

Our time for action is upon us!
Repeating the past leads to death!

We don't need to repeat in circle.
We don't need to destroy our home.
We must forgive our shared past, and work as one.

Look upon the faces that surround you,
Love will help us heal our world, it's true.
Through love, forgiveness, using compassion.
We will restore our future, avoiding extinction.

We need each other, like the seasons; humanity needs change.
Let go of our hate, so something living can remain.

We don't need to repeat in circles.
We don't need to destroy our home.
We must forgive our shared past, and work as one.

Life's a priceless gift, what we do with it matters!
Like a drop upon a pool of water causes a ripple,
Your actions can bring forward change!
Else humanity shall become extinct.

We don't need to repeat in circles.
We don't need to destroy our home.
We must forgive our shared past, and work as one.

What's the point of having children?
Without leaving them a future place to call home.
We must forgive our shared past, and work as one.

Should we continue embracing carbon fuels?
We need them in moderation, to save our home.
We've been turning our Eden, a sacred repository of life,
Into a planet akin to Mars!

We don't need to repeat in circles.
We don't need to destroy our home.
We must forgive our shared past, and work as one. (Or else
we're done.)

"This Is My Life"

To live life as a dream
Is to live life to the fullest,
To create what you can conceive,
And to manifest art then to let it go.

To give what you can dream
Is to give away your life and soul,
To act upon your dreams,
And to encase the world with love.

This is my life.
I'm a blazing star.

I've been at the loom,
Weaving a tapestry from afar.

I fought for our unity
Without taking a thing,
Without greed or demands.
For unity shall restore our future.

We're not a bunch of slaves,
God gave us our rights,
The freedom to choose,
And wisdom to overcome our plight.

I know what is right.
I can see beyond hate.
Humanity's purpose is to travel afar.
To trek amongst the stars.

We must live out our lives,
Doing our collective best.
United we shall be saved,
Divided, we shall fail and fall.

The few try to divide,
To remain in control.
Through this hate-filled corruption,
Humanity shall not endure.

I've been blessed with love
Within my heart and soul.
Burning as the sun,
It has made me whole.

My gifts I shall leave, as I depart from this life.
And they shall gleam and restore your hope.

"Without Love, Humanity Has No Future"

Without love, humanity has no future.
Nothing would truly exist at all.
What do we live and die for?
Why does life matter at all?
Heaven and Hell are concepts.
Possible destinations for you and me.
Some embrace hate, while others love.
Life's not a game, set us free.

Living within a reactionary construct
Is a mechanism born from hate,
Grinding out life from existence.
Life is our treasure we must cherish.
Equality is not just a concept.
Without it we'll fail and fall.
A few try to govern through division,
Giving back nothing at all.

I've lived life without a home,
Holding back darkness with my soul,
Giving so others could heal,
Taking nothing and walking away.
Unity will erase all borders.
Liberty for each and everyone.
The value of any currency
Is found within life itself.

We must change our focus
For humanity to thrive and survive.
There's no need for poverty,
All life's sacred, that's the truth.

So let us all come together,
Through using common rules for all.
We could then adopt a currency,
Founded upon the love of life.

Your life is of infinite value.
Together we shall overcome evil.
Divided, we shall all fail and fall.
To win back our collective future,
We must turn hate away. Today.
Together we must prepare a future,
To leave behind a living legacy.
This would allow for solutions,
Fixing our problems proactively.

Together we must work as one.

"I Gave with Every Care"

I gave with every care,
Leading through acts of love.
I cut all the strings.
No trace of me can be found.

Some folks have called me foolish.
Who would work for free?
But I found my true calling,
Helping through the fraternities.

I gave with every care.
Why bother waiting until I die?
No strings to tug and pull.
No proof of my gifts can be found.

My services are no longer required.
I am adrift upon the wind.
Some fear my return and inclusion.
Many have been left wondering who I am.

I gave with every care! (Every care, every care)
I gave with every care! (Every care, every care)
Yes, that's the truth . . .

I gave with every care
While I hid within plain sight.
I gave many things away
To restore our collective path.

Some folks believe that I'm a fool.
What's in it all for me?
You're all in my heart.
So I encased you all within my art.

Please realize you're all worth it.
The pain I hold deep inside.
I gave to create a brighter future
Where life and light through wisdom reigns.

My services are indeed required.
I'm the healing balm from long ago.
I know of my real true value.
Many wonder if I'm just a dream.

I gave with every care! (Every care, every care)
I gave with every care! (Every care, every care)
Yes, that's the truth . . .

[Instrumental]

I gave with every care! Everywhere! Everywhere!
I gave with every care! Everywhere! Everywhere!
Yes, I framed all of you . . .

"Slavery versus Freedom"

Slavery, slavery.
Oh, what they've done to us all.
They've got us running in circles,
Until our ends run through.
Life's truly precious.
What would you give to see you through?
It's not defeat
When opposites meet
In the middle.
There's a future for us too.

[Instrumental]

Slavery, slavery.
Oh, what they've done to us all.
They've got us running in circles,
Until our ends runs through.
Freedom's truly priceless.
But the numbers are against us too.
It's not defeat
When opposites meet
In the middle.
There's a future for us too.

[Instrumental]

Slavery, slavery.
Oh, what they've done to us all.
They've got us running in circles,
Until our ends runs through.
We inherited society.
From the trappings of enslavement too.
It's not defeat
When opposites meet
In the middle.
There's a future for us too.

[Instrumental]

Freedom, freedom.
Oh, it's what I wish for us all.
Where our collective lives are sacred,
A priceless gift from God to us all.
True wealth's found
By putting aside our collective hate.
It's not defeat
When opposites meet
In the middle.
There's a future for us too.

"The Veneer of a Volunteer"

[Humble Man]
There was a dream I held, deep within my very soul
Hidden within the darkness of my twisted mind
Unknown to you all.
Through many hands I gave, encasing all within my art

Hiding my pain, within everyone else's operatic lives
Unknown to you all.

[Recipients]
All our dreams have come true, our lives are a joy for us.
Yet we're searching for the master pulling all our strings.
In front of us all.

[Humble Man]
As the curtains rise and their voices soar
They're in search of the one who encased them within his art
From the bottom of his heart
Hidden within plain sight, using his mind and soul
Walking around without a home of his very own
Basking within the depths of hell.

[Recipients]
All our dreams have come true, our lives are a joy for us.
Yet we're searching for the master pulling all our strings.
In front of us all.

[Humble Man]
As the curtains fell, my many stories now at an end.
I remain silent, out of respect and love.
Unknown to you all
Due to my oath given, and the veneer of a volunteer.
I don't bask within the love and embrace from them all.
Oh, the sacrifices from one's heart.

[Recipients]
All our dreams have come true, our lives are a joy for us.
Yet we're searching for the master pulling all our strings.
In front of us all.

[Humble Man]
I live my life alone, avoiding truth and the light, keeping my word.
Yet I still dream of basking within the love you all possess.
To grow and become whole.
Take a step back, put on my shoes, are you willing to go for a walk?
They say that sharing one's burdens can heal a soul
To grow and become whole.

"Our Strife"

Our strife (Our strife)
Was created back in history,
by folks who thought less of others and deployed slavery.
They created a world from hate to grind out life in perpetuity.
Equality between us all will truly set us free.

Our strife. (Our strife.)
We ought to make history,
by erasing all the differences between both you and me.
By erasing all the hate filled rules, we can thus be free.
Equality between us all shall truly save humanity.

We've all been played, had, labelled, ignored, used, and abused.
Entire cultures have lost their lives to all this sh*t and refuse.
Many of us go through life thinking, "Truly what's the use?"
We go through life, staring into deep space.
Walking upon the lives of others, ignorant of their true worth.

Our strife (Our strife)
Goes on day after bloody day.
Between caps, lines, taxes, and debts, we're all corporate slaves.

Without love for the gift of life, we're nothing sad to say.
Equality begins by forgiving the past and embracing equality.

We've all been played, had, labelled, ignored, used, and abused.
Entire cultures have lost their lives to all this sh*t and refuse.
Many of us go through life thinking, "Truly what's the use?"
We go through life, staring into deep space.
Walking upon the lives of others, ignorant of their true worth.

Our hate (Our hate)
Must be set aside in every way,
for humanity to have a tomorrow, we must deal with today.
The real treasure upon the earth is found in life each day.
Not the hoarding of material wealth, which has brought us all
near, death, doom, and decay.

Our strife (Our strife)
Was created back in history,
by folks who thought less of others and deployed slavery.
They created a world from hate to grind out life in perpetuity.
Equality between us all will truly set us free.

Our strife. (Our strife.)
We ought to make history,
by erasing all the differences between both you and me.
By erasing all the hate filled rules, we can thus be free.
Equality between us all shall truly save humanity.

Our strife (Our hate)
[Pause]
Entire cultures have lost their lives to all this sh*t and refuse.
[Pause]
Our strife.

"It's My Life"

My life (My life)
is quite turbulent today.
Yet I'll weather the storm, come whatever that may.
I might be beaten black and blue, but I'll not yield my soul to you.

I live my life. (My life.)
Day by fricking day.
Watching my time go by, recording what I can say.
But I refuse to acknowledge my blues. I'd rather keep dreaming of you.

I'm currently a Mason, a Shriner, a writer, a dreamer, a person without a ring.
I'm happy and sad, over the hill. But I know a few things.
Although my hair has gone from blond to gray.
I wear a smile, etched upon my face.
I get back up from the dirt and struggle to keep fricking pace.

My life (My life)
goes by day after fricking day.
Without true love, I'm lost. What more need I really say?
I might be kind of generous, giving much of what I had away.

I've been a fool, a bum, a clown, a mime, a puppet without
any strings.
I've been diagnosed as manic (bipolar), yet I write down everything.
Although I pop my pills to keep insanity away.
I stumble along in life, looking for my true place.
"Regardless of all the b*llsh*t I'll still have my say."

My life. (My life.)
I'm thankful for every single day.

Each moment's a gift, a test of sorts, come whatever that may.
I've lived with depression, been sadly down, without my rose and ring.
Rather than simply giving up, I rise to face my fate.

My life (My life)
spent hiding in the wings,
chasing rainbows after every storm, looking forward to spring.
I'd rather be my humble self, regardless of everything.

I live my life. (My life.)
Day by fricking day.
Watching my time go by, repeating like ground hog day.
Sure, I'm sad and lonely, but my honor shall see me through.

My life (My life)
[Pause]
"Regardless of all the b*llsh*t, I'll still have my say."
[Pause]
It's my life.

"Once Upon a Dream"

Once upon a dream (It's all about you).
Through the power of love (I came to you).
My finest writing, I gave (Framed you for life).
I encased you within my art (From my heart, from my heart, from my heart).
A sacrifice for all (No strings or demands).
Born from my soul.

[Whispered softly:] (A place, a time, a dream.)

Once upon a dream (I gave my heart).
I've nothing to show (But love within my soul).
I've encased all the world (Through the sacred fraternities).
My temples within my mind (Built with love, built with love,
built with love).
Paying through acts of kindness (For all to see).
Born from my heart.

[Whispered softly:] (A place, a time, a dream.)

Once upon a dream (I silently walked away).
I spent my time as king (In a humble way).
Teaching all forgiveness through love (Asking for love's return).
Giving for humanity with humility (The best of me, the best of
me, the best of me).
God deserved my service (Given for free).
Back whence I came.

[Whispered softly:] (A place, a time, a dream.)

Once upon a dream (It's now about me).
Embracing my art and creativity (For all to see).
My story's just beginning (From a fork in the road).
I create from my heart (From my soul, from my soul, from my soul).
My kingdom's within my mind (Born from nothing at all).
Though love I'm whole.

[Whispered softly:] (A place, a time, a dream.)

[Read out at the end:]

Oh to dream, oh to dream.
Thoughts flow by of my dream.
Whereby the few shall truly know.
Time does fly out the window.

Yet, there's hope though my mind,
By leaving gestures, the thoughtful kind.
That perhaps one shall eventually find:
"A place, a time, a dream."

"Until We Meet Again"

For you, I don't exist at all.
Just another face within a crowd.
I've given for free in the hope that you'd see me,
And that you'll ask for my name out loud.

For you, I've gave away my art,
Setting you free upon the world.
I've been waiting you see, for you to need me.
And that you'd turn my world upside down.

I've turned all my dreams into reality.
I've turned all my focus unto myself.

For you, I've embraced my own art
For you to recognize me. (Setting me free.)
I'd rather wait for you see, than embrace another for me,
Being patient for my true love's return.

I've turned all my dreams into reality.
I've turned all my focus unto myself.

For you, I've embraced my own art
For you to recognize me. (Setting me free.)
I'd rather wait for you see, than embrace another for me,
Being patient for my true love's return.

Today, I still hide in the shadows.
Just another fan with any crowd.
I've given for free in the hope that you'd see me,
And that you'll ask for my name out loud.

For you, I've gave away my art,
Setting you free upon the world.
I've been waiting you see, for you to need me.
And that you'd turn my world upside down.

I've turned all my dreams into reality.
I've turned all my focus unto myself.

Until we meet again, I'd rather be alone.

"Fight, Fight, Fight"

Fight the fight (Fight)
Talk the talk (Talk)
Walk the walk (Walk)

[A boxing ringside bell is hit three times]
[Have the round cards displayed with the infinity symbol
appearing after every round]

Hiding in plain sight.
Within our urban jungle, that's right.
Life spent living within a pendulum.
Opposing opinions, opposing laws.
Fight, fight, fight.
Swinging to the left, swinging to the right.
Swinging to the left, swinging to the right.

Trapped within a perpetual fight between wrong and right.
Wake up!

Fight the fight (Fight)
Talk the talk (Talk)
Walk the walk (Walk)

[A boxing ringside bell is hit three times]
[Have the round cards displayed with the infinity symbol
appearing after every round]

There's one thing we can all agree on
Round after fricking round
Opposite opinions never agree
Swinging to the left, swinging to the right.
Swinging to the left, swinging to the right.
Trapped within a perpetual fight between wrong and right.
Wake up!

Fight the fight (Fight)
Talk the talk (Talk)
Walk the walk (Walk)

[A boxing ringside bell is hit three times]
[Have the round cards displayed with the infinity symbol
appearing after every round]

On occasion, someone hits the canvas
[Ref shouts] One, two, three
Up on their knees
[Ref shouts] Four, five, six
Back to their feet
The fight resumes again

Fight the fight (Fight)
Talk the talk (Talk)
Walk the walk (Walk)

[A boxing ringside bell is hit three times]
[Have the round cards displayed with the infinity symbol
appearing after every round]

"Will I Be Remembered?"

Work ends, life begins, heading home for dinner.
Allow me to rest please.
Week ends, life grows, heading out for coffee.
Allow me my only vice.

All these moments, I take solace.
Regardless of the date and time.
And my enjoyment grows every time.
Sadly, we must return to work in due time.

Every morning, I'm greeted with true love.
Sometimes I hear purring and the odd meow for a feeding.
I stare in appreciation out of love for my cat.
Someday his name will be spoken by those that he doesn't know.

This repeats over and over as our daily routine.
Funny and very true.
I'm blessed with his love
It helps me from being blue.

Time never stops, these moments do pass.
I will always cherish these memories.

Someday I too shall leave,
Will I be remembered?

Work ends, life begins, heading home for dinner.
Allow me to rest please.
Week ends, life grows, heading out for coffee.
Allow me my only vice.

All these moments, I take solace.
Regardless of the date and time.
And my enjoyment grows every time.
Sadly, we must return to work in due time.

Every morning, I'm greeted, with true love.
Sometimes I hear purring and the odd meow for a feeding.
I stare in appreciation out of love for my cat.
Someday his name will be spoken by those that he doesn't know.

This repeats over and over as our daily routine.
Funny and very true.
I'm blessed with his love
It helps me from being blue.

Time never stops, these moments do pass.
I will always cherish these memories.
Someday I too shall leave,
Will I be remembered?

"We Crave Love and Affection"

We crave love and affection.
We crave love and affection.

Just because we do, we do, we do.
We crave love, we crave love.

When I'm walking down the street.
Looking at all the homeless people.
All looking for a hand up.
Cardboard signs made with hope.
That society will give them change.

We crave love, oh yeah, yeah, yeah.
But little comes from society today.

We crave love and affection.
We crave love and affection.
Just because we do, we do, we do.
We crave love, we crave love.

I don't bother watching the news.
It's all negative without any hope.
Always talking circles around death.
It always reaches the same conclusions.
That society will wake up and change.

We crave love, oh yeah, yeah, yeah.
But little comes from society today.

We crave love and affection.
We crave love and affection.
Just because we do, we do, we do.
We crave love, we crave love.

Fast forward to the next day.
The media keeps repeating the negative.
As we slave to make ends meet.

Bombarded with every form of hate.
Turn the keys, press the button already.

We crave love and affection.
We crave love and affection.
Just because we do, we do, we do.
We crave love, we crave love.
We crave love and affection.
We crave love and affection.
Just because we do, we do, we do.
We crave love, we crave love.

"Love and Reason Returning?"

[Sing with sadness and determination.]

Austerity's come alive, through the tightening of the markets.
With hate, they've embraced throughout these many years.
The markets fill our lives, with the things that we need.
Our survival is based upon love and reason returning.
(Love and reason returning.)

By tightening the screws, they are tying up our hands.
Unable to react in a proactive way. (A proactive way.)
Our society's rules were born from out of enslavement.
Austerity's used so the few can remain in control.

The clash of views, fighting to gain or maintain control.
This has been going on for thousands of years. (Thousands
of years.)
When will they see? That our lives represent our true wealth.
Instead, they invent many ways to destroy ourselves.

The sum of our lives combined represents our treasury.
Instead, they enslave through the creation of different laws. (Of different laws.)
Why can't they see? That we are all of us equals.
We must embrace and forgive each other for our survival.

History repeats, so the few can retain their controls.
Riding the waves through the accumulation of great sums of wealth. (Sums of wealth.)
The markets fill our lives, with the things that we need.
Our survival is based upon love and reason returning.
(Love and reason returning.)

By tightening the screws, they are tying up our hands.
Unable to react in a proactive way. (A proactive way.)
Our society's rules were born from out of enslavement.
Austerity's used so the few can remain in control.

The clash of views, fighting to gain or maintain control.
This has been going on for thousands of years. (Thousands of years.)
When will they see? That our lives represent our true wealth.
Instead, they invent many ways to destroy ourselves.

The sum of our lives combined represents our treasury.
Instead, they enslave through the creation of different laws. (Of different laws.)
Why can't they see? That we are all of us equals.
We must embrace and forgive each other for our survival.

"Austerity Hides the Hands of Fate"

Austerity hides the hands of fate.
Tying society up so we react to late.
Our lives are the treasury.
Hate acts through justifying austerity.
Blood fills our streets through misery.
Rotting decay.
Encased within caps and lines.

Throughout my life, I spend time dreaming.
While others hide in plain sight scheming.
Some walk following their marks late at night.
Looking to fill their pockets and have a fight.
No one knows when this play will end.
Everyone knows life's not a game of pretend.
My eyes have seen a friend pass away.
Heard his last breath.
With heavy hearts we carried on.

Life's a circus of choices made.
Many realize that they've been played.
Will society come together at last.
Forgiving our mutual shared collective past.
Building a future that will last.
Born from our combined collective past.
Starting anew.
Erasing all the caps and lines.

"Wisdom" is gained as we grow old.
When embraced, it does take hold.
Listen to what others have to say.
Life isn't simply a drama or play.

Through my words, I shall leave behind.
What I've learned for others to find.

"I Simply Don't Bother Dreaming of You Anymore"

You don't need any flowers
You don't want true love
You're into chasing and making money
There's no room in your life for more

I chased you with flowers
Fresh roses in full bloom
And encased your life with art
I made your life a love-filled fantasy

Being a very old soul
I know my real worth
You couldn't see beyond my art
So I walked away and closed the door

You appreciate the finer things
You cherish 24-karat gold
But my love's a blue diamond
Freely given, but can't be bought or sold

Although I have been taken
You've been framed for life
I was looking for a beginning
But was sadly set aside in the end

I gave you my hand
Wiped away all your tears

Created for you a living opera
But you chose material wealth over true worth

I have retained my honor
My fraternal family's love too
I don't speak of gifts given
For my word is more solid than stone

[Speaking part]
My services are no longer given.
I simply don't bother dreaming
[Pause]
About you
[Pause]
Anymore.

[Videography:]
He is wearing a black tuxedo, Shrine Fez, and black facial mask,
walking in a sacred grove at night in winter. (Film on February
14.) Throughout the song, he is holding a red rose in full bloom.
At the end of the song, he arrives to a Masonic temple and
removes his Fez upon arrival and is invested with his apron by
several brethren. The scene shifts to the cover of my novel.

"Our Beloved Hockey Game!"

Welcome back again, to our hockey game.
See our legends take to the ice.
Every passing play,
Going either way,
Brings excitement to our lives.
The players glide,

Bump and collide,
And the fans roar in the rink.
Our passions rise,
When the puck flies,
At every hockey game!
Yes,
There's no other game, that anyone can name
That compares in any way
To our beloved hockey game!

As time goes, the whistle blows.
Both teams face off in the rink.
Play by play,
Flowing either way,
Our game will make you think.
A passing play,
A break away,
And the fans take to their feet.
The puck soars,
Someone's scored!
In pursuit of Lord Stanley's cup and ring!
Yes,
There's no other game, that anyone can name!
That compares in any way!
To our beloved hockey game!

As stats compile, we recall and smile.
Our heroes from the rink.
Game by game,
With passions aflame,
They stole our hearts in a blink.
Within our Hall,
We joyfully recall,

Our icons from our game.
Yes,
There's no other game, that anyone can name
That compares in any way
To our beloved hockey game!

"We Want to Fill Our Stands"

We shall bring you something
That's in high demand.
We shall give you something,
Cherished memories of pretend.
We want to fill our stands.
We want to fill our stands.
We want to fill our stands.

With passion, sharing our voices,
You'll be moved by our show.
With fashion, flair, and design,
We'll entertain you for awhile.

Our performance shall touch your hearts (Deep inside)
Our passion and words will hit you
Behind your eyes
Behind your eyes
Behind your eyes

Through art, we'll leave you
Happy in the end.
Though art, created with heart,
You'll approve our friends.
We want to fill our stands.

We want to fill our stands.
We want to fill our stands.

[Instrumental]

[Back to the top, repeat]

"The Sounds of Youth"

The schools come alive with the return of children.
With bright eyes, they learn from our collective past.
Their halls are all filled with the sounds from our future.
Their minds are all filled with the wonders of youth. (The wonders of youth)
Oh, to live life without the taint of bias.
That rises from that which they're taught. (Which they're taught)
Our love shall return, from all our children,
Like birds flying by on warm summer day.
Growing up and learning that we're all equals.
Our differences set aside for the greater good. (The greater good)
Through our youth we pass on
What wisdom we have gained.
Our homes come alive with the return of our children.
With their voices, they share what they have learned.
Our rooms are all filled with the sounds of our future.
Hearts are filled with wonder, thankful for their lives.
What's the point of life without the inclusion of children?
They return our love, as they grow before us.
Their hearts are all filled with dreaming of their futures.
They develop and grow, before they fly away. (Before they fly away)
Our future is bright, resting in the hands of our children.

They rise and take our places as we age. (As we age)
We all fly away, returning where we came from,
Leaving the world behind, within those caring hands.
Their homes shall come alive with the arrival of their children.
With their hearts, they share what they have learned.
Their homes are all filled with the sounds of the future.
Hearts filled again with wonder, thankful for their lives.
Growing up and learning, that we're all equals.
Our differences set aside for the greater good. (The greater good)
Through our youth we pass on
What wisdom we have gained.
What's the point of life without the inclusion of children?
They return our love, as they grow before us.
Their hearts are all filled with dreaming of their futures.
They develop and grow before they fly away. (Before they
fly away)

[Fade out after the inclusion of the instrumental]

"All The Homeless People"

I'm sad, gazing upon all our homeless people.
I'm sad, gazing upon all our homeless people.

John Oross
Although my pockets are empty my hearts filled with love,
Living out my dreams,
My eyes are windows,
Tears held back inside my mind behind my pseudo façade.
Societies broken.

All the homeless people,
Where have they been driven from?
All the homeless people,
Why hasn't help come along?

God above
Has given words out of love but few read them.
His many devout servants
Look upon us all
What's the point of life without love? A precious gift.
Choices build over time.

I'm sad, gazing upon all our homeless people.
I'm sad, gazing upon all our homeless people.

John Oross
Would rather live a modest life, pursuing his true love.
She's framed.
God above
Would rather forgive us all, securing our bright rightful future.
But no one listens.

All the homeless people need our love and care.
Where have they been driven from?
All the homeless people need our love and care.
Why hasn't help come along?

"Hate vs. Love, Death, or Life"

We're all free so how can it be
That most of us just don't get by in society?
We're all free so how can it be
That most of us just don't get by in society?

Between, currency differentials, borders, caps, and lines,
We're all struggling almost all the time.
Taxes go up and the debts go high.
The powers that be focus on managing our time.

I do understand
Life's no game.
Hate versus love,
Death, or life.

We're all free so how can it be
That most of us just don't get by in society?
We're all free so how can it be
That most of us just don't get by in society?

Because of different rules, wealth replaces worth.
Why must we turn the other cheek?
Inequality breeds hate without an end.
Lives are too precious to waste it negatively.

I do understand
Life's no game.
Hate versus love,
Death, or life.

I do understand
Life's no game.
Hate versus love,
Death, or life.

I do understand
Life's no game.
Hate versus love,
Death, or life.

I do understand
Life's no game.
Hate versus love,
Death, or life.

I do understand
Life's no game.
Hate versus love,
Death, or life.

"My Love Has a Price, Baby"

I gave from my soul,
Being kind takes a toll.
I gave towards all freely.
Will love return to me?
I'm waiting in the dark.
I'm hidden from actual view.
My love has a price, baby.

Although I gave with love,
Some sadly fear my heart. (Fear my heart)
So, I now hold back
What was once given away.

Here I start once again,
Embracing art for my own.
I'm walking sadly all alone.
So, my soul can mend.
I've light within my heart,
Encased within all my art.
My love has a price, baby.

Although I gave with love,
Some sadly fear my heart. (Fear my heart)
So, I now hold back
What was once given away.

In silence, I walked away,
Yet I've more to say,
Determined I'll return to you.
So, tell me my friends
Will our love overcome hate?
Will insanity seal our fate?
My love has a price, baby.

Although I gave with love,
Some sadly fear my heart. (Fear my heart)
So, I now hold back
What was once given away.

We must forgive the past,
healing the wounds we hold.
We must all come together
Before it's sadly too late.
Nukes will seal humanities fate.
Carbon returns all into sand.
My love has a price, baby.

Life's no game of pretend,
Hate's reign must truly end
For humanity to have a future.

"Be Sincere & Apply Forgiveness"

We're tired of the hate.
Apply forgiveness before it's too late.
Acknowledge whether wrong or right.
Do you stoke the flames of hate, rather than forgiveness and love?
Love and life can't be replaced with anger and hate.

Why can't they simply see there's no difference between you
and me?
Applying forgiveness is a treasure to held onto above all.
Is your heart hard as stone, will you reap what you sow?
Be sincere and apply forgiveness, that's right.

Forgiveness is a treasure beyond compare.
Imagine embracing anger, hate, death, and darkness rather than
forgiveness and love.
Our fate dances between our decisions we make.
Humanity must unite for our future to burn bright.
Forgiveness will bring peace to your soul.
Read between the lines and act upon these clues.

Will the curtain fall?
Will it be the end of us all?
Embracing hate will lead us all into the arms of death.
Why embrace hate and darkness?
Wouldn't you prefer love and light?
Lying to yourself will not bring warmth back into your heart.

So, close the book on hate before its sadly too late.
Be sincere and apply forgiveness, that's right.

"Many Wandering Thoughts"

Life is precious, beyond any physical material worth.
Some do things, throwing away their priceless soul.
Some do things for another making them whole.
Although I face my life with empty hands,
I will continue throughout whatever God silently demands.
There are many challenges along life's twisted path.
Do you succumb to defeat or rise and take a stand?

Many loose lips spill lies along the way.
Many are bitter trying to have a say.
Many are corrupt trying to drag everyone down.

[Instrumental]

Some pray for selfish things taking a knee.
When your backs turned, some deploy a knife.
Greed and selfishness do swallow many lost souls.
Regardless of what I lack, I'm truly whole.
I've carried many burdens deep within my soul.
Some weave their desires through another's bloody hands.
What's your religion, your belief in any faith?

Many live their lives in silence, day after day.
Many trip and fall while using broken crutches.
Many are simply used, lost in another's design.

[Instrumental]

Consider, are you presently who you really are?
Consider, every person has their wants and needs.
Do you sacrifice your worth, honor, and soul?
Many faiths twist words to enslave a believer.

We each have opinions held close and dear.
Morality shouldn't be policed, it's a personal journey.
The individual determines their own precious life's worth.

Many are the issues we all must face.
Many will move forward leaving most others behind.
Many wandering thoughts have indeed swallowed me whole.
[Pause]
Would you trade your soul for material gain?

[Pause]
The decision is truly in your two hands.

"In Our City"

As another crow cries,
On a typical average Winnipeg day,
Many homeless I pass along my way.
In our city. (In our city)

We live our lives.
Some run towards those in need,
While other succumb to devilish greed.
In our city. (In our city)

Why can't they see?
Money shouldn't be used to define.
Life is a gift without compare.
Yet many lose their way.
Laying down in utter defeat,
Another lost soul living on our streets.
Too many of us turn away.

Soon they become desperate.
Some learn how to take,
Some learn how to kill.
In our city. (In our city)

As both the innocent and guilty die.
How many more chalk or yellow tape lines,
Until we mend our self-serving ways?
In our city. (In our city)

As another crow cries,
On a typical average Winnipeg day,
Many homeless I pass along my way.
In our city. (In our city)

We live our lives.
Some run towards those in need,
While other succumb to devilish greed.
In our city. (In our city)

[Pause]
[Ask] What's it like in your city?

"Welcome All of You to Hell!"

Sadly, my sanity left me.
My world turned into Hell.
Taking my pills sustains me
In this perpetual Hell.
Waking up daily, swimming in hate,
Welcome all of you to Hell!

Although we're all fallen angels,
There's always room for more.
Games between sin and salvation,
No one's here to keep score.
Waking up daily, swimming in hate,
Welcome all of you to Hell!

Where is all the love gone, baby?
Where is all the love?
We've turned our Eden into Hell!

White angel wings are history,
Singed by the flames of Hell.
Many are devils in disguise,
Welcoming us all into Hell.
Waking up daily, swimming in hate,
Welcome all of you to Hell!

A devil hides deals in detail
Within their actions and deeds.
These prankish imps know the score.
It's a fine line between us all,
Between those in Heaven versus Hell.

Trying to live in balance, baby.
Trying to live in balance.
Undermining life in pursuit of death.

"Have You Ever?"

Have you ever held depression at bay?
Waiting for a light to enter your life each day.
Have you ever simply given things away?

Holding onto your words as your internal pain held sway.
Have you ever held onto your despair?
Smiling, carrying on no matter the negativity coming your way.
Have you ever?
[Pause]
Holding on while letting go.

[Instrumental]

Have you ever given your love away?
Holding onto memories shared as your time slowly slips away.
Have you ever faced complete, utter loss?
Holding back all your tears to carry on for all.
Have you ever seen someone sadly pass?
Their last breath expelled as their light left their eyes.
Have you ever?
[Pause]
Holding on while letting go.

[Instrumental]

Have you ever been homeless and alone?
Swallowing back your tears clinging onto your
internal self-worth.
Have you ever lost your fricken mind?
Strapped in a bed without knowledge of your own name.
Have you ever acted as a clown?
Regardless of your own personal issues cheering up
everyone around.
Have you ever?
[Pause]
Holding on while letting go.

[Instrumental]

Have you ever had someone help you?
As most of your acquaintances turned and walked quietly away.
Have you ever turned away from wealth?
Avoiding all contracts offered hiding their true motives
and intentions.
Have you ever witnessed acts of hate?
Inequality leads us all towards it sad to simply say.
Have you ever?
[Pause]
Holding on while letting go.

[Instrumental]

Have you ever?

"Problems & Secrets"

We've got our problems aired out on the news.
We've got our problems, some win while others lose.
We've got our problems after we depart work at five.
We've got our problems just trying to stay alive.
[Pause]
We've got our problems, yeah. We've got out problems.

Some problems come up while others drive us down.
Other problems come up, wearing us all down.
Some folks win while others lose, that's the truth.
Yeah, that's the truth.

[Instrumental]

Some spill their secrets while other dream and scheme.
Some air their secrets, making other folks truly scream.

Some keep their secrets, taking them to their graves.
Some hide their secrets, making other folks their slaves.
[Pause]
Some bury their secrets, yeah. Some spill their secrets.

Some secrets trip you up, while others let you down.
Many secrets come up, making you into a clown.
Some secrets remain in the dark, that's the truth.
Yeah, that's the truth.

"Nothing"

We're all struggling to escape the big bad machine.
Taxes and the bottom line have all become obscene.
When you then apply a cap to top it all off,
What then do you have?
[Pause]
[Sing] S-L-A-V-E-R-Y

We're all equals and the currency we ought to use is love.
Instead, the powers that be divide us between below and above.
When you then apply love vs. hate to top it all off,
What then do you have?
[Pause]
[Sing] W-A-R

We're all divided between parties with the label "Us vs. Them."
Divided by using everything imaginable, of this I don't pretend.
When you apply hate, it eventually promotes division
and inequality,
What then do you have?

[Pause]
[Sing] D-E-A-T-H

We're all doomed to fail collectively as a race.
Entire generations will fail, and their lives will be thrown away.
Life is the precious gift we have which can't ever be replaced.
What then do you need?
[Pause]
[Sing] F-O-R-G-I-V-E-N-E-S-S

[Back to the top, repeat for a second run-through]

[End with]
Aren't you all tired of being ignored, used, and abused?
Aren't you all FED up with this system of utter inequality?
What are the differences between both you and me?
[Pause]
N-O-T-H-I-N-G

"Got it? Get it? Give it! Live it!"

Got what I want? Then flaunt it baby!
Got what I need? Then show me baby!
Talk the talk, walk the walk
[Pause]
Earn my love.

[Spoken] Are you up to it? Give it your all. Got it? Get it? Give it.
Live it.

Get into the ring. Get up and sing.
Let your voice soar. Let the crowd roar.
Go with the flow. Let it all go.

[Pause]
Earn my love.

[Spoken] Are you ready for it? Give it your all. Got it? Get it?
Give it. Live it.

Give in to the need. Let your heart feed.
Let your soul loose. It's your life, choose.
Move my heart, deliver your art.
[Pause]
Earn my love.

[Spoken] Are you in the game? Give it your all. Got it? Get it?
Give it. Live it.

Got what I want? Then flaunt it baby!
Got what I need? Then show me baby!
Talk the talk, walk the walk
[Pause]
Earn my love.

[Spoken] Are you up to it? Give it your all. Got it? Get it? Give it.
Live it.

Get into the ring. Get up and sing.
Let your voice soar. Let the crowd roar.
Go with the flow. Let it all go.
[Pause]
Earn my love.

[Spoken] Are you ready for it? Give it your all. Got it? Get it?
Give it. Live it.

Give in to the need. Let your heart feed.
Let your soul loose. It's your life, choose.

Move my heart, deliver your art.
[Pause]
Earn my love.

[Spoken] Are you in the game? Give it your all. Got it? Get it?
Give it. Live it.

Got it? Get it? Give it! (Live it)
Got it? Get it? Give it! (Live it)
Got it? Get it? Give it! (Live it)
Live it! Live it! Live it!

"Time Never Slows as Time Flows"

Staring at my image within a mirror
Looking through my sore, tear-filled eyes
Memories fade as the time goes by
Many friends I've lost along the way
All the while I've kept my devil at bay
At times my depression has held sway

Time never slows as time flows
Time ever flows and never slows
Make time count as it goes
Time is sadly short, Heaven knows

I've got bright red, blood-shot eyes
Sadly, many of my dreams have died
Yet I keep trying come what may
To live life fully in every way
My hope's still burning in my heart
It still does infuse all my art

Time never slows as time flows
Time ever flows and never slows
Make time count as it goes
Time is sadly short, Heaven knows

At times life goes down a drain
Embrace your dreams, cast aside the pain
Life's the sum of your decisions made
Sure, there's times when you're truly played
What's it worth without love, my friend?
All is left behind in the end

Time never slows as time flows
Time ever flows and never slows
Make time count as it goes
Time is sadly short, Heaven knows
[Pause]

Time never slows as time flows
Time ever flows and never slows
Make time count as it goes
Time is sadly short, Heaven knows

"Sin or Salvation"

Gaze at the truth within my eyes
Silent and used as time flies by
Waiting in pain silently
Polaroid stills taken for all to see
Yet there's no room beside you for me
Waiting in utter agony

Forsaking sin for salvation (Ah ha)
Forsaking sin for salvation (Ah ha)

I encased many with my heart
Framed for an eternity with my art
Many dreams do come true

Forsaking sin for salvation (Ah ha)
Forsaking sin for salvation (Ah ha)
Life's no game

Some throw their souls away
Some lie and cheat every day
Yet I gave
Yet I gave
Yet I gave all I could away

My scars I do wear with pride
I've been battered, bruised, and I've cried
Life's no game
Life's no game
I still smile walking the extra mile

Sin or salvation
Sin or salvation
Life's not a game

We're all slaves to the bottom line
Chasing money all the time
Benevolence versus greed
You must choose
You must choose
Win or lose (Oh yeah)

I've been homeless many times
I've stared down sadness deep inside
Feeling worthless and cast aside
Yet I gave towards all

Forsaking sin for salvation (Ah ha)
Forsaking sin for salvation (Ah ha)

"I'm GA-GA over GA GA"

Oh yeah—Oh my Gaga
Oh yeah—Oh my Gaga
I'm mesmerized, caught in a trance
Oh yeah—Oh my Gaga

Oh yeah—Oh my Gaga
I'm mesmerized, caught in a trance

I'm GA-GA over Gaga
I'm GA-GA over Gaga
[Spoken in a passion-filled voice, SULTRY] (OOH-LA-LA)
I need your love in life's dance

I've given freely without any strings
To heal my soul deep down inside
I walked away from money and gold
Wishing for your presence by my side

I've my reasons, that I hide,
One of which is true love
I'm in need of your love
Love, love, love I need your love (Yeah)

I want your passion, fashion, and design
For you I'm waiting to make you mine
You're ICONIC, talent, and flare
I've need of it in my life
Love, love, love I need your love (Yeah)

[Spoken in a passion-filled voice, SULTRY]
I know that you want me
And realize that you need me
We want this bad, give us a chance

I'm passion filled, and I need your love
Combined we'd have a great chance in life
Together we'd rule this dance
Leaving everyone else caught in a trance

Oh yeah—Oh my Gaga
Oh yeah—Oh my Gaga
I'm mesmerized, caught in a trance
Oh yeah—Oh my Gaga
Oh yeah—Oh my Gaga
I'm mesmerized, caught in a trance

I'm GA-GA over Gaga
I'm GA-GA over Gaga
[Spoken in a passion-filled voice, SULTRY] (OOH-LA-LA)
I need your love in life's dance

I've given freely without any strings
To heal my soul deep down inside
I walked away from money and gold
Wishing for your presence by my side

I've my reasons, that I'd confide,
One of which is made up of art that I hide
I'm in need of your love
Love, love, love I need your love (Yeah)

I want your confidence, truth, and word
For you I'm waiting to make you mine
You're ICONIC, talent, and flare
I've need of it in my life
Love, love, love I need your love (Yeah)

[Spoken in a passion filled voice, SULTRY]
I know that you want me
And realize that you need me
We want this bad, give us a chance

I'm passion filled, and I need your love
Combined we'd have a great chance in life
Together we'd rule this dance
Leaving everyone else caught in a trance

I'm GA-GA over Gaga
I'm GA-GA over Gaga
[Spoken in a passion filled voice, SULTRY] (OOH-LA-LA)
I need your love in life's dance

I'm GA-GA over Gaga
I'm GA-GA over Gaga
[Spoken in a passion filled voice, SULTRY] (OOH-LA-LA)
I need your love in life's dance

You're the talk of the town, baby
You stole my heart, so come and claim it, baby
You're the talk of the town, baby

You stole my heart, so come and claim it, baby
You're the talk of the town, baby
You stole my heart, so come and claim it, baby
You're the talk of the town, baby
You stole my heart, so come and claim it, baby

I hide in darkness, wearing my pseudo façade
So come on, baby, let us resume our dance
What's life without taking a chance?
Qu'est-ce que la vie sans prendre de risqué?
This isn't no game of pretend
Towards you all my love I do send
Towards you all my love I do send
All my love I do send
All my love I do send

Oh yeah—Oh my GA-GA
Oh yeah—Oh my GA-GA
I'm mesmerized, caught in a trance
Oh yeah—Oh my Gaga
Oh yeah—Oh my Gaga
I'm mesmerized, caught in a trance

Caught in this perpetual dance
Caught in this perpetual dance
[Pause]

Let's put this charade to an end
We don't have to pretend
We don't have to pretend
[Pause]

I'm GA-GA over Gaga
I'm GA-GA over Gaga

I'm GA-GA over Gaga
I'm GA-GA over Gaga
[Spoken with passion] (OOH-LA-LA)

[Video]
The scene opens up in an empty theater lit entirely by candles (1895 New York, USA). The red with gold trim velour curtain is up, and a custodian is sweeping up on the stage. Red roses litter the stage. A film projector is situated in the orchestra pit, facing the empty white theater walls at the back of the stage. As the custodian looks up as he departs the stage, the projector begins to play. He takes a seat in the empty theater to watch the film. The era is purposefully chosen to depict a scene of the past which is the opposite of the scenes of GAGA playing out of her ICONIC videography. A magazine cover of *Bad Romance* followed with brief scene references.

End the video with a still of GAGA wearing her ICONIC lightening bolt dress with a teacup upon her lap.

Fade to black as the custodian picks up a rose from the floor and smells it, looking with love at the screen. Custodian is wearing a mask.

The song plays out with scenes of GAGA and her career being displayed.

End.

"Words I've Given Have Hit Home"

My full blond crown has turned gray for all to see.
My slight frame has expanded outwards like a tree.
I'm framed in darkness through other people's slights of hand.

No one truly knows,
As the saying goes,
That life's a gift
And I've cherished every day that I've seen.

Someday, I'll know the true love from my rose born from
my dreams.
Until then, nothing that appears in my life's what it
seems. Honestly.
And so now I encase myself with my art.
Its light shines out from the dark,
Outwards for all to see.

I'm sworn to my words that 've given away, silent am I.
Waiting out my days hoping for her love, hiding all my pain.
The wounds from which I bleed are upon my very soul.
I'm honor bound, no trace of a string from my gifts can be found.

No one truly knows,
As the saying goes,
That life's a gift
And I've cherished every day that I've seen.

Someday, I'll know the true love from my rose born from
my dreams.
Until then, nothing that appears in my life's what it
seems. Honestly.
And so now I encase myself with my art.
It's light shines out from the dark,
Outwards for all to see.

My words I've given have hit home in every way,
My words I've given have hit home in every way,
My words I've given have hit home in every way,

If I should die before she comes my way,
My words I've given have hit home in every way.

[Back to the top, repeat]

Perhaps the day of her arrival into my life's today.

"Dead to the World!"

Dead to the world! Eyes closed in slumber,
Dreaming of a better tomorrow!
Without love all seems quite hollow.

Life's a gift bound with love.
Life's a gift bound with love.
Time's a gift treasured by God above.

Dead to the world! Our time's upon us.
Our deeds shall determine tomorrow!
Between sin and salvation
Exists a fine line.
Repeating this perpetual play.
Repeating this perpetual play.
Will you trade sin for salvation?

Cast aside sin for salvation's embrace.
Secure your future before it's too late.
Life and light or death and darkness.
Salvation or damnation? You decide.

[Back to the top, repeat]

"Lovesick Serenade"

I've walked many miles with you held within my heart and soul.
My heart is heavy with the burden of my word given long ago.
Many roses have I sent to you along the way,
Encasing you within my lovesick serenade.
Throughout these many lonely years I've kept my faith,
Hiding my feelings within my creativity, revealing
outwardly nothing,
Encasing everyone within my lovesick serenade.
My hands are empty and heart heavy from sacrifices.
The embers within my hearth and heart glow upon hearing
your voice.
Your breath's a long passionate kiss fanning the flames.
Moments are precious and time ever flowing with change, a
constant friend.
My thoughts of your love glow akin to stars within our night sky.
All you must do is open the door to your heart.
My heart has already encased you within my lovesick serenade.
We don't have forever, just these few precious moments,
Yet our story will live on through eternity
As a perpetual play found within this lovesick serenade.

"My Life Goes on like This"

I'm holding back my words
Out of heartfelt respect
Humanities in my heart
Trust me of this I do attest
Take a walk with me
Down the path I tread

Perception's a funny thing
Some are hard to believe
I've framed many
Within this fricken show
I've taken nothing
My life goes on like this:

I hold back my tongue
Pretending that I've nothing to say
Keeping my silence
Framed within honor's embrace
My apron and fez I truly adore (Adore)
Many mistake my silence
As a flaw of someone of who's weak.

Passing my time away
Giving my art away in the dark
Through other people's hands
I've helped many along the way
I've taken nothing for myself
Except the love that they hold
My years have been blessed
Living out my life filled with dreams
Walking a line made from truths
Nothing's really written out
I've figured things out on my own
My life goes on like this:

I hold back my tongue
Pretending that I've nothing to say
Keeping my silence
Framed within honor's embrace
My apron and fez I truly adore (Adore)

Many mistake my silence
As a flaw of someone of who's weak.

[Spoken at the end]
The life I possess is its own reward and I've given my word,
bound by love and light.

"Everyday Is Hump Day"

It's five a.m. all over again
Working life away wishing upon a star
Sipping upon an espresso
Looking for something sweet
It doesn't really matter
Living out the day moving along to the next
These days keep repeating
I'd rather be asleep back in my bed
It's just another workday
Chasing money all the time
For you make ends meet

Every day is Hump Day…(Sad to say)
Wishing for better days (In every way)
Where is all the fun today? (It's gone away)
Drinking to chase my blues away…(Each and everyday)
Every day is Hump Day

I slowly walk to work
Trying to arrive on time
With my stomach on empty
For I don't have a dime
Dreaming throughout my life

For someone's hands to hold
Sadly, time keeps rolling on
And before you know it you're now old
Nothing seems to be real
All of it the stuff of dreams
Living life without love working for someone else's needs

Every day is Hump Day…(Sad to say)
Wishing for better days (In every way)
Where is all the fun today? (It's gone away)
Drinking to case my blues away…(Each and everyday)
Every day is Hump Day

Looking within my mirror
My golden hair is now all gray
Devoid of all its color
Wasting away with nothing to say
Life's a gift but it must be lived all the time
So come on and let loose,
Hiding out won't change a darn thing
Working out your issues
For a simple prenup and ring
I've given out many roses
Framed with my words of love

Every day is Hump Day…(Sad to say)
Wishing for better days (In every way)
Where is all the fun today? (It's gone away)
Drinking to case my blues away…(Each and everyday)
Every day is Hump Day

All my life,
I've given towards making dreams come true

Lifting people up,
Lending them a helping hand out of the blue (Out of the blue)
My challenges today,
I'm facing them down all the time
Like a fish out of water
That swallowed the bait left on the line

Every day is Hump Day…(Sad to say)
Wishing for better days (In every way)
Where is all the fun today? (It's gone away)
Drinking to case my blues away…(Each and everyday)
Every day is Hump Day

"The Bears Are Back in Town!"

Money, we made the other day,
Sadly, has been taken suddenly away,
Waiting for the bulls to return someday.
Hate's driving the world crazy presently
With this "Us versus Them" mentality.
Where can all the love be found?

The bears are back in town. (The bears are back in town.)
The bears are back in town. (The bears are back in town.)
The bears are back in town. (The bears are back in town.)

Our stocks we bought just the other day
With the hard-earned money from yesterday
Are now worthless sad to simply say.
What's the sense of dreaming?

We're trying hard every single day,
Coping, hoping for a better, brighter day.

Chasing money in every single way.
Why the games of hate?

The bears are back in town. (The bears are back in town.)
The bears are back in town. (The bears are back in town.)
The bears are back in town. (The bears are back in town.)

The FED they keep on taking,
Giving their reasons for our torment.
Set aside the hate for love.
What's the point of all the scheming?

Lives are being slowly taken away,
Thrown aside using greed in every single way,
To justify their lack of morals.
Isn't it better to give then receive?

The bears are back in town. (The bears are back in town.)
The bears are back in town. (The bears are back in town.)
The bears are back in town. (The bears are back in town.)

"You're My Dream"

I've been played, yeah, walking alone in my daily life.
My years I wear, and I keep on crying deep down inside.
All I wanted from you
Is acceptance and love
Allow for my presence
Within your daily life
Silently waiting,
I framed your life with my light and love.

You're my dream, yeah.
Place your hands in mine.
You're my dream.
I refuse to believe that I've wasted my time.

I've kept to myself, waiting for my dream to arrive.
Through all these lonely years, I've kept silent as a mime.
All I asked from you
Is acceptance and love
I wait to receive
With humility,
Hoping that your life will again allow for my love.

You're my dream, yeah.
Place your hands in mine.
You're my dream.
I refuse to believe that I've wasted my time.

For your love I gave
For your love I tried
For your love I cried
For your love I died
I've nothing from you
Except personal pain

You're my dream, yeah.
Place your hands in mine.
You're my dream.
I refuse to believe that I've wasted my time.
You're my dream, yeah.
Place your hands in mine.
You're my dream.
I refuse to believe that I've wasted my time.

[Pause]
I refuse to believe that I've wasted my life.

"Poppies, Sunflowers, & Roses"

[Part 1]
Everyday is a blessing for tomorrow may never come.
Look for love within all people, situations, and things.
For peace to reign we must forgive our collective past
And eliminate differences in law along with currency.
The few try to divide us all, it's a form of control.
So, let's end slavery once and for all.
[Pause]
Give poppies, sunflowers, and roses in remembrance of love.
Yes, apply forgiveness and give each other:
[Pause]
Poppies, sunflowers, and roses in remembrance of love.

[Part 2]
We can't survive within an apocalyptic world.
The above must be embraced before its too late.
Humanity's true potential and our lives are at stake.
A nuclear holocaust doesn't eliminate divisiveness.
Embracing carbon-based fuels is also leading us to our end.
We can't survive through an ice age or within a desert.
[Pause]
Give poppies, sunflowers, and roses in remembrance of love.
Yes, apply forgiveness and give each other:
[Pause]
Poppies, sunflowers, and roses in remembrance of love.

[Part 3]
Forgiveness is required and is an extension of true love.
Without embracing each other, humanity is doomed to fail.
This "US vs. THEM" mentality must come to a swift end.
War occurs when there is a conflict of values and ideals.
This is the absence of love within each and in every field!
War solves nothing for the issues remain unresolved.
[Pause]
Give poppies, sunflowers, and roses in remembrance of love.
Yes, apply forgiveness and give each other:
[Pause]
Poppies, sunflowers, and roses in remembrance of love.

[Video: Part 1]
The singer's walking within the war memorial at Vimy Ridge
(FRANCE/EUROPE). Honor guard with the UN flag unfurled
to follow the artist.

[Video: Part 2]
The singer's walking within the war memorial at Arlington
National Cemetery (USA/NORTH AMERICA) Honor guard
with the UN flag unfurled to follow the artist.

[Video: Part 3]
The singer is walking about the Human Rights Museum
Winnipeg, Manitoba, Canada (CANADA/NORTH AMERICA)
Honor guard with the UN flag unfurled to follow the artist.

[Video: Part 4]
Singer shown entering the International Peace Gardens carrying
a wreath and placing it at the front of the garden entrance. This
signifies that peace needs to be embraced for our collective
survival. Throughout the video, the singer is placing a mixture of

wreaths comprised of poppies, sunflowers, and roses. Dressed in black (primary) and red (trim) in remembrance. Wreaths: green, signifying life and hope. No guns or salutes. Honor guard with the UN flag unfurled to follow the artist as they kneel placing the wreath. End focusing upon the wreath placed in front of the poem I created "In Every Field!"

Fade to black after a minute of silence.

"She's a Sinner!"

She will take whatever she wants,
Spending cash just to flaunt.
She'll eat you for dinner.
She will take you to her place,
Put a smile upon your face.
Yeah, she's a sinner.
[Pause]

She'll drive you crazy, yeah, yeah, yeah. Real crazy.
Making you scream, making you shout, that woman ain't fine.
She will always get her way,
Making cash in every way.
She'll make them fricken quiver.
Never ever is she alone, there's always someone new within her home.
Yeah, she's a sinner.
[Pause]

She'll make them jealous, yeah, yeah, yeah. Real jealous.
Making them scream, making them shout, that woman ain't mine.

Well, I'm truly sad to say
She'll never have her way.
The few through cash control her.
She might have a fancy place.
She might have panache and grace.
Yeah, she's a sinner.
[Pause]

She'll drive herself crazy, yeah, yeah, yeah. Truly crazy.
Making some scream, making some shout, that woman
ain't mine.
What she's got isn't hard to find:
Being loose, immoral, and unrefined.
She'll never get to know me.
I would smile in her face,
Put her kindly in her place.
Yeah, she's a sinner.
[Pause]

She's nothing to me, yeah, yeah, yeah. Truly no one.
I'd make her scream, making her shout, that woman ain't fine.
Yeah, yeah, yeah, she's a sinner.
Listen to me, she's got no hooks in me.
Yeah, yeah, yeah, she's a sinner.
Nothing in life's free, take it from me.
Yeah, yeah, yeah, she's a sinner.
Yeah, yeah, yeah, she's a sinner.
Yeah, yeah, yeah, she's a sinner.
Yeah, yeah, yeah, she's a sinner.
[Pause]

[Spoken firmly at the end while shaking your head sadly] She's
a sinner.

"My Life"

My life (My life)
Has been full of dismay,
Dreaming about true love, every single day.
Sadly, I've been battered and bruised.
Looking for love, left worn and used.

My life (My life)
Has been empty until today.
This is my story, I must convey.
Chasing after my dreams, alone, and totally confused.
If it comes back, I'll be happy and amused.

I've been a sad clown, a vagabond, a mime, a ghost, and a king.
I've been used, abused, ignored, and kicked living without
a thing.
Every time I find myself caught in last place,
I realize that there's always another vying to take my place.

My life (My life)
I've been caught in a play,
Hoping for a love filled tomorrow, to fill my day.
Hiding all my sad love filled blues.
Wearing a smile, regardless how I've been used.

My life (My life)
At times it does fall apart.
Yet sadness takes cover when I frame others with my art.
Hiding away all that I can do,
Taking nothing for granted, staying humble and true.

I've been a sad clown, a vagabond, a mime, a ghost, and a king.
I've been used, abused, ignored, and kicked living without

a thing.
Every time I find myself caught in last place,
I realize that there's always another vying to take my place.

"We Enjoy All These Pleasures"

We look forward to any game.
We look forward to some fun.
Taking time out to enjoy ourselves,
Boredom is now on the run!

[Instrumental] [Refrain]

Some folks love to wager,
While others watch for fun.
Regardless of our personal preferences,
Together bearing witness as one!

[Instrumental] [Refrain]

We need our times together.
We seriously need all the fun.
Taking in special moments to treasure,
Witnesses of all that was done!

[Instrumental] [Refrain]

We admit to enjoying these things,
Trading in our problems for fun.
Some recall games from the past.
Through love, we have already won!

[Instrumental] [Refrain]

We enjoy all these pleasures.
They provide memories to hold.
It matters not win or lose,
Whether we're young or old!

[Instrumental] [Refrain]

Our time lasts for the moment,
Since time waits for no one,
Leaving behind some things to remember.
Enriches us all, yes, everyone!

[Refrain]
So, let's cheer, cheer, cheer for our teams
Regardless of who has finally won,
For the efforts of all involved in these games
Have won our hearts through their play.

"Someday"

Someday my love will return to me.
Perhaps soon, I'll take a knee.
I've framed many with love, without any strings.
For their love is worth more than any piece of paper.
Their love blinded my eyes as it healed my heart.
So, I gave away some of my priceless art.

Someday their love will set me free.
Perhaps soon, they'll truly recognize me.
I've dreamed about their love, healing my soul.
For their love is worth more than any material gain.
Their love has encased my soul, inspiring my art.
So, I gave away some from my beating heart.

Someday with love, they'll understand me.
Perhaps soon, they'll know true liberty.
I've suffered without their love, living all alone.
For their worth is heavenly, nothing can compare.
Their love has set my path, I'm upon today.
So, I gave towards all, keeping my depression at bay.

Someday through love, it will find me.
Perhaps soon, for all of eternity.
I've paid from my loving soul, giving it my all.
For their worth is priceless, beyond what I say.
Their love fuels my art that I've hidden away.
So, I gave towards all, a simple and modest start.

Someday God's love will return from above.
Perhaps soon, they'll unite as one.
I've paid throughout my life, without any rewards,
For their collective love, trying to restore its return.
Their love found its mark, it struck home.
So, I gave it my all, as the king of nothing yesterday.

Someday, without love, I will be called away.
Perhaps soon, I'll face judgement day.
I've considered many different things, opinions I truly have.
For life is our true wealth, not any material hoarding.
Their love has made me whole, returning it is my goal.
So, I gave it my all, while keeping focus upon the light.

Someday our love will reunite our humanity.
Perhaps soon, they'll again be free.
I've pleaded from my soul, serving as our king.
For all life shines bright, beyond the stars above.

Their love has set me free, in service with humility.
So, I gave to all love, this is my only currency.

"Take a Sip of Whisky and Pretend You're Me"

I've given you many reasons hoping that you'd see me.
It's been many lonely years, sad that you've set me free.
I'd give you my creativity if we were meant to be.
I've turned from all my hopes and shattered dreams,
Living my life alone in sadness since you've turned from me.
There's no time for us, no longer reasons to discuss, you simply
have let me be.
So, take a sip of whisky and pretend you're me.
Think of me now and then perhaps you'll again have need of me.
It stands to reason that without true love, life's just so plain.
I've shed enough tears chasing you in perpetuity.
Now to frame myself with my art for all to see.
Perhaps there's someone out there who has need of my creativity.

[Instrumental]

I've written many things hoping that your love was for me.
Upon this world together as one for all to see.
I've framed you with my creativity in order to set you free.
I gave from my soul, hoping that you'd see and want me
Since the beginning of your career, yet you simply just can't see.
There's no longer any reason for me to give my art away.
There never was an us, no need to fuss, I've truly set you free.
So, take a sip of whisky and pretend you're me.
Think of way back when as you turned from me.
It stands to reason that without love, nothing's in it for me.
I've lost enough of my years chasing you in perpetuity.

Now to face myself and my art for all to see.
Perhaps there's someone out there who has need of my creativity.

[Instrumental]

I've suffered through homelessness, sadness, along with despair.
I've lived through much in the way of personal tragedy.
I'd have sacrificed all my art in exchange for a prenup and ring.
You healed my soul, regardless of how things stand between you
and me.
I'm thankful to have known true love even if it's not meant to be.
There never was an us, nothing truly to discuss, you simply don't
want me.
So, take a sip of whisky and give a toast to me.
Think of what I've given you, hoping that you'd face me.
It stands to reason that without true love, life has no reason.
I've given enough away for free chasing you in perpetuity.
Now to embrace my art to heal myself for all to see.
Perhaps there's someone out there who has need of my creativity.
[Pause]

Yeah, perhaps there's a woman out there waiting for a guy like me.
Who'd sacrifice her own life and art out of love for all to see.
Without regard to herself, embracing words given for humanity.
In the name of the one above walking away from the monetary.

"Waiting for You to Enter My Life"

I've made my list
I've checked it thrice
I've truly been good

Like whisky on ice
Waiting for you to enter my life.

I've been patiently waiting
It's the simple truth
I've been silently praying
My dreams simply all about you.

I've seen you while singing
I've watched you on TV
You've healed my broken soul
And through art, set me free.

I've kept my word
I've truly been nice
I've kept many secrets
Of this, you need not think twice.

So, you better look about
You better really try
By giving towards another
I'm the reason why
I've been kind, giving away love.

"Many Stories"

Many stories begin from pretend.
Some are fairy tales, while others sad, without end.
For many years, I destroyed all my art
Without considering the benefit to others,
Hiding my feelings within my soul.

My pain did grow, with nowhere to go.
Sadness and despair filled my life.

I'm now sharing all I create.
Some things are real, how I feel, not pretend.
For my future, I'm now facing my past.
Born from art, facing my heart.
Regardless of fear from the unknown.

My fears I know, I've let them go.
Happiness and joy now fill my soul.

My story begins from the unknown.
These many years, my soul's healed, and I have grown.
Fear's no longer holding back my being kind.
I've spent time crafting for others their dreams,
Ignoring my simple wants and needs.

My joy did grow, through others I know.
As King, I've given towards all with love.

Many years in my life have now passed.
I've lived in silence, along with despair, without end.
For a future to begin from every end.
I no longer hide out of fear.

My love's grown with what I know.
Through kindness, loves made me whole.

"I've Spent My Time"

My problems they keep coming
Weighing heavily upon my mind

Trying to simply move forward
Through acts of being kind
I've turned and walked away
Hiding what I can do
Trying not to take anything
Remaining humble, silent, and true
[Pause] I've spent my time, walking my imaginary line.

[Instrumental]

My issues they keep coming
Making me sad and blue
Dreaming of a better tomorrow
By spending time with you
Looking for my true love
To have and to hold
Building through love a family
As moments keep moving on
[Pause] I've spent my time, making a fricken dime.

[Instrumental]

My thoughts they keep coming
As I see them through
Trying to turn them over
Making other things come true
I've spent my time alone
Living life on the road
Selling tickets truth be told
A circus to simply behold
[Pause] I've spent my time, wishing you were mine.

[Instrumental]

My dreams they keep coming
No matter what I do
They have me truly hoping
That I'll make my way to you
I've given many things away
To heal my bruised soul
Giving your all takes a toll
[Pause] I've spent my time, yeah, I've spent my time.

"We Keep on Repeating Our Past Mistakes"

We're a bunch of slaves working in life for free.
We're a bunch of slaves working in perpetuity.
The few through money have our lives in their hands.
This isn't funny and this abuse must truly end.
Our treasuries built from the time of enslavement.
Its true values found within the lives it represents.
When we print what's required can we truly become free?
This is love towards us all yet hate sadly reigns over humanity.
[Pause] What's the point of it all if we keep repeating our past mistakes?

[Instrumental]

We'll never progress far enough and prevent our demise.
We'll never see our future; it will leave us all behind.
The trust is comprised of our lives which are of infinite worth.
The few have twisted it causing suffering and death.
It goes beyond our deaths towards the extinction of humanity.
This abuse must end before our end comes upon us all.
Unity and equality are human rights that we must possess.
Presently we have inherited a world based upon the opposite.

[Pause] What's the point of it all if we keep repeating our
past mistakes?

[Instrumental]

We need to come together and forgive the things left in our past.
We need to see each other though the lens of true love.
Sadly, hate reigns over us to the detriment of life itself.
The few keep their places this way by maintaining the status quo.
Leading us blindly towards war, the same processes as before.
Death is not a reward and can't compete with life itself.
We must eliminate laws and physical things which confine.
We must have a single currency to promote fairness for all.
[Pause] What's the point of it all if we keep repeating our
past mistakes?

[Instrumental]

War will occur if we allow the few to manipulate us all.
War will occur if we the people don't unite once and for all.
Hate truly knows no reason and can't see life's true worth.
Our governmental systems been twisted out of our care
By the accumulation of wealth and the use of debt collection.
Taxes should not exist under the conditions set forth currently.
Common rules and standards build trust and equality for all.
One constitution designed to promote love and equality for all.
[Pause] What's the point of it all if we keep repeating our
past mistakes?

[Instrumental]

Life's a precious commodity which when destroyed can't
be replaced.
Manipulation of our sacred trust must be set to rights for love

to reign.
If left unchecked they will continue to throw our lives down
the drain.
This path leads us all towards death which is not a reward.
Let us stop and ponder our history of what has gone on before.
This "US vs. THEM" mentality must be set aside; divided
humanity will fail.
This ploy's outdated and it should be set aside.
Equality and unity of purpose will overcome this circle of death.
[Pause] What's the point of it all if we keep repeating our
past mistakes?
[Pause] What's the point? Our lives can't simply be replaced.
[Pause] Life's our treasure not the accumulation of money.

"A Metaphor for Hope & Love"

Love of life must hold sway.
Giving is the light holding darkness at bay.
A metaphor for hope and love.

I get high off giving things away,
For positive cause and effect to hold sway.
Giving another a heart-felt hand.
Nothing in return, no pleas or demands.
Giving's an act of love.

Love of life must hold sway.
Giving is the light holding darkness at bay.
A metaphor for hope and love.

I've been hurt giving away my art.
It's out of love I gave others a start.

Giving's a way of living life.
Nothing in return, no pleas or demands.
Giving's the art of sacrifice.

Love of life must hold sway.
Giving is the light holding darkness at bay.
A metaphor for hope and love.

Although I'm known as sacrifice,
I'm a humble man, my name Johnny will suffice.
Giving towards a better tomorrow.
Nothing in return, no pleas or demands.
Giving's a form of utter humility.

Love of life must hold sway.
Giving is the light holding darkness at bay.
A metaphor for hope and love.

Some I have framed with my love of life,
Hiding my heart's hurt and strife.
I've given much away as focus can see
For our collective future, yes, you and me.
Nothing in return, no pleas or demands.
Giving to serve with utter clarity.

Love of life must hold sway.
Giving is the light holding darkness at bay.
A metaphor for hope and love.

"I Have Nothing to Show for My Brilliance"

"I'm alone lately.
Nowhere to go.

Nothing to do.
Resting all alone.
Basking within the sounds of my breathing."

My pain lingers without her embrace.
I've tried reason, I've tried kindness.
Tried to give, trying to live.
Blinded by the love within my heart
And the realization that I was used and cast aside
Without any love and someone to confide.
[Pause] Sadness remains. I have nothing to show for
my brilliance.

[Instrumental]

My dream's alive, yet I'm alone.
All I wanted was to earn her love.
I framed her for all to see
With my creative art and imagery.
Yet, she has turned sadly away,
Just like a nightmare within a play.
[Pause] Sadness remains. I have nothing to show for
my brilliance.

[Instrumental]

Through other people's hands I gave.
One can't take credit for gifts given.
People hide their intentions through cash.
People use their cash to associate.
People try to live out their dreams.
Yet no one cared to lend a hand.
[Pause] Sadness remains. I have nothing to show for
my brilliance.

[Instrumental]

My pain lingers, festers, and grows.
What I've truly suffered only Heaven knows.
Hear my plea filled with strife.
I've given my word as a bond.
I've framed many for all to see.
All in service towards helping humanity.
[Pause] Sadness remains. I have nothing to show for
my brilliance.

[Instrumental]

I wear my mask with a smile.
What I truly know I've set aside.
Some take while I chose to give.
Love is my currency I give with pride.
Helping others without a reason why.
Just to give another a reason to smile.
[Pause] Sadness remains. I have nothing to show for
my brilliance.

"Yet No One"

Giving my love away, more than I could stand.
Everybody took some, yet no one heard my heart-filled demand.
[Pause]

Giving my art away, more than I can say.
Nobody saw me, yet no one gave me a helping hand.
[Pause]

Giving my heart away, more than I could give.
Somebody help me. No one heard my love-filled prayer.
[Pause]

Giving my creativity away, more than I could bare.
Everybody knows me, yet no one chose to truly care.
[Pause]

Basking within my silence, my words all ring true.
Anybody hear me? No one has answered the call.
[Pause]

Giving my future away, yet more I must give.
Everybody's worth it, yet no one has given their all.

[Refrain]
Blinded by my love, deep within my old soul.
Giving away art is my calling; I now know my true role.
My heart has returned home, yet I'm still living life alone.

[Back to the top for another run-through]

[Spoken at the end of the second run-through with conviction along with sincerity]
I'd rather have no hands to hold than to own another person's sins from the days of old.

"Will Her Love Come Back to Me?"

I dreamt of a girl; sadly, my hopes went up in flames.
I gave from my soul, my art, heart, and imagery
'Cause I wanted her love.
But sadly, she didn't see.

I'll never be the same.
Will her love come back to me?

So, now I'm gone, and I've left her all alone.
Without my art, she struggles on her own
'Cause I need her to see
Just who she is to me.
I'll never be the same.
Will her love come back to me?

I gave my life away, hidden beneath it all.
My gifts were ignored; so, sadly, I walked away.

Sadly, my love. Yes, sadly my love.
Sadly, my love. Yes, sadly my love.
Without my love, your career shall never be the same.
Never will it be the same.

"Nothing in Life Is Truly Free"

[Open with the sound of our stock markets opening for business; setting of the video can be on the NYSE floor.]

The ringing of the bells.
Our collective worth does swell.
When our profits rise lining our wallets.
[Pause] Nothing in life is truly free.

Fueling the market's bottom line,
Our hopes rise and shine
When our profits soar funding our dreams.
[Pause] Nothing in life is truly free.

A sudden negative market turn
Has all our stomachs churn
As we all experience the Fed's rising rates.
[Pause] Nothing in life is truly free.

As our collective profits fall,
Some experience a market call.
For every profit loss, there's a hidden reason.
[Pause] Nothing in life is truly free.

[Spoken at the end of the first run-through only] This process
repeats every business day.

[Instrumental]

[Back to the top, repeat for a second run-through]

[Spoken at the end]
Some millionaires are indeed made,
Yet, some end up broke and played.
Because, win or lose, this is about control.

"Hope & Love"

I've known what to do without someone to hold.
I've known true love yet I'm still living life alone.
I've known the truth behind many different things.
I've known how to still smile without her love, prenup, and ring.
I've known utter sadness when death took people away.
I've known depression's grip and darkness along the way.

[Instrumental]

I'd rather walk alone without her love to call my own.
I'd rather starve myself than to be someone else.
I'd rather face my future with an open mind.
I'd rather give my prose towards helping others along the way.
I'd rather live alone than to embrace hate; it's the simple truth.
I'd rather wait for her love and hand to enter my life someday.

[Instrumental]

It brings me pleasure and hope, fueling my love-filled dreams.
It brings my art to life as I ponder many different things.
It brings me joy to give with love lending a helping hand.
It brings us all closer together and has divisiveness on the run.
It brings to mind that life's precious and shouldn't be
thrown away.
It brings its own rewards by sharing what I know.

[Instrumental]

[Speaking part]
Hope and love are timeless gifts in life, used to feed our
precious souls.
Without giving towards another and hoarding what we know,
We shall live in darkness, reaping what our ignorance has
truly sown.

"I've Been Waiting All This Time"

My dream takes her stage.
My heart can't turn the page,
Looking upon her, walking about.
Just for her hand, I've given more than I can stand.
She's my true love. This I'll scream and shout!

She drives my art, drives my heart, drives me crazy.
Wow, wow, wow…Truly crazy.
[Pause] I've been waiting all this time.

[Instrumental]

I've infused her life with art.
From the bottom of my heart
Right from the very start.
Just for her love that fits like a glove.
She's my true love. This I'll scream and shout!
She drives my art, drives my heart, drives me crazy.
Wow, wow, wow…Truly crazy.
[Pause] I've been waiting all this time.

[Instrumental]

My dream knows her place.
My heart she can't replace,
Looking about for her true love.
Just for her kiss, I filled her life with bliss.
She's my true love. This I'll scream and shout!
She drives my art, drives my heart, drives me crazy.
Wow, wow, wow…Truly crazy.
[Pause] I've been waiting all this time.

[Instrumental]

The way she simply talks,
The way she truly rocks, drives me wild.
The way she moves around.
Turning my frown upside down, I hit the ceiling.
She my true love. This I'll scream and shout!
She drives my art, drives my heart, drives me crazy.

Wow, wow, wow…Truly crazy.
[Pause] I've been waiting all this time.

[Instrumental]

The way she delivers art,
The way she twists my heart, makes me dizzy.
The way she makes me feel.
I can't any longer conceal, it's not been easy.
She my true love. This I'll scream and shout!
She drives my art, drives my heart, drives me crazy.
Wow, wow, wow…Truly crazy.
[Pause] I've been waiting all this time.

[Instrumental]

The way she meets my stare,
The way she wears her hair, knocks me out.
She has us all talking, she's a dream.
She was looking for me, for an eternity.
She my true love. This I'll scream and shout!
She drives my art, drives my heart, drives me crazy.
Wow, wow, wow…Truly crazy.
[Pause] I've been waiting all this time.

[Instrumental]

From the sound of her voice,
My beating heart does rejoice, I'm on fire.
I'm down on the mat, knocked out at that.
For many of these years,
I wiped away her tears with my art.
She my true love. This I'll scream and shout!
She drives my art, drives my heart, drives me crazy.

Wow, wow, wow…Truly crazy.
[Pause] I've been waiting all this time.

[Instrumental]

The way she simply talks,
The way she truly rocks, drives me wild.
The way she moves around,
Turning my frown upside down, I hit the ceiling.
She my true love. This I'll scream and shout!
She drives my art, drives my heart, drives me crazy.
Wow, wow, wow…truly crazy.
[Pause] I've been waiting all this time.

[Instrumental]

The way she delivers art,
The way she twists my heart, makes me dizzy.
The way she makes me feel,
I can't any longer conceal, it's not been easy.
She my true love. This I'll scream and shout!
She drives my art, drives my heart, drives me crazy.
Wow, wow, wow…truly crazy.
[Pause] I've been waiting all this time.

[Instrumental]

The way she meets my stare,
The way she wears her hair, knocks me out.
She has us all talking, she's a dream.
She was looking for me, for an eternity.
She my true love. This I'll scream and shout!
She drives my art, drives my heart, drives me crazy.

Wow, wow, wow…truly crazy.
[Pause] I've been waiting all this time.

[Instrumental]

From the sound of her voice,
My beating heart does rejoice, I'm on fire.
I'm down on the mat, knocked out at that.
For many of these years,
I wiped away her tears with my art.
She my true love. This I'll scream and shout!
She drives my art, drives my heart, drives me crazy.
Wow, wow, wow…truly crazy.
[Pause] I've been waiting all this time.

[Instrumental]

Wow, wow, wow…truly crazy.
Wow, wow, wow…truly crazy.
Wow, wow, wow…truly crazy.
[Pause] I've been waiting all this time.

"Peace through Forgiveness and Love"

How can it be that peace shall not reign
Between us all in this life?
History repeats, have you ever asked why?
Inequality breeds hate between you and me.
Life's the most precious of commodities,
But those in charge treat life as if it were a game.

Peace can truly reign, through forgiveness and love.
Provided we all forgive our collective past.

Why must the few try to control our lives
Between both a cap and a line?
Our treasuries are all tainted with the blood from our dead.
For we inherited a system built from hate.
If we could see through another person's eyes,
Equality would then overcome all forms of hate.

Peace can truly reign, through forgiveness and love.
Provided we all forgive our collective past.

Why do the few try to divide us all
With borders, conflicting laws, and other means?
The true value of any currency can be found within life itself.
The few are trying to retain their controls.
Unities are required for peace to reign, but that requires equality
for all.
But to do so, we must change our ways.

Peace can truly reign, through forgiveness and love.
Provided we all forgive our collective past.

"Eternal Love"

Eternal love…

I've travelled many miles during my life
Looking for the one to call my wife
These many empty years I wear with pride
For in truth, I've finally found my bride

[Refrain]

Eternal love…

The years have quite simply flown on by
I've lived alone and I've my reasons why
When you've found the one you truly love
Another can't compare I swear by God above

[Refrain]

Eternal love…

I know my role in this life of mine
Like the stars above this knowledge does shine
Yet I don't have her in my arms
But for her I'll wait to cast my charms

[Refrain]

Eternal love…

My heart just will not turn the page
Come whatever that may, including the Ice Age
Some things are of infinite value and dearth
While others have no real value or worth

[Refrain]
Just like a river connects to a sea
There's no other in this life for me
For her I'll propose down upon my knee
In this life and the next unto eternity

[Spoken]
What you'll come to realize within time is that infinity runs an
awfully long time.

"Facing My Art and Embracing the Music"

My time has arrived and I'm following my dreams,
Pause/whisper: It's true.
My art will shine bright, like the stars in our night sky.
I've been walking within my shadows' embrace.
It's time for my voice to be heard,
My feelings of love to be released.
For many years, I've embraced my silence,
Listening to the needs of the world,
And sacrificing my art by giving it all away.
Wearing my mask made of love.

[Speaking part] Facing my art and embracing my music.

I must follow my heart and face the music.
Armed with my art, I have saved for myself.
[Pause/whisper with a smile while pointing to oneself]
What, myself?
Our world fills my soul with love for I know my role:
To encase you all with the love within what I create.

My soul has been freed, by the love within my heart.
Our art shall take wing and shine for all to embrace.
My temple of love is within my heart and mind.
Just like a wall, it's built with art and creativity.
My words shall hit home, freeing our true potential,
Freeing us all from the trappings of enslavement,
Brought out of the darkness into our collective light.

[Speaking part] Facing my art and embracing my music.

I have followed my heart and faced the music.
Armed with my art, I have saved for myself.

Our world fills my soul with love for I know my role:
Encasing all with love through the power of creation, making
us whole.

"I Did It with Humility"

As of now, my future's quite clear.
I've given my life serving humanity freely.
The TRUST needs my love, of this, I'm most certain.
As king, I gave my heart and encased those I love with my art.
But more, much more than this, I did it with humility.

I've made some mistakes, of this I'm quite certain.
But through it all, without any doubts,
I remain myself, free from the taint of their sins.
For the TRUST's sacred, it has my love and heart.
But more, much more than this, I did it with humility.

With a humble heart, and my love-filled soul,
I heard your call: I healed your artistic soul.
I've made no demands from anyone of you.
I severed all strings and avoided any money.
But more, much more than this, I did it with humility.

Yes, there were times that I became unglued,
That they threw at me more, but I pulled through.
Through it all, without any doubt,
I served you all, from my heart.
And so, I live alone, waiting for her love.

Yes, I'm waiting for her love.

"Tried"

You've tried to hold sway over my love-filled dreams
You've tried to take away that which is not yours
I've tried to give away all that I could create
I've tried to walk away for love to come today
We've tried to simply unite through the confines of slavery
We've tried to undo hate through the use of love
They've tried to divide us through the use of differences
They've tried to separate us through the use of currency
[Pause] You've tried, I've tried, we've tried, they've tried, yeah.

[Instrumental]

You've tried to hold back my future over their past
You've tried to make decisions based upon your personal greed
I've tried to show you through my love and heart
I've tried to give you the love I have inside
We've tried to work together with common purpose and reason
We've tried to create together a living legacy through love
They've tried to remove me from my service towards all
They've tried to take credit for the love inside me
[Pause] You've tried, I've tried, we've tried, they've tried, yeah.

[Instrumental]

You've tried to simply rule through the pulling of strings
You've tried to replace me through my unrealized dreams
I've tried to heal inside by working freely without love
I've tried to simply hide that which I hold inside
We've tried to undo hate through the use of it
We've tried to undo fate before it's simply too late
They've tried to rule perpetually through the use of cash
They've tried to sever innovators from their creations

through greed
[Pause] You've tried, I've tried, we've tried, they've tried, yeah.

[Instrumental]

You've tried to simply hide through using another person's hands
You've tried to simply deflect my future due to their mistakes
I've tried to remain silent and accept that nothing's perfect
I've tried to remain humble through treating everyone with love
We've tried to focus humanity on its future through repetition
We've tried to see reason through the use of opinions
They've tried to gain time through the use of carbon
They've tried to push forward through the repetition of mistakes
[Pause] You've tried, I've tried, we've tried, they've tried, yeah.

[Instrumental]

Yeah, much of it has been tried…(Tried)

"I'm Living Out My Dreams"

So now, my dream draws near.
And I shall rejoice, within her embrace.
My friends, dreams do come true,
I'm telling the truth, I'm truly certain.
I've given away in this life,
Helping others, without any strings.
And more, with love in my heart,
I gave my art away.

The regrets I have
Are not worth the time to mention.
I sacrificed for the greater good,

And I did so, with the best of intentions.
I tried to erase my pain
By facing my creative side.
And more, with love in my heart,
I gave in every single way.

Yes, the time is now, of this I know.
I must share the light from within my soul.
And say out loud, through all my pain,
That the greater good, through love, must reign.
I will face it all and share out loud.
And within my heart, my treasure's found.

I'm a humble man of modest means,
Who stumbled upon love within his dreams.
So now, I'm sharing how I feel.
Embracing my art that I've concealed.
Just so, that you all know…
I'm living out my dreams.
[Pause] Yes, I'm living out my dreams.

"Peace"

Why do people fight throughout each day and night?
Throwing away their lives, weighs heavily upon my mind.
Life's a priceless gift, nothing else truly does compare.

I'm writing this piece, for peace to once again reign.
Love's to be embraced, for war and hate solves nothing.
I gave my art to heal everyone's hearts.

Reasons for their fights are due directly to inequality.
Forcing people to migrate, to improve their lives.
If it were up to me, I'd setup things differently.

It's truly sad, you know: people reap that which they sow.
Currency differentials sadly enslave entire cultures,
Diminishing the infinite value of our collective lives.

[Refrain]
We must simply unite; there's no reason then to fight.

"Remarkable"

Remarkable, your voice has touched my soul.
Remarkable, with your love I'd become whole.
Like a fairy tale, with love my heart set sail
Just from a thought of your hand in mine.
We've yet to have met, but upon you, my heart is set.

Remarkable, I've given towards you from my art.
You're my dream, my love-filled fantasy (Fantasy)
That's who you truly are to me,
You're beyond remarkable, it's true.

[Instrumental]

So, take a moment and look back on your life,
I've given you mine, as a husband towards a wife.
It's all been simply remarkable (Remarkable)
For eternity, I've built your life's love-filled fantasy.
A living opera of which I'm your benevolent phantom.
Because you stole my heart, right from the very start.
Think on this woman, my love's remarkable too…

"Don't Try Looking for Rainbows"

Don't try looking for rainbows
While the rainclouds are thick in the sky.
They'll appear when they depart,
And the sun is shining way up high,
Though many tears have fallen,
and many lonely years have passed on by.
Rainclouds don't hang around forever,
Many rainbows shall appear for you and me.

Our love is a metaphor,
And the rainclouds are issues which pass by.
You're in truth my rainbow,
And your love is my pot of gold.
Spend your love upon me (Baby),
And spend your time as we grow old.
Our faith shall lead us,
And tears of our happiness shall indeed fall.

I've been blessed with abilities,
And I've given many pieces of art away.
Healing folks with my love,
Taking nothing, and then I simply walked away.
My soul cries for you,
Without you, I'd rather continue living life alone.
Since I've walked away,
Do you miss me now that I'm gone?

I'm not able to settle,
For nothing else really can compare to you.
I've been alone for years,
Waiting for my dreams to all come true.

I'm a king of old,
My kingdom rests within my heart and mind.
I believe within you all,
And towards most of you, I've been kind.

[Refrain]
I've left you many clues,
And it's within you that my heart resides.
Together we've already been one,
Working in unison for this is our time

"Bitter Pills"

I've much to say
Yet I'm utterly silent
Looking for my future
Stumbling on my past
I've opened up inside
As the doors closed
[Pause]

Take this, take that
Do this, do that
Swallow this, swallow that
Yet another bitter pill...

Trapped in the dark
Walking in the light
Much time has passed
Finishing the race last
I've opened up inside

A door swung wide
[Pause]

Take this, take that
Do this, do that
Swallow this, swallow that
Yet another bitter pill...

Holding back my tears
Swallowing all my fears
Though the empty years
Drinking many bitter beers
Just to cope inside
Heart is open wide
[Pause]

Take this, take that
Do this, do that
Swallow this, swallow that
Yet another bitter pill...

Bitter are my tears
As hope draws near
Looking towards the future
While forgetting my past
Walking down the aisle
Going the extra mile
[Pause]

Take this, take that
Do this, do that
Swallow this, swallow that
Yet another bitter pill...

[Refrain]
Bitter pills
Multiple reasons to swallow
Bitter pills
Making me fricken hollow
Yeah...

"Put It to the Match"

Walking towards my future
With nowhere to go
Looking forward to life
Yet I'm dead inside
Damn...Put it to the match

Sadly I'm on empty
Yet my soul's full
I sadly went wrong
But I was right
Damn...Put it to the match

God knows my future
Healing my broken past
One foot to go
Yet miles off track
Damn...Put it to the match

Gone through my Hell
Just to enter Heaven
Lost my fricken mind
Just by being kind
Damn...Put it to the match

Burning with passion inside
Without any foolish pride
Looking for Mrs. Right
Morning, noon, and night
[Pause]

Damn...Damn...Damn...Light another fricken match

Gone are many yesterdays
Facing my empty days
Looking for her hand
Was my heart's demand
Damn...Put it to the match

My pilot lights lit
But alone at night
Framed many with art
Direct from my heart
Damn...Put it to the match

Treading softly in life
Yet surrounded by death
Never broke the line
Pass me more wine
Damn...Put it to the match

I wrote many things
For that single ring
Filled with much pain
Hit me yet again
Damn...Put it to the match

Damn...Damn...Damn...Where's my damn match?

You're my love match
Simply my prized catch
You're that simple itch
That I can't scratch

Damn...Damn...Damn...
[Pause]

Can you spare a match?

"Equality is a Human Right!"

Living within my mind is just a game.
Hiding in plain sight is just the same.
Living upon the extreme edges of this game.
Hiding what I do is just so lame.
[Pause] Without money do you really exist? [Pause]

Sharing with others though out my entire life.
Giving's what is needed to prevent world strife.
Sharing my creativity freely robbed me of life.
Giving's its own reward cost me a wife.
[Pause] Without flowers can you make honey? [Pause]

Hurting without an existence cost the world peace.
Healing pain will give my life a release.
Hurting others through war shall not bring peace.
Healing only comes through extending life a lease.
[Pause] Without purpose does life have meaning? [Pause]

Love in my heart has healed many situations.
Hate set aside has filled me with solutions.
Love is required to heal our current situations.

Hate extinguishes life without unity in the solutions.
[Pause] Without forgiveness can you have harmony?

[Back to the top for a second run-through]

[Instrumental]

[Refrain]
Common rules will weather any storm.
Without reason we have no rules.
Equality is a fundamental human right.
This will lead humanity to unite.
We must set aside our hate.
Else we will seal our fate.

"Art From the Heart"

[Part 1/ Singer A/ Male]
Love is my spark
It lights my way
The sight of it blinds me
Cautions thrown aside

I gave freely
Without strings or rewards
The only thing that lingers
The beat of my heart

[Part 2/ Singer B/ Female]
I've been touring around for a long time now
Love has eluded me yet I have my art
I'm not the same woman when I'm at home

Nor while I'm under the covers, baby (*sultry laugh*)
It's too bad that you'll never know...

[Instrumental]

[Part 3/ Singer B/ Male]
You're my *Mona Lisa*
Captured for all time
The mention of you blinds me
Has me unhinged

I gave freely
Encased you with art
The absence of you lingers
Yet your still my heart

[Part 4/ Singer B/ Female]
I've been touring around for a long time now
Love has eluded me yet I have my art
I'm not the same woman when I'm at home
Nor while I'm under the covers baby [Sultry laugh]
It's too bad that you'll never know...

[Instrumental]

[Back to the top, repeat once only then end with the following]

[End part 5/ Singer A/ Male: sing with sad realization]
Art from the heart in exchange for your love...
Although I've been had, you've been framed.
For all time...

[Closing statement to be read softly]
You never could see beyond the value of my art.

"Many Roses and Rainbows"

Chasing after the money
Where does it hide?
Working many a day
Taken for a ride
Spending all I have
Just to let go
This is my issue
Hard breaking your hold

Tripping over past decisions
Swallowed many bitter pills
Drank down much alcohol
Just for some thrills
It's never been money
That drove me wild
Simply for true love
I'd wait for a while

Chasing after my dream
Where does she hide?
I've given much away
In you I'll confide
Spent all I have
Just so you know
This is my issue
This story's old

Tripping over past decisions
Swallowed many bitter pills
Drank down much alcohol
Just for some thrills

It's never been money
That drove me wild
Simply for true love
I'd wait for a while

Chasing after my memories
Where did they go?
My heart still roams
Looking for a home
Spending all my time
Just to lose you
This is my issue
Let my story unfold

Tripping over past decisions
Swallowed many bitter pills
Drank down much alcohol
Just for some thrills
It's never been money
That drove me wild
Simply for true love
I'd wait for a while

[Refrain]
Many roses and rainbows
Clouds in the sky
Remind me of you
As my days. . .
Pass on by. . .
Time spent dreaming
With love in my heart
So I could frame you
With love through my art

"Can You Hear It?"

Can you hear it? My soul crying throughout my life. God knows.
And I have never sacrificed my soul for your love. God knows.
Can't you see that I gave away my life? To make you whole. God
knows, God knows.

And, so, I left you. Alone, without my love-fueled art in your life.
Although I still love you, you're not directly within my life.
It's true.
Would you ever do as I have done for you? Sacrifice your art
for love?
I haven't been a recipient of the gift of your love, a sad truth.

So, I live my life. Without someone to have and to hold, my
love's gone.
If you never, never, never, never, ever appear within my life.
My help will never, ever return…return.

I do try to remember that I have made a great difference without
a reward.
For God's love to shine upon my life and heal my very soul.
I can never forgive or forget the pain of the lessons in life I
have learned.
But I know… know, know…
that you love me… within the heart of my soul.
But they control your life, through contracts, money, and
associations. God knows, God knows.

Can you hear it? My soul crying throughout my life. God knows.
And I have never sacrificed my soul for your love. God knows.
Can't you see that I gave away my life? To make you whole. God
knows, God knows.

Although I have been offered
To leave with your heart and hand at our show, many years ago,
It was a game of dishonor, where I'd have to sacrifice my
very soul.
They're see-through paper gangsters controlled by the pull of
a string.
Although I have love for them, I'm no fool—a romantic, but not
a fool.

So, remember!
That you get back in life what you give, it's the truth.
There will come a day when I shall have my love returned,
by you.
That "Meet and Greet" that never occurred within Radio City
because of you.

Can you hear it? My soul crying throughout my life. God knows.
And I have never sacrificed my soul for your love. God knows.
Can't you see that I gave away my life? To make you whole. God
knows, God knows.
Yes, God knows. . .
[Pause]

[Speak with a sad yet determined voice] You reap that which
you sow.

"Keep Your Cool No Matter What"

I first saw her today on the TV
A plate of salad the focus of her ire
Secretly, she was being goaded
A local game show was capturing the play at hand

They finally made the woman lose her cool
The waitress was rewarded with a swear

[Refrain]
I saw her the other day in concert
Dancing and singing to what I wrote
I found my dream... Oh, yes!
I found my dream!

Fast forward to today, looking back
Upon my life's sad direction
Illness has robbed me of my true love
So, I'm confronting my hollow past
[Pause]

You never can tell when true love will appear
But without it, you're nothing, least of all whole
My heart will eventually sing in celebration
When I have her to hold within my arms
Oh, yes...

Gone is my youthful appearance
My blondish hair is now fully gray
I've gained weight due to my depression
All the while I've hidden what I've needed to convey
Money has controlled her directions
Sadly, she hasn't seen this simple truth
I monthly must go into Costco
Swallowing prescriptions galore for my sanity

Gone are many of my memories
Dead are many of my friends
Sad that my love's been rejected

Alone I shall live my life until the end
For true love isn't a game of pretend

[End with repeating the refrain then fade out]

[Refrain]
Never can you get all that you want
Never can you get all that you need
But if you keep your cool, no matter what
You'll win in more ways than one

"My Heart Aches Deep Within"

I look all around and realize that something's missing
My heart aches deep within
I ponder what went wrong, altering my path toward true love
Still, my heart aches deep within

I don't know who you truly are
Or what you look like
Or where you're going
Yet my love for you is true

As my lonely years pass along slowly
And old age creeps up on me
My heart's filled with love
Still, my heart aches deep within

As life moves along and my heart is still beating
I'm still hooked upon you (True)
I yearn for true love to share my life and my love
Yet my heart still aches deep within

I look all around and realize that something's missing
My heart aches deep within
I ponder what went wrong, altering my path toward true love
Still my heart aches deep within

I shall wait for your love to come and heal my soul
Our hearts would join, beating finally as one
I know that no one else can ever replace you
So, I'm still waiting with outstretched arms

Sad. . . and very lonely
Yes. . . I'm in need of you
Yet. . . only you will do

Yes. . . it's the truth that I'm still waiting
For your true love to come back home
Oh . . how I have, need for your love
So, I'm going to wait some more

Sad. . . and very lonely
Yes. . . I'm in need of you
Yet. . . only you will do
[Pause]

Only you will ever do. . . true

"Life Isn't a Game of Pretend"

. . . Everyone
. . . What would you do if I disrespected you?
Or said something rude and inhumane?
Lend me your time and on you, I'll drop my dime
And I'll try to treat you all the same.

. . . Oh, what's life without love between us?
Hmm? Would peace between us be alright?
How do you cope with bombs dropping like rain?
Oh, how this world has truly gone quite insane.

. . . Why didn't you all tell me the simple truth,
That although I'm king, I'm to live my life alone?
Wouldn't you all feel sad and truly, deeply blue?
If I stopped my giving and simply walked away.

. . . Oh, it's not life to be without love in the end.
Truth. Bringing peace to this planet so life don't end.
. . . Sad that my life shall eventually come to an end.

. . . Don't you have dreams and aspirations?
But they're all hollow without love and someone to hold.
. . . Doesn't she see that I gave away my life?
All I wanted was for her to become the one I'd love and grow old.

How would you feel if those you loved had died?
Would you care or simply shrug it off and move along?
Or would you want to pay them back for whatever they
had done?
Forgiveness is truly for oneself but is a gift for all.

. . . Oh, it's not life to be without love in the end.
Truth. Bringing peace to this planet so life don't end.
. . . Sad that my life shall eventually come to an end.
. . . Oh, why must we live to only die, without true love?
Sad. To be alone in this life without her love.
. . . Life is to be lived with the realization that it's a gift in the end.

Some are blessed to live lives as if they were a game of pretend.
Some are capable of helping another, but they turn them aside in

the end.
Some bring forward children to love and pass along that which
they know and own.
Some do lie and hide, lurking in shadows and stabbing people
they know.
Trying to get ahead they most often don't remember that things
come back around.

Oh, what is life without love in the end?
You still must leave it all behind in the end.
Life isn't a game of pretend.
Truth. Life isn't a game of pretend.

"All That You Do Will Come Back to You!"

Why do they hold onto hate?
Turn aside, forgive before it's too late.
Remember that love must see you all through.
Why do they try to take away
That which is sacred in every way?
God truly has love for all of you.

All that you do
Shall return to you. . .
All that you do
Will come back to you.

Why must they throw their lives away?
To confront your hate in every way.
Isn't life precious to all of you?
Aren't we all beyond the past?

Forgive and build a future that will last.
God truly has love for all of you.

All that you do
Shall return to you. . .
All that you do
Will come back to you.

Why do they fight every day?
Equality's a requirement in every single way.
A few hold onto behaviors of old.
We're all slaves to the bottom line,
The currency of life is life itself.
God truly has love for all of you.

All that you do
Shall return to you. . .
All that you do
Will come back to you.

All that you do. . .
All that you do. . .
All that you do. . .
Will come back to you.
Yeah. . .
Will come back to you.

"Broken Dreams"

So will my true love
Ever come back to me?
I have given love away,
Taking nothing; can't you see?

It was a brighter world,
Serving for the greater good.
It was costing my life
In humble service to humanity.
So, I played my roll,
As king up on high.
In service for you all,
A puppet without any strings.
It has taken from me,
My true love in life.
To have and to hold,
As husband for a wife.
I kept my battles inside,
Yet the pain still grows.
For she is my dream,
My heart's only true rose.
I've lost yet I've won,
Giving to all who asked.
And so, I walked away,
Letting go of my dreams.
Faces, places have all changed,
Because I was ill inside.
It cost me many years,
Yet I've kept this inside.
I'm caught within a play.
What must I give away?
I truly didn't really fail,
My soul isn't for sale.
Blood, sweat, and many tears
Throughout all my empty years.
Can she not see me?

The stuff of broken dreams.
[Pause]

[Speak with a sad, sorrow-filled voice at the end] Broken Dreams,
Broken dreams. . . Nothing's as it seems.

[Videography]
A masked man (*Phantom of the Opera* mask), standing facing
the audience with one outstretched hand and the other upon his
heart, clasping a red rose, wearing a Shrine fez, Masonic apron.
The stage is filled with a low-level fog. The backdrop is many
shattered mirrors (*Phantom of the Opera*-style, with red velour
curtains behind. A mirror disco ball spins, casting light onto the
mirrors (Illuminate the fog in places underneath). End with all
the light sources fading to black.

"Death Brings Darkness, Life Brings Light"

Through the thick fog of war
Lives are checked at the door
As the guns all do sing
From blood poppies once again spring

Our lives are precious, you know
Sadly, evil deeds we do sow
Equality will eventually once again rise
Unity in this life's our prize

Bullets are cheap and life priceless
Sanity must reign in every field
We need to forgive the past
In order to secure our future

The beauty of roses in bloom
Versus shadows, darkness, and doom
Corpses used to build a wall
Life's a gift for us all

By forgiving these issues of old
We can bring all into the fold
Life can't be bought or sold
We must break this repetitive mold

[Refrain]
Death brings darkness; life brings light
Do what's right, let us unite
Lives can't be replaced with death

[Pause]

[Soft firmly with resolve and conviction] Sanity and reason must meet, in every field!

[Pause briefly, then read the poem I wrote titled "In Every Field!"]

[Videography]
Opening scene:
Have soldiers in full gear marching across the fog-filled stage (illuminated underneath), followed by the singer all dressed in red; she will pause at the side of the tomb facing the audience as the soldiers disappear off stage.

Closing scene:
Lower the lights in the house slowly throughout the performance, ending in complete darkness. Have a spotlight shining down upon the tomb of the unknown soldier on the stage; a widow dressed in black carrying a bouquet of red roses

and holding the hand of a small child shall then appear and kneel in front of it, placing the roses at the foot of the tomb.

"Can't They See? Fools!"

Fools never think beyond the here and now.
As the meaning of their lives escapes them.
Living in the circles of their repetitive actions.
Bullets, bombs, ignorance are the tools of war.
War occurs when there is no common ground.
[Pause] War brings death, peace brings life, "What's your preference?"

Fools, they always covet what their neighbor has.
They forget the true wealth on this planet.
Living in the circles of their own folly.
Everywhere they bring disease, suffering, strife, and death.
War occurs when you try to bully another.
[Pause] War brings death, peace brings life, "What's your preference?"

Fools most often mistake material wealth for true worth.
Forsaking life is akin to autumn leaves signaling change.
The seasons repeat in order to sustain life.
The collapse of democracy through a gun barrel.
War occurs when you promote inequality and inequity.
[Pause] War brings death, peace brings life. "What's your preference?"

Fools try to possess all through monetary hoarding.
The lack of reason brings about true insanity.
If we but respected the life of another.

Alas, it's "Us vs. Them" through opposing opinions.
War occurs when you have no real solution.
[Pause] War brings death, peace brings life. "What's
your preference?"

Fools hide from the truth, hate breeds hate.
We're supposed to be all of us equals.
Presently our global governments are inherited
from enslavement.
We disrespect entire cultures through our many differences.
War occurs when you try to treat others unfairly.
[Pause] War brings death, peace brings life. "What's
your preference?"

[Refrain]
Can't they see. . .
The writing upon the wall?
The red velour curtain fall?
The many forms of death?
Life is our true wealth!
Can't they see. . .

[Statement to be read at the end] War solves nothing, it breeds
hate, and then the cycle repeats through the children who now
have hate in their hearts twenty-five years later.

"Follow Your Dreams, Follow Your Hearts"

I always put off today,
What I could've done yesterday.
I was dreaming away life,
Rather than facing my life.

Living my life in the past,
Dreams die often real fast.
Have you ever looked back,
Trying to find your lack?
Mirrors only works with light.
Wisdom is earned, that's right.
Procrastination, yeah. . . procrastination.

Procrastination. . .
Is a circle of pain.
Procrastination. . .
Is fear facing your pain.
Procrastination. . .
Much will you sadly lose.
Procrastination. . .
Your destiny, you must choose.

Many people, places, things repeat.
Obstacles designed you must defeat.
One must overcome one's pain
In order for happiness to reign.
Listen to your heart's purpose,
Allow the future to surface.
Some marry their career path,
Searching for their true path.
Greed causes many sad disruptions,
Leading toward war sadly erupting.
Follow through, yeah. . . follow your heart.

Procrastination will cause you pain.
Procrastination, who bears the blame?
[Pause]

Follow your dreams, follow your hearts.

"We All Need Love"

Abandoning my sadness that keeps me in pain.
Applying a Band Aid to a mortal wound.
Why rub salt into these festering wounds?
When all it requires is love-filled cure.
Abandoning my sadness that keeps me in pain.
Applying a Band Aid to a mortal wound.
Why rub salt into these festering wounds?
When all it requires is love-filled cure.

We must do more than sit back and repeat.
Every wrong's amplified when it's repeated in perpetuity.
Ignorance is born from a lack of thought.
Ignorance is a weapon too, born from wrongs of the past.
Stop and consider what your life's worth.
Don't mistake wealth for worth.

All too soon we lose our youth, life wasted, spent chasing
circles. . .
All too soon we lose our youth, life wasted, spent chasing
circles. . .

Abandoning my sadness that keeps me in pain.
Applying a Band Aid to a mortal wound.
Why rub salt into these festering wounds?
When all it requires is love-filled cure.

Abandoning my sadness that keeps me in pain.
Applying a Band Aid to a mortal wound.
Why rub salt into these festering wounds?
When all it requires is love-filled cure.

We must do more than sit back and repeat.
Every wrong's amplified when it's repeated in perpetuity.
Ignorance is born from a lack of thought.
Ignorance is a weapon too born from wrongs of the past.
Stop and consider what your life's worth.
Don't mistake wealth for worth.

All too soon we lose our youth, life wasted, spent chasing
circles. . .
All too soon we lose our youth, life wasted, spent chasing
circles. . .

How can you build a future upon the sins of our past?
Death is our legacy within this construct.

Like a preacher, asking for forgiveness (We need this!)
Like a politician, speaking in truths (We need this!)
Like an order, applied against chaos (We need this?)
Like a soldier, applying death's solutions (We need this?)

We all need love. . . Put aside the lies. . .

"Can't You All See?"

Can't you all see?
That we're all wasting our time.
Chasing money in perpetuity, casting aside our liberty.
Will reason not prevail?

Or will our futures set sail?
Liberty's found by embracing everyone as an equal.
Inequality only breeds hate.
Help each other before it's too late!
Forgive those who have trespassed against you.
So we can move forward together in unity.

So, can't you all see?
Love of life's greater than hate.
Set aside our differences, for life is not a game.
Will reason truly prevail?
Or shall we simply fail?
Only through forgiveness can we reconcile our past.
In order for life to prevail,
We must help each other, else we all shall fail.
Common sense is based upon reason,
No matter the time, place, or specific season.

Can't you all see?
That time's running short.
We must set aside carbon fuels, which cause mass extinctions.
Will cooler heads prevail?
Will reason lift the veil?
Thankfully it's not too late to change our collective fate.
Wisdom's only found through true love,
God already has enough angels up above.

So, will you yield your hate?
Before it's simply too late.
We must set to right our path and reach for the stars above.
Will truth truly prevail?
Will humanity simply fail?
So it's up to you and me, do you want humanity to simply die?

We must stop repeating the same old play,
Or humanity shall succumb to death and decay.

"A Broken Master of Puppets"

I'm caught up within a play
Much of which I can't say
Use or be used,
That's the way

He tries to get us all
Answering to his beck and call
I bid farewell to you,
Along with your games

I've cut the strings of fellowship
I've walked away from you today
You're nothing more than. . .
A broken master of puppets

No matter what we do
No matter where we go
My door has been closed to you. . .
Forevermore

Trust is something earned
The truth of this I did learn
I have replaced my focus. . .
And walked away

So take a look around,
What have you truly found?

You're gazing toward your future
Through a broken rearview mirror

Since our friendship's died
Our paths no longer coincide
I return to working,
Upon my life's dreams

Can't you see the cost,
Of what truly you've lost?
Self-delusion shall not carry you far.
A broken master of puppets

Sure, you're great upon the loom
But you can't see beyond your own tomb
It's a fine trap constructed
From the remnants of. . .
Broken people, places, and things
[Pause]

Farewell.

"My Heart"

I'm still yearning for you.
Waiting for the day our paths will collide and our dream will
come true.
My heart is yours, no matter what I've tried to do.
So come back to me, no one else will ever do.

I've thrown my art at you.
Framed you with gifts of prose in order for your dreams to
come true.

I've paid the price by walking away from all of you.
Preserving my soul, no matter what others have tried to do.

We're finally together at last.
Our hearts now one, built upon our mutual treasured past.
This monstrous dream has now passed, burning bright and fast.
Healing our wounds through our love that has come to pass.

It's been a plethora of years.
Sharing life together, building our place, overcoming our mutual tears and fears.
Time has flown and we both do show the passage of many years.
Our hearts still beat in rhythm filled with love that's cherished and held dear.

It's now my time to go.
Toward a place we know within our souls that I pray you'll wait to follow.
Please lead a long life filled with love from within your heart.
It's now time for us to part, please don't dwell within sorrow.

Although you shall shed many tears,
Worry not for me, I shall wait for you, regardless of the number of years.
I hope you'll find your way forward, regardless of all your internal fears.
Release my hand, depart, and know that he's calling unto me, my dear.

[Brief pause]

My path is clear, bright, filled with love and light. . .

"This Is My Story"

I dream of her constantly
Yet I live life alone
From the very first moment
I've had nowhere to turn and nowhere to go

I fight using my soul
Against the confines of circumstance
Although I've swallowed much sorrow
Reaching out toward all with love

This is my story,
I'm following my heart
No matter what happens,
Right from the start.

I fought back the night
By giving away my art
Turned down all the money
To reap that which I've sown!

And I know what I need to do
To mend my very soul
I must honor my love-filled heart
Giving my all, embracing my art

And this already improved our world
How one man's story healed many hearts
One doesn't live forever
What are you leaving behind, before you go?

This is my story,
I'm embracing my art

No matter what happens,
This is my start
To overcome that which you fear
Setting aside hate by embracing love

"Someday, My True Love"

Someday, my true love will come back to me
Although much time has passed
For her, my heart still sings
Someday, I'll bask in love, from another soul
Upon that very day, she will make me whole

Somehow, my love, we'll eventually have a chance
Until that precious day, you'll always be my bad romance

You'll have to find your way into my daily life
And I'll marry you and make you my heart's only wife
Stefani, can't you see, that you're never alone
For I have framed you with more than mere words

You'll have your day, all dressed up in white
Walking down the aisle, wearing a smile so bright
Stefani, can't you see, you're my heart's only rose
And it will be a breath of spring when you finally propose

Although our lives will end, our souls shall carry on
This is no game of pretend, when two join into one
For me there's no one else, all others pale compared to you
So, I'll wait for you, for our love is true.

[Back to the top, repeat for a second run-through]

"Omicron"

We're all living for the day that Omicron will simply fade away
Scientists are searching for that way, to put the lid upon what
needs to be done
Every life lost was precious, lights that cannot be replaced
But, by working each day well into the night, we will eventually
win this fight!

Omicron will take your life away
God already has enough angels dwelling with Him today
Wars are fought in order for our freedoms today
Omicron, we will win against you, that's right!

Most of us line up, row on row; our lives are precious, don't
you know?
Vaccines are created to keep our deaths at bay, but some are still
being lost anyway.
Some may think this is perpetual waste of time, trying to save
lives, yours and mine.
The day will come that we will all work for free, giving with
kindness to secure our liberty.
It's up to each of us to answer freedom's call.

We're all living for the day that Omicron will simply fade away
Scientists are searching for that way, to put the lid upon what
needs to be done
Every life lost was precious, lights that cannot be replaced
But, by working each day well into the night, we will eventually
win this fight!

Omicron will take your life away
God already has enough angels dwelling with Him today

Wars are fought in order for our freedoms today
Omicron, we will win against you, that's right!

Most of us line up, row on row; our lives are precious, don't
you know?
Vaccines are created to keep our deaths at bay, but some are still
being lost anyway.
Some may think this is perpetual waste of time, trying to save
lives, yours and mine.
The day will come that we will all work for free, giving with
kindness to secure our liberty.
It's up to each of us to answer freedom's call.

What's the real difference between you and me? Eliminate these
differences in order to become free.

"Every Day Is Christmas"

Every day's Christmas, I know this in my heart
But the world's run with hate and has turned our love away
Each day, this tears me apart [Whisper] (Tears me apart)
For our lives are precious and special

So, Merry Christmas, toward one and all
May all our burdens be lifted away
I'm telling you: can't you all see?
That hate must turn into love

Each day's Christmas, deep within my old soul
I framed everyone with my art from my heart
Each day, their absence is hidden with a smile
Without living my life with that someone special

Those in power, don't play fair
I'm determined to be myself

Every day's Christmas, I know this in my heart
But the world's run with hate and has turned our love away
Each day, this tears me apart [Whisper] (Tears me apart)
For our lives are precious and special

So, Merry Christmas, toward one and all
May all our burdens be lifted away
I'm telling you: can't you all see?
That hate must turn into love

Each day's Christmas, deep within my old soul
I framed everyone with my art from the heart
Each day, their absence is hidden with a smile
Without living my life with that someone special

Those in power don't play fair
I'm determined to be myself

There's a rift between those who hold sway
Over our lives come whatever that may
We need to treat everyone like ourselves
Before the circle of hate repeats

So, Merry Christmas, toward one and all
May all our burdens be lifted away
I'm telling you: can't you all see?
That hate must turn into love [Whisper] (Love)

"All My Giving"

As I lay my head in rest
My life has been truly blessed
For my love for you is absolutely true
I gave my love away, toward all who came my way
Yet I'm still living life alone; I'm blue.

Life's no game of pretend; therefore, my sadness has no end
For my soul is not for sale, that's true
So, I waste my life each day, giving my heart away
Toward making other people's dreams come true.

All my giving is hidden from your view
All my giving has made me sad and blue.

As I lay my head in rest
My life has been truly blessed
For my love for you is absolutely true
I gave my love away, toward all who came my way
Yet I'm still living life alone; I'm blue.

Life's no game of pretend; therefore, my sadness has no end
For my soul is not for sale, that's true
So, I waste my life each day, giving my heart away
Toward making other people's dreams come true.

All my giving is hidden from your view
All my giving has made me sad and blue.

All my giving. . .
All my giving. . .
Oh, all my giving has kept me from all of you.

"Let Hate Go"

Oh, regardless of the time of season
Through wars, we lose our reason
Since life's precious, you all know
Let hate go, let hate go, let hate go.

Sadly, there's no way of healing
This issue from simply repeating
Without forgiveness applied to the past
So, let hate go, let hate go, let hate go.

Embrace each other as an equal
War needs truly no other sequel
But if you keep up this fight
Humanity will die, yes, that's right!

My love for humanity is genuine
Finer than any produced fine wine
And I still do love you so
Let hate go, let hate go, let hate go.

God doesn't use hate, but love
Life is his treasure up above
He's willing to forgive us all
So, let hate go, let hate go, let hate go.

[Firmly whisper] Let hate go.

Our future's built upon our past
Hate leaves us dead and last
So, stop to think long and slow
Let hate go, let hate go, let hate go.

[Firmly whisper] Let hate go.

[Back to the top, repeat]

"I Did It for Her Love"

As of now, she's not in my life.
And so, I live my life alone.
I've confessed my heart many times,
I'll wait for her, of this I'm certain.

I've encased many with my art.
Paid with kindness from my very soul.
And more, way more than this,
I did it for her love.

Although I suffer in silence,
I smile every time I see her face.
I did what I could for all of you
And am waiting for my love to return.

I wrote her business plan,
And dressed her with my art and prose.
And more, way more than this,
I did it for her love.

Yes, I've paid the price for all of you,
And I walled away all my pain.
But though it all, there was never any doubt,
My soul cries for her and I will wait.
I served as king without any strings,
And did it for her love.

I've given toward all of you,
Free from my soul; I've paid with love.
And now, my tears I hide,
I find it all so darn confusing.

To think, I've given away my life
And I did it in a humble way.
I haven't taken from the trust
For the trust is truly sacred.

Who I truly am, just a humble man
With love in his heart and soul
To convey those things that I truly feel
And for this love I will never yield.
My life does show, I have given my all,
And did it for her love.

"Reason, Rhythm, and Rhyme"

I'm badly hooked upon your love
I've seen you at your best
Cared for you at your worst
Framed you within my precious art
Placed upon you my entire life
All in the name of love
Lifted you up with caring hands
I've never taken anything from you

You're my reason, rhythm, and rhyme

I'm badly bruised, battered, and blue
Living life without any of you
One step forward, three steps back

Many shades of gray in layers
Then it all fades to black
I've set all my broken pieces
Coming back at you with love
You're my reason, time after time

You're my reason, rhythm, and rhyme

I'm badly wanting to start again
Oh, to have my first chance
One step left, three steps right
Dreaming of you in my arms
My life's been a perpetual fight
They try to keep you down
With many shallow and false pursuits
Circling the drains, a constant strain

You're my reason, rhythm, and rhyme

[Back to the top for a second run-through]

"Will You Be Calling?"

I should have stayed home playing upon my cell phone
Instead I went to your home, and you gave me your big bone
[Laugh with sarcasm]
I should have stayed at home and played upon my cell phone
Instead I went to your home, and you tried to claim me for
your own
[Laugh]
I'd rather pursue my art and sacrifice, all that I own
Than be trapped without a love for my very own

[Sing with sincerity]
I turned left when I should have gone right
I should have simply rolled over and turned off the light

I've been the one on the losing end
Gave up on love in order to find it again
I've given my heart away, this ain't no play
Will you be calling?

Focus of my affections
You know you can have your way with me
However you want it
It's up to you to call
I'm tired of hanging on the other end
Waiting for my phone to ring

I should have stayed home playing upon my cell phone
Instead I went to your home and you gave me your big bone
[Laugh with sarcasm]
I should have stayed at home and played upon my cell phone
Instead I went to your home, and you tried to claim me for
your own
[Laugh]
I'd rather pursue my art and sacrifice, all that I own
Than be trapped without a love for my very own

[Sing with sincerity]
I turned left when I should have gone right
I should have simply rolled over and turned off the light

Waiting at home for you to phone
I'm trying to be patient, you know
I'll give you a bit longer
Don't take too long.

"Oh, Man"

I used to go through life hiding in plain sight
Walking in the light but trapped in the dark
Giving away what I could say through my art
But, oh, man, the pain was too great without you

Although I appear to be unmoved by your heart
I've got love for you deep down within my soul
I always knew that I just couldn't hide from you

But, oh, man, why must I sit here and wait?
You captured my love when you swore over your salad
But I shall not sacrifice my soul for our first kiss
There will never again be another like you
I tried to rule through my love and art
But all the while I was chasing you through others
But, oh, man, your absence within life has taken a toll
Must I chase you all over again?
Must this game go on without end?
Must I lose you to win again?
But, oh, man, this ain't no game of pretend

I've cried out loud but no one heard it
Living life without your love is no fun
I live life alone rather than give up on you

But, oh, man, why must I sit here and wait?
You captured my love when you swore over your salad
But I shall not sacrifice my soul for our first kiss
There will never again be another like you
I tried to rule through my love and art
But all the while I was chasing you through others
But, oh, man, your absence within life has taken a toll

Must I chase you all over again?
Must this game go on without end?
Must I lose you to win again?
But, oh, man, this ain't no game of pretend

Although I'm a very old soul
I found you with my art
I need you to make me whole
'Cause you're the one that I need
Oh, I concede, oh, I concede
This is no game
But, oh, man, must I lose in order to win?

I used to go through life hiding in plain sight
Walking in the light but trapped in the dark
Giving away what I could say through my art
But, oh, man, the pain was too great without you

Although I appear to be unmoved by your heart
I've got love for you deep down within my soul
I always knew that I just couldn't hide from you

Although I'm a very old soul
I found you with my art
I need you to make me whole
'Cause you're the one that I need
Oh, I concede, oh, I concede
This is no game
But, oh, man, must I lose in order to win?

"You're My Life"

You're always upon my mind, I wish to make you mine
Yet I had to walk away although I won your heart zillions of times
I had to encase your love with my precious art
I'm sadly recalling
In the past you came upon me like a moth unto a flame
I'm mesmerized and this time it's my way
All I want from you is that prenup and ring
I'm a calling!

You're my life
You won my heart many years ago; come and find me
Have it your way, baby
I'm back within your life
Now I stand ready to live my life by your side
You've always known it was true, baby
I'm going to take you home
And claim you for my own
I'm going to take you home
And never leave you alone
Many years ago, I had heard your call
I came to your aid as a lovesick puppet
You cut all my strings and cast me aside
I'm still madly in love
So come back to me and repair my heart!
Oh, yeah, I'm going to take you home
And claim you for my own
I'm not going to accept no
For it's my heart that you already own.

You're my muse
When I see your face, I get stars in my eyes

It's always been your way, baby
Can you feel my words and the rhythm of my love?
Care to let me in, baby?
I can't leave things alone
I'm claiming your love for my own
I'm going to take you home
And never leave you alone
Because there's no way I can lose
I'm madly in love
With the one who has won my heart!

Yeah, you're my life
Yeah, you're my life
Yeah

I'm madly in love
With the one who has won my heart!
I'm going to take you home
And claim you for my own
I'm going to take you home
And never leave you alone
Many years ago, I had heard your call
I came to your aid as a lovesick puppet
You cut all my strings and cast me aside
I'm still madly in love
So come back to me and repair my heart!
Oh, yeah, I'm going to take you home
And claim you for my own
I'm not going to accept no
For it's my heart that you already own.

"Listen to Your Heart"

One, two, three, four
Get upon this floor
You know the score
Come dance some more
[Pause]

Four, three, two, one
Our dance has begun
Time for our fun
Under the setting sun

Get into my rhythms
Hooked upon my rhymes
Love is my crime
This is our time
Listen to your heart
Right from the start
Let your feelings soar
Dance like never before
Move both your feet
Sway to my beat
It's time to unwind
You're upon my mind
Look upon me dance
Don't miss this chance
Let your passions ignite
Mother Monster is right
Always try being kind
Ignorance is truly blind

Love from your heart
Framing another with art

[Back to the top for another run-through]

"Forgiveness"

I've been through Hell,
Waiting here for you.
Every time I turn,
Waiting for your return.
Seconds turned into years.
Are you coming back?

I've been waiting here,
Looking out my windows,
Watching the sun rise,
Watching the darkness fall,
Watching the shadows play,
Waiting night after day.

I appear to be
Caught within a trap,
Born from my past.
We all make mistakes.
Forgiveness begins with self.
Settling within my situation.

I've found my calling,
My purpose in life:
To encase with art,
Those whom I love

By my own hands,
Basking in their love.

[Back to the top for a second run-through]

"Oh God. . . Why Do They?"

They tried to:
Keep me down
Make me blue
Give me pain
Label me manic.

Affixed to my fate,
It's never too late.
Oh God. . .
Why do they keep coming back for more?

They tried to:
Keep me silent
Bring me down
Feed me lies
Saddle me down.

Affixed to my dreams,
Nothings as it seems.
Oh, God. . .
Why do they keep to the same old game?

I've been taken:
For a fool
To the door

For a ride
To the cleaners.

Affixed to my pain,
Life's not a game.
Oh, God. . .
Why do they keep breaking the rules they make?

I'm in utter darkness.
My prison's without walls.
I'm upon the truth,
I've lost my youth.
Oh, God. . .
Why do they keep performing the same play?

[Back to the top for a second run-through]

"Darkness"

Lost in the sea of life, walking in the light.
Drifting from one place to the next.
Don't want to give up my soul.
Because of inequality, greed, an extension of absolute hate.

Everywhere I turn, there is another sign of you.
(Caught in my darkness, just caught within my darkness)

Life has become so lame.
Chasing money, chasing greed.
People throw away their purpose.
Just for a taste of you.

I'm tired of all this.
Chasing shadows, chasing death.
People living life without you
When you're right in front of them!

Can't they see that life is so much more?
Hiding behind another, afraid of their own worth!
If we looked at each other as equals, all would fall into place.
How many more will lose their life for you?

Everywhere I turn, there is another sign of you.
(Caught in my darkness, just caught within my darkness)
And every moment we don't realize this is a waste.

Life has become so lame.
Chasing money, chasing greed.
People throw away their purpose.
Just for a taste of you.

I'm tired of all this.
Chasing shadows, chasing death.
People living life without you
When you're right in front of them!

And I know I once was blind, too.
Aren't you tired, too?
History repeating, history repeating!
All seems so hopeless!
[Shout] That's what hate wants you to believe!

[Back to the top for a second run-through]

"Heaven Knows"

Heaven knows
I've been through Hell, as the old saying goes.
Heaven knows
I've fought for love and was dealt many blows.
Oh, the pain, there's nothing in this world without you.
I've given away my entire world for all of you.

Heaven knows
I've fought back my tears through these many years.
Heaven knows
I was the king up on high, yet I passed on money—why?
Oh, the games they played upon me and upon you.
I've given my heart until it turned black and blue.

Heaven knows
I've shaken all the foundations of power with love.
Heaven knows
I've given away my future. Now ask yourselves: why?
Oh, the sadness, there's nothing left for me to do.
I've given priceless art from the bottom of my heart.

Heaven knows
I've taken nothing but was asking for your love.
Heaven knows
I served as sacrifice, a mime, jester, and king.
Oh, the deception they played upon me—and you, too.
I've given you my life, that's the very simple truth.

Heaven knows
I've fought back the darkness, as this play continuously unfolds.
Heaven knows
Yes, Heaven knows.

"I'm Bothered"

I'm bothered.
I gave to you my heart and art without any strings.
I wonder,
How long it will take for you to find yet another?
Oh, the pain, sad and blue, that your love wasn't true.

Why bother?
You're missed but sadly you've embraced another.
I wonder,
What went wrong between us? Still I do wonder!
Oh, the pain, sad and blue that your love wasn't true.

Why bother?
Trying to hide my sadness is a blunder.
I wonder,
What it was about me that made you choose another?
Oh, the pain, sad and blue that your love wasn't true.

Why bother.
You've moved along, tearing my soul asunder.
I wonder,
Why you decided that you'd go and love another?
Oh, the pain, sad and blue that your love wasn't true.

I heard and answered your call!
My pain, I no longer hide behind.
I've dropped my mask of pain.
I live a life sadly alone.
There's nothing left for me to do for you.

"Take My Words to Heart"

Take my words to heart
Let them dance within your mind
Let me chase away your tears through love
I worked freely
To earn your love and respect
To pave the way with love

Fill my life with songs
Let me hear your lovely voice
My precious words from your lips
All my words, for your love
All my dreams are of you

Fill my life with art
Let my love warm your soul
Allow for me again to fill your life with love
With my words, comes my heart
With my words, comes the world
With my words
Yes, with my words
I would again encase you.

"Oh, My Gaga"

I was ignored by you ever since way back when
So I made up my mind, my pain must come to an end
Looking upon you now, I haven't really learned!
I chased you around many parts of the globe
You're a part of my very soul

Your many looks all dressed in white
One more look and I'll come unglued, oh. . .

Oh my Gaga, here we go again. . .
My, my, I could never resist you
Oh my Gaga, will our show ever end?
My, my, I could always assist you
Yes, I'm determined and true
Happy since I found you
No, no, I never could let you go
Oh my Gaga, it's you I love

My, my, I couldn't stop my pain!

I was angry at you for being set aside
I lost count of all the times that I've cried over you
Looking upon you now, I haven't really learned!
I chased you around many parts of the globe
You're a part of my very soul
Your many looks all dressed in white.
One more look and I'll come unglued, oh. . .

Oh my Gaga, here we go again . . .
My, my, I could never resist you
Oh my Gaga, will our show ever end?
My, my, I could always assist you
Yes, I'm determined and true
Happy since I found you
No, no, I never could let you go
Oh my Gaga, it's you I love

My, my, I couldn't stop my pain!

Oh my Gaga, here we go again. . .
My, my, I could never resist you
Oh my Gaga, will our show ever end?
My, my, I could always assist you
Yes, I'm determined and true
Happy since I found you
No, no, I never could let you go
Oh my Gaga, it's you I love

My, my, I couldn't stop my pain!

Oh my Gaga, here we go again. . .
My, my, I could never resist you
Oh my Gaga, will our show ever end?
My, my, I could always assist you
Yes, I'm determined and true
Happy since I found you
No, no, I never could let you go
Oh my Gaga, it's you I love

My, my, I couldn't stop my pain!

"Our Love Brightens This World!"

[Male vocal]
I have given away my world
Much of what I had to say
Tell me, brethren, why the fear?
Let's get our show back on the road!

I have opened my heart
Encased you all within my wonderful art

I repeated this over and over
And never taken you all for a ride!

All for our world!
To push humanity ever forward
I never refused, any of you
And I did this all for free!

Our world's truly priceless!
With all life on this planet being sacred
But I was severed from my place
As your rightful king

Our love brightens this world!

[Female vocal]
Immeasurable love
Euphoric feelings
Flying, climbing, uplifting
Throughout many years out of sight!
Your love brightens our world!

[Male vocal]
Don't ever look back in defeat

[Duet]
Why repeat our mistakes
Over and over, endlessly
Humanity has come so far!
We must never go back to the way that it used to be!

[Male vocal]
Your love's my world!

[Female vocal]
Your love's my world!

[Duet]
Every moment's a rainbow
And love's our pot of gold!

[Male vocal]
All for our world!
To push humanity ever forward
I never refused, any of you
And I did this all for free!

Our world's truly priceless!
With all life on this planet being sacred
But when I was severed from my place
As your rightful king

Our love brightens this world. . .

"Ours Is the Real Theatrical Show!"

Your pulse quickens as you walk on through the door.
The anticipation and excitement climbs like never before.
And your soul is restless with excitement that you can't ignore.
Your eyes fixed upon the ring,
Suddenly our ringmaster starts to sing:

"Ladies and gentlemen, it's the moment you've been waiting for. . .
You'll bare witness to our show that you've never seen ever before. . .

It will make you dream, make you sing, due to our acts within this ring!"

Nowhere to run, nowhere else to go, we're coming for you.
It's our time together that truly really does matter.
Your heart beats faster as we burst onto the scene.
It's real, it's live, it's our time.
We spend our lives living life to the fullest in our ring.
Watch our story unfold before your very eyes.
With love in our hearts we perform and sing within our ring.
All causes related as you all already know, so happy at the end you'll never want to go!

[Crowd] (Wow) Immortal, the reason we come, these performers in our ring!
[Crowd] (Wow) Where our imagination's crowned as our true king!

Don't worry, we're here for you, chasing after our dreams.
For these moments are precious, don't miss what comes after.
We'll open your minds and brighten all your eyes.
Helping others is our reason we are chasing after.

Our multicolored lights surround our theatrical ring.
Living for these precious moments, sharing our dreams.
The unimaginable comes alive, thrilling you.
[Crowd] (Wow) Ours is the real theatrical show!
We ignite our fires within our very souls.
Living out our dreams by healing others.
Watch us over and over as we tour around.
[Crowd] (Wow) Ours is the real theatrical show!

Our multicolored lights surround our theatrical ring.
Living for these precious moments, sharing our dreams.

The unimaginable comes alive, thrilling you.
[Crowd] (Wow) Ours is the real theatrical show!
We ignite our fires within our very souls.
Living out our dreams by healing others.
Watch us over and over as we tour around.
[Crowd] (Wow) Ours is the real theatrical show!

Ours is the real theatrical show! [Crowd] (Wow)
Ours is the real theatrical show! [Crowd] (Wow)
Ours is the real theatrical show! [Crowd] (Wow)
Ours is the real theatrical show. . .

"I'm So Lonely"

(Hmmm, hmmm, hmmm, hmmm)
I'm so lonely
I'm so lonely

I'm so lonely (Yeah, yeah, yeah, yeah)
Because you're not in my life (Sad and very blue)
I'm so lonely (Yeah, yeah, yeah, yeah)
For I don't have you to hold tight (Sad and very blue)
You're my dream
My true happiness
My heart forever
Torn all apart. . .

I'm so lonely
You're the reason why. . .
I'll continue to try
I'm still lonely (Sad but very true)

(Hmmm, hmmm, hmmm, hmmm)
I'm so lonely
I'm so lonely

I'm still alone
Yet I still dream of only you (Yeah, yeah, yeah, yeah)
I encased you with my art (Gifts for only you)
You're being unfair, so we're through (I'm not giving my life)
You were my muse
I was the king
All I ever wanted
Was a prenup and ring

Perhaps my sorrow
This bad romance
The clouds will part
So, I can have my first chance. . .

(Hmmm, hmmm, hmmm, hmmm)
I'm so lonely
I'm so lonely

"Someday Soon. . . That Day Is Today!"

Someday soon
You'll come my way
I've been hoping and dreaming
Of you every day
Waking up each morning
With you by my side
To have and to hold
You as my bride

Oh, every morning
Every morning
Your eyes shine like the sun
When you're hurting
I'll simply be there
To chase them away

Someday soon
I'll hear you say
Your two words of love
To have and hold
Come whatever that may
Building upon our future
A home of our own
Let's fill it today

Every single day
In every single way
You chase my blues away, yeah
But when the clouds do come
We will face whatever that may
Together we are one, yeah

You warm my heart
You're part of my soul
With you I see rainbows
Wherever we both go
The sun shines in your eyes
Don't you know?

For many years
They've kept you from me
Sure, I gave you love

But there was nothing in it for me
For without your love
I became bitter and sore
So, I simply stopped giving
All my art away
I left you alone
Come whatever that may

It finally dawns,
That I'm your man
So, come and find me
To have and to hold
As soon as you can

Today shall be the day
That you find me, yeah
Today shall be the day
Today shall be the day
That you'll be mine
For all of time

Someday soon
I hope and pray
Perhaps that day is today. . .
Perhaps that day is today. . .
That day is today
That day is today
That day is today

"On with Our Amazing Show!"

[As you enter the live theater, all the paths are illuminated but the seats are left darkened. The overhead house lights are left off.]

[Instrumental]

(Ohhh, ohhh, ohhh, ohhh)
They've said it all before as you walked on through the door
(Ohhh, ohhh, ohhh, ohhh)
You've been looking for thrills that will leave you with total chills
(Ohhh, ohhh, ohhh, ohhh)
Bound by the traditions of generations from our collective past
(Ohhh, ohhh, ohhh, ohhh)
Bringing you memories that you'll cherish and that will truly last
(Ohhh, ohhh, ohhh, ohhh)
Awakening your imagination by opening up all of your minds

[Rolling thunder three seconds with illuminated fog from underneath flowing in the ring covering the floor.]

The pioneers of our circus will mesmerize you within our ring
Each pulse-driven moment greater than what passed before your very eyes

[Build song from this point]

[Pause]
Now, the moment you've all been waiting for is finally upon us all. . . "On with our amazing show!"

"Baby, It Has All Been from Me!"

I'm sorry that you don't love me
I'm hurting because you want nothing from me
I'm hurting but you won't see me
Shed a single tear for thee
[Pause]
You're a fool without my visions
You'll wander about without any of my directions
You're blind and I've set you free
So, baby don't bother thinking of me
[Pause]
As your light fades, mine still shines
Sure, I love you, but you wouldn't give me the time
You're selfish and now all alone
You've been simply unfair with me
[Pause]
I've encased you from within my art
All I wanted from you was a humble start for us
Sure, I hurt, so I've written this down
And framed my sorrow for eternity
[Pause]
Your love fades within my heart
Because you ignored my gifts of love from the start
Sure, there's still time for us
But you'd better act in time
[Pause]
Until then, keep dreaming of me
Until we meet, I'll keep on hoarding my art for me
Can't you see that we're bound by love
Sent from God up above
[Pause]

I'm filled with sadness in my heart
What's taking you so long to find my heart?
I've left a trail, but I've cut all the strings
So, baby, can't you now find me?
[Pause]
Don't you realize that my love is true?
All I need is one opportunity and then I'd be with you
Spending my life encasing you within art
So, baby, sent my love for you free
Baby, it has all been from me. . .

"Said Johnny to All of Humanity"

Said Johnny to all of humanity
Let us free our true potential
By abandoning all the remnants of slavery
Let us free our true potential
Equality, equality
Unite us all with love
And bring about peace in this world
And bring about peace in this world

Said Johnny to all of humanity
We are all of us truly equals
Let us unite against all our differences
Unity, unity is possible for us all
By treating each other with respect and love
By treating each other with respect and love

Said Johnny to our God up above
The trust is truly sacred
And for your love I've worked for free

I pray that this wisdom finds them
For our lives are the greatest gift of all
For our lives are the greatest gift of all

Said our God above to all of humanity
Listen to each other with love
Treat each other with the same
Free yourselves from deception
Unity, unity
The concept is a human right
And forgive each other of the past
And forgive each other of the past
And forgive each other of the past

"Over and Over"

You're all a bunch of crooks, you're all on the take.
You've all made decisions to line your pockets.
You're all disingenuous, wearing your pseudo facades.
I state my case, based upon the lack of progress.
The people's lives are sacred, within our mutual care.
It then stands to reason, that you've lost your reason.
Our lives are priceless, their worth beyond any measure.

The trust owes no one. Debt is a false pursuit.
Brought about by inequality, born from out of hate.
When will you all see? That our lives are precious?
You serve by our will, born from out of love.
You're all a bunch of crooks, you're all on the take.
You've not seen reason, time after time.
Again, and again, over, and over.

[Back to the top and repeat]

[At the end, have a record of Luciano singing with his voice skipping saying over and over. FADE OUT.]

Inspired by global politics based on the swinging pendulum methodology between left and right, blue, and red, liberal, and conservative, etc.. ENOUGH—too many lives are being lost in this process, we are failing the sacred trust this way.

Inspired by the opera "La donna è mobile" sung by the iconic Luciano Pavarotti.

"A Dream, A Fantasy"

I'm not. . . really happy.
Without your love,
All is just a dream.
A Fantasy.
You're the one for me.
You must know what I mean.
I was searching for you,
And you for me.
In this love-filled fantasy,
I found you and you found me.
I have need of you,
And you for me.

Please, my dream and fantasy, come for me, and you will see.
My heart. I'll encase you with love, sent from above.

You came for me,
A long time ago.

But that was yesterday.
I was caught in a play.
I couldn't break away
Due to contracts.
You simply walked away,
Without confronting my love.
It's just a game,
Without your love.
Nothing else truly matters.
My dream.

Please, my dream and fantasy, come for me, and you will see.
My heart. I'll encase you with love, sent from above.

My soul is restless
Without your love.
Nothing matters to me,
Without you, my dream.
My soul still hungers
For your love.
But you walked away.
Honey, this isn't a play.
I'm trapped in darkness,
Filled with light.
Caught in place,
Hear my plight.

Please, my dream and fantasy, come for me, and you will see.
My heart. I'll encase you with love, sent from above.

"I Do"

There's a kind of rush. . .
That I get by watching you, that's right.
As you travel the world, in search of me and my true love.
It's always been from me.

Imagine the two of us. . .
United at last by our fates, that's right.
All I ever wanted was your love and to be married to you.
You have my heart completely.

I've been waiting for you. . .
For your precious love of me, that's true.
As you performed your art, no one else will ever do.
For that's the simple truth.

Just imagine us both, united at long last.
Together, we are one, written in the stars.
This we both know, on with our show.

So read this note carefully. . .
You're my true love.
I donated my art
To enter your life,
A husband to a wife.

What I need from you. . .
Is your precious love, that's right.
As you again travel the world, performing our art,
I just need to spend my life upon only you.

The only word I need hear. . .
Is "I DO" from you, my dear

You're the spark in my eyes
And within my soul.
No one else will ever do.

"The Reality of Your Absence Lingers On"

It was in the dead of night
The sky lit up by the stars
The moon was casting its cool glow
As you quietly were walking on by

Oh, how I wanted to hold you
To hear your voice within my ears
And listen to your heartfelt plea
Baby, what have you done to me?

I remember that dream within my mind
Framed you were with the stars above
The moon's glow reflected within your eyes
As you had quietly walked on by

Oh, how my thoughts of you linger
I didn't even get your first name
Too stunned to chase after my dream
The realty of your absence lingers on.

Back to the top for another run-through

Yes, the reality of your absence lingers on. . .

"Oh God, Bless Us All"

Oh, God, bless our United Nations of our world.
With the grace of Your love,
and the wisdom of ages past.
Extend us Your guiding light.
Long have we been torn by war.
Bring to us what we sow.
Allow for equality to reign.
Forgive us of our sins and transgressions.
Oh, God, bless us all. . .

Each culture is to be commemorated.
Each breakthrough to be celebrated.
And Your bounty shared by all.
Extend to us Your helping hand.
Allow for us to dance and sing.
Let us overcome being corporate slaves.
Allow for forgiveness to reign.
Forgive us of our sins and past.
Oh, God, bless us all. . .

Oh, God, life is our true wealth.
And kindness ought to be our currency.
Through forgiveness and common laws,
We would then overcome our common flaws
And pave the way for Your return.
Our individual nations must unite.
Through love we'd discover ourselves.
Forgive us of our divisive past.
Oh, God, bless us all. . .

Each life is to be appreciated.
Each birth is to be commemorated.
We must set aside our hate.
Before our end comes; it's never too late.
Allow for us to redeem ourselves.
Let us overcome our wrongs through love.
Allow for abundance to reign.
Forgive us of our ignorance.
Oh, God, bless us all. . .

[Refrain]
Oh, God, we have seen the light.
Please save us from our perpetual fight
So we may rediscover the joys of peace.
Please come back to us all. . .

"Peace Screams"

As I lie resting
Trouble follows me around
As she lies resting
Peace screams; no sound

She wanted to go dancing
Drinking and to have fun
She was now expecting
I wanted to save some
She wanted her friend
To move right on in
A house built on love
Let the end now begin

As the moments passed
The farther she walked away
Less did I now see her
As she danced nights away
She now found old feelings
That drove her his way
My dream, my dream. . .
Oh, what I'd do to you.
For you I've written,
A fantasy that's for two.
I'm sadly missing.
From your life, that's true.
But this isn't a defeat,
Or a mass fricken retreat.
For my life's incomplete without you.

My dream, my dream. . .
Oh, how I have need of you.
For you, I'm smitten,
You're my fantasy, that's true!
I'm still sadly missing,
From your life, that's true.
But I won't retreat.
I won't admit to defeat.
For my life's still incomplete without you.

My dream, my dream. . .
All that I want is you.
You can have my writing,
If your love for me is true.
For me, the ballgame's over,
You've pitched a perfect game.
So, for you, I wait.

It's never too late.
So, baby, please say "I do."
So, baby, please say "I do."
Baby, I'll never tire of you... Let us overcome being
corporate slaves.
Allow for forgiveness to reign.
Forgive us of our sins and past.
Oh, God, bless us all...

Oh, God, life is our true wealth.
And kindness ought to be our currency.
Through forgiveness and common laws,
We would then overcome our common flaws
And pave the way for your return.
Our individual nations must unite.
Through love we'd discover ourselves.
Forgive us of our divisive past.
Oh, God, bless us all...

Each life is to be appreciated.
Each birth is to be commemorated.
We must set aside our hate.
Before our end comes; it's never too late.
Allow for us to redeem ourselves.
Let us overcome our wrong's through love.
Allow for abundance to reign.
Forgive us of our ignorance.
Oh, God, bless us all...

[Refrain]
Oh, God, we have seen the light.
Please save us from our perpetual fight

So we may rediscover the joys of peace.
Please come back to us all. . .

"In This Simple Song"

Gone are many of my memories. . .
I filled in many blanks with my words. . .
Looking around for my true love. . .
Where can she be?
Sadly, she's eluded me.
Can you hear my words?
Can you hear my words. . .
Within this simple song?
In this simple song.

Gone are many of my friends. . .
Changes to my life I've made. . .
I look around, realizing that I'm still unhappy. . .
My dream has me!
It's sadly eluding me.
Can you see into my eyes?
Can you read into my words. . .
Within this simple song. . .
In this simple song?

Gone are many of my years. . .
I've filled in my hollow life with benevolence. . .
Thankfully, I've realized who it is that I love. . .
But she keeps turning. . .
Into other men's arms.
Can you feel my pain?
Can you see my tears. . .

Within this simple song?
In this simple song.

She came upon me within dreams, promising me the world.
I had to leave behind my pain, my memories of sadness.
I prayed that she would come for me, but, sadly, it's just a
fantasy. . . a fantasy.

[Back to the top for a second run-through]

"Incredible"

Incredible, my heart's been left ajar. . .
Incredible, I'm still here, wherever you are. . .
Like a love-filled fantasy, that's who you are to me.
Through art and love I've set you free.
No one ever before has been so dear to me.

Incredible, in every single way. . .
I've been praying that you'll come back to me. . .
Making my dreams a love-filled fantasy.
For someone such as you, you're beyond unforgettable.
I pray the feelings are mutual too.

Incredible, you still haven't come my way. . .
Incredible, I'm still waiting for you to this very day. . .
Like an opera filled with love, you've been sent by God above.
The secret is that I have heard the call.
And I'm waiting for only you.

"My Dream"

My dream, my dream. . .
Oh, what I'd do to you.
For you I've written
A fantasy that's for two.
I'm sadly missing.
From your life, that's true.
But this isn't a defeat,
Or a mass fricken retreat.
For my life's incomplete without you.

My dream, my dream. . .
Oh, how I have need of you.
For you I'm smitten,
You're my fantasy, that's true!
I'm still sadly missing
From your life, that's true.
But I won't retreat,
I won't admit to defeat
For my life's still incomplete without you.

My dream, my dream . . .
All that I want is you.
You can have my writing,
If your love for me is true.
For me, the ballgame's over,
You've pitched a perfect game.
So, for you I wait.
It's never too late.
So, baby, please say "I do."
So, baby, please say "I do."
Baby, I'll never tire of you. . .

"It's Beginning to Look a Lot Like Hell Here"

It's beginning to look a lot like Hell here. . .
Everywhere I go.
I've taken a look around; no one can be found.
Culture and entertainment are gone.

It's beginning to look a lot like Hell here. . .
With COVID on the loose.
There's no end in sight for our perpetual plight.
Everyone's wearing a mask.

It's beginning to look a lot like Hell here. . .
With austerity in full bloom.
We keep track of debts; we live with regrets.
Everyone's a corporate slave.

It's beginning to look a lot like Hell here. . .
With all the empty windows.
People try to justify war, the same as times before.
Repeating our historical mistakes.

It's beginning to look a lot like Hell here. . .
With most folks now unemployed.
Sad with nothing to do, dreams set aside anew.
As we lose our lives.

If we looked upon each other as equals. . .
We would then eliminate war.
Break the cycle of hate before it's sadly too late.
And we would then know peace.

With war, we erase entire cultures. . .
Because we just don't get along.

I pray we sees the light, before God turns from our plight!
And walks away from us all.

"Waiting for Love to Draw Near"

Placing my heart into all that I create
Trying to give love in order to receive
Extending my two hands to pull others up
Asking for nothing in the hopes for love
I was told many times not to care

The things which I've given encased us all
Yet I gave my all though many hands
Taking no credit, sowing the seeds of love
Waiting for true love to come on back
I was told many times not to care

Sure I've made mistakes, no one's truly perfect
I never wrote myself into our living opera
In order to express my love through charity
So Cupid's many arrows could hit their marks
I was told many times not to care

I'm great at weaving words into our play
Forsaking my emotional self, come whatever that may
Although my service was cut sort from fear
I've been waiting for love to draw near

I've been a puppet. I've been a mime. I've been a king. These are
my crimes.

"My, My, My. . . Time Does Fly."

I can hear her coming now
Right from out of the blue
I can see her coming now
A rose that's in full bloom

I've hardly been wrong now, right?
My heart won't turn the page
I've changed with the many seasons
Yet my soul has truly grown

Why is it that we're losing time?
They've truly not been really fair
I've given my career away truly
Why do you not seem to care?

I found you in this world
Filled with all of our sins
All I've truly ever really wanted
Was your hand, where to begin?

My eyes mist with many tears.
My mind plays upon many fears.
My hair's now showing many years.
My, my, my. Time does fly.

Back to the top and repeat a second run-through

My, my, my. Ask yourself why?
Love's my reason. . . Why did you. . . pass me by?

"I Shall Abide My Time"

I gave toward all with an open heart
With eyes wide open but I didn't see.
I was chasing you through other people's hands.
Sure I was benevolent, but filled with pain.
Because you're divine, I shall abide my time.

I found it easy giving my career away,
Yet to this day, I am sadly alone.
Longing for your love, prenup, and wedding ring.
But you all were totally unfair with me.
Because you're divine, I shall abide my time.

So I took myself out of the line
Although I have given to all of you.
My longing has always been your sweet love.
Unfortunately you turned and walked away from me.
Because you're divine, I shall abide my time.

I lost more than you can ever imagine.
I've lived without a place to call home.
Yet I have not given away to despair.
Sure, I have made my share of mistakes.
Because you're divine, I shall abide my time.

I've had my fill of spending life alone.
Wallowing within my heart's pain silently at home.
Unable to get beyond my hurt-filled past.
Cast aside like any pair of worn shoes.
Because you're divine, I shall abide my time.

"Can't You See My Tears in My Eyes?"

Writing is a part of my healing process.
To bring forth what's hidden underneath the surface.
My experiences are many, but friends are few.
Yet we all get to where we're needed?

I wear my smile to deflect my sadness.
I remain hidden beneath the surface in truth.
"Can't you see my tears in my eyes?"

I used to simply give my art away
To try and heal through many other voices.
My art's all over the world through others.
But my brilliance is owned by many others.

I wear my smile to deflect my sadness.
I remain hidden beneath the surface in truth.
"Can't you see my tears in my eyes?"

I was extremely elated, making others very happy.
But I was very sad deep within me
For they have kept her from my life.
You can't live life from a rearview mirror.

I wear my smile to deflect my sadness.
I remain hidden beneath the surface in truth.
"Can't you see my tears in my eyes?"

Many years have passed, my abilities are honed.
Nowadays, I hoard that which I have created,
Wanting to make it on my own through art.
But publishing takes money which I don't have.

I wear my smile to deflect my sadness.
I remain hidden beneath the surface in truth.
"Can't you see my tears in my eyes?"

[Back to the top, repeat]

"Can't you see my tears in my eyes?"

"Come Save Me"

Are you to be my wife?
I'm tired of all the lies!
Caught in a web so fine.
Not born from out of reality.
So please open up your heart,
Look upon my art and see.
I may appear a humble man
With nothing much to offer you.
But look at what I've given.
Can't you see? It's all been from me.
I've walked within the darkness, craving the light.
Can't you see? You really do matter to me.

Father, they keep on ignoring me.
Without her love I'm truly dead.
Living alone is what I dread.
Father, my dreams have just begun.
Sadly, they quietly turned, walking away.
Ohhh, how all my pain grows.
I've been hiding in plain sight,
Trying with all of my might,
To humbly exist in your life.

Can't you see? It's all been from me.
I've fought with an open mind, giving it all I had.
Can't you see? They really do matter to me.

Father, sadly your time had come.
It was many, many years ago.
I still have nowhere to turn.
I still have nowhere to go.
Father, ohhh. I've died many times.
But I do still truly dream
Of being the king, the king.
But nothing truly does matter.
Without love, it meaningless to me.
Can't you see? It's all been from me.
I've fought with an open heart, working for all for free.
Can't you see? Life really does matter to me.

I have been a shadow of a man.
Longing you your love, encased within silence.
I took nothing to prove a point.
Heaven knows!
Heaven knows!
I'm caught within a bad romance.

Although I am a humble man, kind as the wind,
Although I have given away, much as the king,
Please spare my life from this obscurity.
Nothing in this life is truly free. . .
Someone has to pay to set us free. . .

Heavens! No—I've nowhere to turn, nowhere to go.
Heavens! Oh—I've nowhere to turn, nowhere to go.
Heavens! No—I've nowhere to turn, nowhere to go.

I can't let you all go, let you go (Ever)
I can't let you all go, let you go (Truly)
Ohhh. . . ohhh. . . ohhh. . . let you go. . . ohhh. . .
Come save me.
Come save me.

So you think you can shun me and allow me to die.
So you think that I'm weak now please ask yourself truly why?
Oh Father—can't you send her into my life?
Oh Father—can't you send her into my life?
Just got to break the pattern
Come save me. . .

Nothing but their love really matters.
Nothing but her love for me.
Nothing but their love really matters.
Nothing seems to really matter

Come save me. . .
Come save me. . .

"Come for Me Now"

It's summer time in my heart blazing like the rising sun.
My dream's real!
And the world outside I'll chase her around for her love.
I'm elated that she's for me.
Please (Come for me now) (Stop your hiding)
'Cause I need you in life, in my daily life.

I'm a meteor falling through our sky burning red hot.
For you inside!
Like a volcano, you burst forth onto the scene.

For everyone to see; encased within my art.
I set you free! (Free! Free! Free!)
For you I'd continue to work for free!
Upon my bent knee, when will you marry me?

You make this lion roar, defying the odds stacked against me.
Like a fighter within a ring! You make my soul sing!
I want my prenup and ring! Not a simple thing!
So, come for me now. . . put your hand within mine.
Our combined love will set us free! (Free! Free! Free!)
I'd continue encasing your life with my art.
It will hit you square within your heart.

Like the running of the clock, my love still flows.
Every moment that you're not within my arms.
Sets off alarms! I need our wedding bells!
It's been a burning Hell, a nightmare encased in darkness.
An endless scene; a Monster Ball! I've heard your call!
For you, I'd take the fall. It's curtains for me.
So come on down and set us free! (Free! Free! Free!)

Come for me now. . . (Why the hesitation?)
Come for me now. . . (I'm getting older)
Come for me now. . . (Soon I'll not be around at all)

I've asked you many times, never directly,
Always through my art-filled dreams.
Crying out silently. . .
Hoping that you'd come for me. . .
And allow for my love-filled creativity.
To encase you with my art. . . right from my art-filled heart.
What's the matter? Funny colored bits of paper are keeping
us apart?

Come for me now. . . (Why the hesitation?)
Come for me now. . . (I'm getting older)
Come for me now. . . (Soon I'll not be around at all)

[Back to the top for another run-through]

"Yes, I Did"

When I was just a child and my heart
Was filled with love
I used to look upon the whole world
Through love-filled eyes. (Yes, I did. Yes, I did. Yes, I did. Yes,
I did)
Suddenly, my father had sadly died.
God had called him away.
The person I was sadly changed inside.

No longer was his love around [Whisper] (Sadly I, too, had died)
But I quietly held all my hurt deep inside.

No one was around to confide.
So I set my art aside.
I was the man at home, yeah.
Mother and Sister needed me, yeah.

When I was twelve and my heart
Was filled with pain
I used to look upon the whole world
Through tear-filled eyes. (Yes, I did. Yes, I did. Yes, I did. Yes,
I did)
Suddenly, my mother sat there and cried.
The man she loved had sadly died.

No longer was his love around [Whisper] (Sadly she, too,
had died)
But she always sat around and cried.

No one was around to hear
To lend their understanding, supportive ears.
I could do nothing for her.
So I helped around the home.

When I was seventeen and my heart
Had healed deep inside
Mother's heart found another man's love
Though tear-filled eyes (Yes, she did. Yes, she did. Yes, she did.
Yes, she did.)
Suddenly, they had married before too long.
Another man that she could truly love.

The day following their wedding,
He called us to have a family meeting.
It was then that we learned
He married Mother for the money. (It wasn't love! It wasn't love!
It wasn't love! It wasn't love!)
Our world went totally dark inside.
Mother confessed that she wished she knew before.

Soon I turned eighteen and my heart
Filled with frustration deep inside.
Just days prior to my birthday,
I could no longer hide my sadness inside.
I went cold inside. (Yes, I did. Yes, I did. Yes, I did. Yes, I did.)
Suddenly, I had quit my job and dropped school.
Just so I could try to heal inside.

I was labeled a bum, yeah!
I stopped paying my rent at home, yeah!
He treated us all wrong, yeah!
Just like a sad country song, yeah!

Upon my eighteenth birthday,
I got my surprise.
I came home from job hunting,
To find my stuff outside upon the lawn.
The locks upon the house were changed,
With a small note upon the door:

[Spoken softly with sadness]
You're no longer welcome here.
Unless it is by written invitation.
Don't bother trying to contact us.
I've taken the family on a vacation.

So I came to terms with being alone,
without a home of my own.
I was sad and blue,
But determined and true.
I never ever did give up.
I just took things by the moment.
Yet again, I had died inside.

"Pressure"

I'm under pressure. It's weighing me down.
Giving me nightmares, nowhere to turn.
I'm under pressure to publish my works.
I lack the funds, sadly, no help's around.

[Whisper] (Sad. Sad. Sad, but it's true.)

I've known pressure. All kinds of it.
It drove me down, I was homeless. . .
I've known pressure. Running many shows.
Living on the road, I was in charge.
Love. Love. Love, drove me down.
It's my world that I'm working upon.
Watching my true dream encased within my mind.
I'm determined for her to come my way. [Whisper] (Yeah.)
Her love's my treasure. Nothing else matters.
I've been sad and blue. Not sure what to do.
Games of honor and dishonor played upon me.
[Whisper] (Yeah.)
I'm under pressure. It's held me back.
Because of love that I lack. . .
I'm under pressure to perform myself.
I lack the love, sadly, she's not around.

[Whisper] (Sad. Sad. Sad, but it's true.)

I've known pressure. Facing their expectations.
It drove me away; I can't yield my soul. . .
I've known pressure. Giving things away.
Living on the streets, without a home.
[Whisper] (Empty. Empty. Empty, but I never give in to despair.)
This has happened, many times before.
No one to turn to, on my own.
I never gave up, I never gave in. [Whisper] (Yeah. . .)

[Back to the top, repeat a second time through]

"The Markets"

The opening bells. . .
The opening bells. . .
Oh, the opening bells are all ringing.
They bring to us. . .
They ring for us. . .
Oh, how opportunity has us all singing.
The markets flow. . .
The markets grow. . .
Oh, how the markets know what to bring!
The rising prices. . .
The many devices. . .
Oh, how our stock markets serve.
The many choices. . .
The many voices. . .
Oh, how our good fortunes sing.
The money flows. . .
The money grows. . .
Oh, how the people's worth goes.
Suddenly, we endure a massive correction. . .
A sudden, profound change of direction. . .
Turning a party into a wake.
Suddenly, the markets again turn. . .
So that we may all again earn . .
And take from the table our bounty.
We have inflation. . .
We have infatuation. . .
As our stock markets soar.
The rising prices. . .
The secret devices. . .
As our rates rise from the floor.

The tickers displayed. . .
Many are played. . .
Some tell lies, that's the truth.
Companies are created. . .
Companies are rated . .
As we expect more profits galore.
Suddenly, we endure a massive correction
A sudden, profound change of direction
Turning a party into a wake.
Suddenly, the markets again turn
So that we may all again earn
And take from the table our bounty.

[Return to the top and repeat]

[Speaking part]
Our markets' true wealth comes from the sum of our lives
governed by it not the collection of material hoarding.

"The End Is but Another Beginning"

I encased you within a living play along with your friends!
Full of money, love, and fame.

Did you think that I'd sell my soul for you to come my way?
I asked for you to come get me many years ago.

My feelings are getting stronger, stronger. . . stronger. . . for the
woman of my dreams.
My loneliness is getting harder, harder. . . harder. . . Nothing truly
is as it seems.
Nothing truly does really matter, matter. . . matter. . . without my

dream in my life.
Nothing truly is ever easy, easy... easy... Love in life isn't a game.

I've been a puppet in a play, a mime with nothing to truly say.
Full of sorrow, hurt, and loss.

Don't think that I've given up on having you each and every day!
You're my queen, love, and life!

My feelings are getting stronger, stronger... stronger... for the
woman of my dreams.
My loneliness is getting harder, harder... harder... Nothing truly
is as it seems.
Nothing truly does really matter, matter... matter... without my
dream in my life.
Nothing truly is ever easy, easy... easy... Love in life isn't a game.

I've been hiding in plain sight, yet you only truly saw me once.
I'm truly patient, filled with hope.

They tried to play me for a fool, because I'm an old soul,
Pinning upon me hate and dishonor.

My feelings are getting stronger, stronger, stronger. For the
woman of my dreams.
My loneliness is getting harder, harder, harder. Nothing truly is as
it seems.
Nothing truly does really matter, matter, matter. Without my
dream in my life.
Nothing truly is ever easy, easy, easy. Love in life isn't a game.

I've been told not to care and to treat them without the same.
But their lives matter to me.

I never took them for granted, to prove it I worked for free.
For the TRUST is truly sacred.

My feelings are getting stronger, stronger, stronger. For the woman of my dreams.
My loneliness is getting harder, harder, harder. Nothing truly is as it seems.
Nothing truly does really matter, matter, matter. Without my dream in my life.
Nothing truly is ever easy, easy, easy. Love in life isn't a game.

The end is but another beginning.

"Can You Figure Out My Dreams?"

I was an innocent child
Looking upon the world with love
Playing with all my friends
Thankful for each moment in time

Suddenly my father was gone
Another angel up in the sky
At twelve I became a man
With a sorrow-filled heart

Time kept on moving along
I was growing into my role
Helping others along the way
Thankful for each moment in life

Suddenly my home was gone
Family had thrown me on out

I was eighteen and homeless
With a wounded, sorrow-filled soul

One day life became a circus
Travelling on the open road
My soul's still filled with purpose
Learning to embrace my dreams

Time kept on moving along
I was growing into my role
Helping others along the way
Thankful for my purpose in life

Suddenly she was upon me
The woman of my living dream
But they played their games
So I simply retired, walking away

Fast forward, it's now today
Gone are my many yesterdays
Gone... Gone... Gone...
Yet I'm still thankful for today

[Refrain]
Can you imagine my true purpose?
Can you figure out my dreams?
Do you know my true calling?
Do you realize love's no game?

"Time"

Time...
Is it time?

To release my love once again!
For I'm the one,
Who simply loves everyone.

[Instrumental]

Time...
It's my time.
To release my love once again!
For it burns like the sun,
But being alone isn't fun.

[Instrumental]

Time...
My precious time.
I've given much of it away!
To heal and grow,
Trying to reap what I've sown.

[Instrumental]

Time...
Turn back time.
To live out these moments again!
So please bring back my love,
For it fits like a glove.

[Instrumental]

Time...
Is it time?
To repeat this doom-filled game.
It seems so lame,
Drives me quite insane!

[Instrumental]

Time. . .
We've little time!
To bring forth my love once again!
For I'm truly getting old,
With no hands to hold.

[Instrumental]

Time. . .
It's my time.
To heal this world once again!
By working for free,
I will free humanity.

[Instrumental]

Love. . .
My precious love.
Pours out of my very soul!
I've answered the call,
But I hit a brick wall.

[Back to the top, repeat for another run-through]

"Not Everything Is as It Seems"

I let my tears fall where they may.
I want true love to come my way.
A true love to have and to hold.
Someone to share my life and grow old.

Yet although I have found my heart's rose.
She has sadly chosen another lesser man's rose.
So, I go on living my empty life.
Without my true love, my heart's chosen wife.

I truly framed her with many a rose.
I really framed her secretly with my prose.
The true king without a prenup.
Without love and his rose ring.

I've lived many years, giving almost everything away.
For her to actually return my love today.
I'm a hopeless romantic—what can I say?
This passion-filled monster is here to stay.

Yet although I have found my heart's rose,
She has sadly chosen another lesser man's rose.
So I go on living my empty life.
Without my true love, my heart's chosen wife.

I truly framed her with many a rose.
I really framed her secretly with my prose.
The true king without a prenup.
Without love and his rose ring.

[Refrain] [Spoken softly]
So that others can have their dreams.
Not everything perceived is as it seems.

"We Get What We Actually Give"

We get many lies to swallow!
Life at times seems so hollow.

Wrong or right, who to follow?
Within our sins we do wallow!

Light, night in an endless fight.
Wrong, right. Endless is our plight.
Through darkness we find our light.
Sin augments our actual true plight.

We get many truths to follow.
Life tends to augment our sorrow.
Within our pain do we wallow.
Wrong or right, whom to follow?

Might, right in an endless fight.
Morning, noon, night. Who's actually, right?
Many fall to darkness seeking light.
Sin frames our actual true plight.

Many approach life as a game.
This to me seems so lame.
Some grasp their fortune and fame.
Only to find love's no game.

[Refrain]
We get what we actually give.
We must learn to truly forgive.
We must learn to actually live.
We get what we actually give.

"Can You Imagine?"

[Refrain]
They simply had stopped to stare

As the world past on by
With the telling of many lies.
They put up all their walls.
Hate simply does try to justify.
Being better than you or I.

People mistake wealth for true worth.
Basing their judgements upon the monetary.

[Main]
Can you imagine working for free?
Taking nothing as a humble king.
Trying to heal the many rifts.
Through gifts given from one's heart.

Can you imagine what I've done?
Living a penniless and humble life.
Trying to avoid creating any sin.
Through benevolent sacrifice from one's soul.

Can you imagine all my pain?
Unable to hold my true love!
We are all of us equals!
Through perceptions from my artistic mind.

Can you imagine the hidden truths?
They would fall down like dominos.
Yet I am sworn to silence.
Born from my true heart's desire.

"Your Sins I Don't Own"

You were unfair toward me
It cuts like a knife
You wouldn't let me in
I asked you for love

Yet no one truly knows
I've taken many hidden blows
Just like we make one
Life without love's no fun

My warm tears have fallen
The bitterness of total isolation
Yet you're still my rose
I bleed from your thorns

I always placed you first
For you alone I thirst
What must I really do?
The hurt keeps on repeating

The fool I've truly been
The devil's in perpetual sin
An angel with blackened wings
I've died so many times

I'm alone in my silence
I'm alone in the dark
I'm torn in many ways
I'm a king without love

Gone is my youthful spark
Taking handfuls of pills galore

Depression bites deep within me
It's never ever really over

Bipolar is my twisted diagnosis
Manic is my true love
Gone is my youthful appearance
Artificial, superficial repeating issues

[Refrain]
Heaven's smiled wide upon me
Although I believe in harmony
Hell's waiting patiently for me
My soul is my own
Heaven's tears have covered me
We're all of us equals
I'm not truly really broken
My soul I do own
My mind's won many battles
I've fought and I've given
Freely without any real strings
Casting aside money for love
Your sins I don't own

"Past, Present, Future"

I've been searching for true love
Sent by you from heaven above
I've been waiting a long time
For you truly to be mine
I've set aside sin for salvation
For you I've faced utter starvation
Going about life quietly all alone

Looking for love for my own
For many years I gave away
For a future created from yesterday

Past. . . repeating the same old play
Present. . . Our collective actions shall define
Future. . . is born from our time

A special person wanted my love
For it fit like a glove
But they set my love aside
My hurt—this I can't hide
I served with the utmost humility
For the sake of all humanity
I live a humble modest life
Without the hands of a wife
They fear their true king's return
Yet, for his love they yearn

Past. . . repeating the same old play
Present. . . Our collective actions shall define
Future. . . is born from our time

Repeating the same mistakes as before
Will bring our death to the fore
The absence of our cosmic spark
The heaven's light would go dark
For life is our real legacy
Not the mindless pursuit of money
Forsaking the planet to retain control
Will eventually cause our bell to toll
For life is on the brink
So stop, change, reverse, and think

Past. . . repeating the same old play
Present. . . Our collective actions shall define
Future. . . is born from our time

I served all with utter humility
In order to save all humanity
I'm just a simple humble man
Doing what in truth I can
Polluting the earth poisons us all
Can't you hear the earth's call?
We must mind our presence
In order to remain in existence
We need to realize this now
And act upon this some how

Past—Will we ever truly learn?
Present—Will we ever truly act?
Future: ???

"Snap to It"

[Refrain]
Sacrifice. . . Sacrifice. . . Sacrifice. . .
Once, twice, thrice

Snap to it and give
Snap to it and live

Sacrifice. . . Sacrifice. . . Sacrifice. . .
Once, twice, thrice

[Main]
Move to your own rhythm

Speak with your own rhyme
I didn't succumb to greed
But I hurt I concede
I took many hidden blows
Starving for love Heaven knows
People used me for profit
And labelled me as prophet
I served my true love
Along with the one above
It's within dreams I'm caught
It's within them I fought

Walking the walk; talking the talk

Swallowing a lot of pain
Tears fell like falling rain
I took nothing for me
I worked endlessly for free
A king of truly nothing
This has a familiar ring
They told their many lies
I simply turned saying goodbyes
I fought back silent screams
Trying to live my dreams
Longing to be simply me
So I worked for free

Walking the walk; talking the talk

They say I must choose
Should I, my soul I lose
Nothing is ever for free
Nothing is simple trust me

My mind is my salvation
My heart is my preservation
No one can understand me
Perhaps God is the only
Regardless of what I lose
I will not ever choose
Love and life are treasures
Money simply doesn't really measure

Walk the walk; talk the talk

[Refrain]

"Over and Over"

[Refrain]
I need her in my life
It's my sorrow I'm hiding
They seem not to really care
It's all about the money
To me it's a bad dream
That keeps on simply repeating
Over and over in my mind

[Main]
I wake up each day bathed in sorrow
Without real hope for a brighter tomorrow
I simply ignore all my pain deep inside
But from it I cannot truly hide
My smile is etched upon my face
I'm stuck caught in my silent lonely place

I go about my day bleeding emotionally inside
Without hands to hold, someone to confide
Hiding all my pain and bitter tears
Days, weeks, months now turned into years
I've made a difference improving many different things
But I'm denied her love, prenup and ring

There is a hidden cost to my charity
This I now do see with clarity
But to truly make a real lasting impression
You must swallow a lot of depression
Acts of true love bring about the same
For love is not an actual game

[Refrain]

"Just Because"

[Refrain]
Just because I served as your king
Just because I want a prenup and ring
Just because all I want is your love
I'm waiting for her is the truth
I'm waiting for so long lost is my youth
I love, I love, I love. . .
Deep from within my soul.

[Main]
You're my world as a whole
You're the reason in my soul
You're the beat of my heart
You're the reason for my art

As the seasons come and go
As the time seems to flow
As my days pass on by
As my art begins to fly

[Refrain]

You're the love within my heart
You're love's hidden within my art
You're the best part of me
You're the reason I gave freely

As the years come and go
As my art seems to flow
As my tears have dried away
As my fears have bled away

[Refrain]

You're the best part of my life
You're the one I need as wife
You're the desire in my soul
You're the one making me whole

As I await your love's return
As I await, I do learn
As I embrace my art myself
As I reinvent my old self

[Refrain]

"I Love You All"

I love, I love my life
And all of those I've helped
And I am thankful to have served
As king, dispensing my art and love
All of it done for free

All that I've asked for was love

I love, I love you all
You're all worth my hurt inside
And I'm thankful to know my purpose
As king, sewing seeds from my soul
All of it done for thee

All that I've asked for is love

I love, I love to help
For giving is my true calling
And I'm thankful to have healed
As king, working upon unity through equality
All of it done with humility

All that I've asked for is love

I love, I love deep inside
My heart and my soul
And I'm a puppet upon a string
As king; I've never asked for the tangible
All of it born from love

All that I've needed is love

I love, I love God above
From the deepest parts of me
And I'm thankful to have been leaned upon
As king, waiting for a prenup and ring
In return for all my art

All that I've wanted is love returned

[Back to the top for another run-through]

I love, I love you all
To me You're all equals
Regardless of sex or race
Common purpose along with reason; life is my justification
And a common currency
Flows within my heart and soul

If we are cut, don't we bleed
Of love, don't we all have need?
Currency differences are a form of hate
Common laws would bring about peace
And increase our life's value without any wars

I love, I love you all
With the utmost sincerity
Nothing's worth more to me
You're all worth it is the truth. . .

"Love Is What Truly Matters"

I can't hide from my many truths
Gone are my memories from my youth

I've set aside pursuits from my heart
Forsaken and hidden my talent for art

Now I'm at war within my very soul
I've heard the call and know my role
Back are my dreams, born from art
On the trail born from my heart

I've had enough of other things
Many of which have a familiar ring
I'm a puppet, yet I'm a king
Without a kingdom, prenup, and ring

Can't you hear my silent scream?
I'm out of breath waiting for my queen
What must I do for her to come my way?
Perhaps she'll realize what's been happening

God, it's love that truly matters

I've helped many with their dreams
In order to bring about love and peace
I've promoted equality for us all
Hate has no place in our hearts

Darkness and Light are truly one

I'm caught within a perpetual play
Waiting for her is not my way
Yet of all the flowers on this earth
I'll show you all my true worth

I'm the rain upon her petals
I'm the sun hidden in the shadows

Yet it's a bright blue sky
None of us knows our time to die

I have left her a blazing trail
But she's not bothered to follow it
Too concerned with playing her role
Yet her love is my only goal

Common laws will bring about peace
Common sense would then reign
No one would then be left behind
Hate swept aside though actual love

God why can't they see our truths

Life is our true wealth that you've given
Many books have indeed been written
Yet we seem the repeat the same things
Why must we put up with all of it

Each life sacrificed unto hate our light fades

I've been writing from my heart
No lies told right from the start
Through hate our world would fall apart
No future generations to remember our lives

So hurt I set aside many things
Trying to deal with life without a ring
But I've never faltered, nor have I failed
I'll not forsake my life or others for wealth

Through politics you have multiple views
Regardless of where you stand they take

Yes we must pay our way forward
Yet who owns the treasury and our love?

If we always set aside self for another
We would then know peace and love
If we gave from our hearts and soul
Nothing would stand in our way

Money must not rule our reality

"Heal The World through Love"

Heal the world through love
By treating each other as equals
Let us do away with war
Upon hate let us close the door.

Can you recall true love?
Can't you forgive each other?
Through hate there is only death.
Our lives are worth so much more.

Heal the world through love
By treating each other as equals
Let us do away with war
Upon hate let us close the door.

If we simply act through love
By helping others freely from the heart
It will eventually come back to you
And make this world a better place.

Heal the world through love
By treating each other as equals
Let us do away with war
Upon hate let us close the door.

The world through love will unite
And our future shall burn bright. . .

"Slaves to the Bottom Line"

What's the difference between you and me?
Equality. . . Equality. . . Equality

What's the reason for all of our wars?
Equality . . . Equality. . . Equality

Some believe in God
While others do not
Some believe in salvation
While others do not

We are all of us slaves to the bottom line.

We must put aside
Hate. . .
We must put aside
Greed. . .
We must put aside
Intolerance. . .

We must put them aside for the betterment of all.

What's the real difference between you and me?
Nothing . . . Nothing . . . Nothing

What's the real reason for all of our wars?
Perception... Perception... Perception

Some believe in money
While others do not
Some believe in hoarding
While others do not

We are all of us slaves to the bottom line.

We must put aside
Hate...
We must put aside
Greed...
We must put aside
Intolerance...

We must put them aside for the betterment of all.

What's the reason for the gold standard?
Justification... Justification... Justification

What's the real value behind any currency?
Life... Life... Life

Some believe in our future
While others do not
Some believe in our past
While others do not

We are all of us slaves to the bottom line.

We must put aside
Hate...
We must put aside

Greed. . .
We must put aside
Intolerance. . .

We must put them aside for the betterment of all.

"Opinions"

Ugh, ugh!
Right!
Ugh, ugh!

Skipping steps, opened your mouth?
Here we go, he's dressed me down!
His words, tearing down my self-esteem.
Opinionated fool, zero friends.
You simply can't see the forest from the trees!
Everyone will simply walk away.
You'll be alone!

Opinions! Opinions!
Opinions! Opinions!

I haven't been playing games, you keep on opening your mouth!
Your opinions all that matters, better move along.
Conscious clear.
His words, tearing down my self-esteem.
I've never been messing around!
You simply can't see the forest from the trees!
Everyone will simply turn away.
You're again alone!
Opinion! Opinions!
Keep them to yourself!

Opinions! Opinions!
Keep silent by yourself!
Yeah, it's difficult keeping your mouth closed, your opinions
to yourself!
Your words are swimming, upon a river run dry.
Ugh huh!
Yeah, we all have opinions, right!
You're blinded by what you see and can't hear.

Opinions! Opinions!
Opinions! Opinions!

Yeah, my temper is boiling hot, that's right!
You've offended me to my core. Your opinions have hit home!
Hey, look in the mirror, keep your opinion to yourself!
Some words can't be erased. . .
You're unloading, I'm silent!
Look back in your mirror at your best friend now.
Got an opinion, speak freely.
Jaws dropping, throw caution to the wind!

Opinions! Opinions!
Opinions! Opinions!
Opinions! Opinions!
Opinions. . .

"FAME!"

I've given much away
What others sing today
Yet I'm all alone
Sitting here at home

They swim in fame
Fortune and red wine
They dine at restaurants
Names said with love

I hear my art
Owned by many others
My brilliance is hidden
On every level imagined

Oh to walk alone
Oh living life alone
Oh repeating this game
Oh seems so lame

[Refrain]

I've helped many folks
Gave without any strings
To heal their hearts
I sacrificed my art

Gifts of grand design
Illuminated paths of light
I'm encased within darkness
A phantom in life

I want their love
Living without her love
Hidden by my circumstances
A perpetual bad romance

Oh to walk alone
Oh living life alone

Oh repeating this game
Oh seems so lame

[Refrain]

[Back to the top, repeat]

[Refrain]
FAME!
Yeah. . .
FAME!
Yeah. . .
FAME!
Life's no game. . .

"Someday, Just as There's Rainbows"

Some day. . . just as there's rainbows
Love will come for me. . .
It doesn't matter where I am. . .
She is the one for me.

As I look upon her from afar. . .
Uncontrollable feelings have me ajar. . .
At the sound of her voice.

When she appears upon the stage. . .
My heart simply won't turn the page. . .
I've found her! My true love. . .

All that I need out of life. . .
Is to have and hold her as my wife. . .
My true love. . .

Some day. . . just as there's rainbows.
She shall set my heart free. . .
Until then, my clouds shall not part. . .
And I await her arrival upon a bent knee.

Can you see her in your minds?
Can you guess who is to be mine?
I've encased her with my art. . . for free. . .

As she sings and dances from my art. . .
From the start, she stole my heart. . .
I've found her! My true love. . .

All that I ask for in return. . .
Is the gift of her love. . .
Which I shall earn. . . by her side. . .

Some day. . . just as there's rainbows.
She will set my heart free. . .
Until then, I live within shadows. . .
Wearing a mask for all to see. . .

Can you walk within my shoes?
Living each moment, living the blues. . .
Separated from her true love. . .

I presently live life utterly alone.
Hiding my feelings silently at home. . .
With a broken heart. . .

Others have trapped me in my place. . .
All I can do is imagine her face. . .
My true love. . .

Some day. . . just as there's rainbows. . .
She shall finally come to me. . .
The clouds shall part,
And I'll shower her with my art.
Framing her for all to see. . .
[Pause]
Yes. . .
And she'll be remembered for eternity. . .

"Christmas Is a Way of Life"

[Refrain]
Christmas. . . Christmas. . .
Is found everyday of the year.
Christmas. . . Christmas. . .
Not just on a chosen day.
Christmas. . . Christmas. . .
Is a way of living life.
Christmas. . . Christmas. . .
It's found within all our hearts.
Christmas. . . Christmas. . .

[Main]
Put aside all of your troubles.
Put aside all of your fears.
Put aside all your hardships.
Put aside all your wants.
Turn to those whom you love.
Give to them with your heart.

Put aside all that material glitter.
Put aside all that you need.

Put aside all of your desires.
Put aside all of your hurts.
Turn to those whom you love.
Give to them with your heart.

[Refrain]

Put your faith in each other.
Put your efforts toward helping another.
Put aside all of your greed.
Put aside all of your anger.
Turn to those you love.
Give to them with your heart.

Put your thoughts within your actions.
Put your heart not within things.
Put aside your funny paper pieces.
Put aside all the loose coin.
Turn to those you love.
Give to them with your heart.

[Refrain]

"Yet I Cast No Stones"

There are many things
That have gone unsaid
There are many things
That I have given
There are many things
Yeah. . . There are many things
[Pause] There are many things
[Pause] Yet, I cast no stones

There are many things
That have made me
There are many things
Which have hurt me
There are many things
Yeah. . . There are many things
[Pause]There are many things
[Pause]Yet, I cast no stones

There is enough greed
There is enough lies
This is not Hell
This is not heaven
There is enough hate
There is enough BS
Yeah. . . There is truly enough
[Pause]There is truly enough
[Pause]Yet, I cast no stones

[Refrain]
Why do others hate?
Why???
[Pause]
Why do others lie?
Why???
[Pause]
Why do others cheat?
Why???
[Pause]
Why do people steal?
Why???
[Pause]
Why do people kill?

Why???
[Pause]
Why do people sin?
Why???
[Pause]
Yet, I cast no stones

[Speak softly with a sad voice] Inequality breeds these things. . .

[Back to the top, repeat]

[Have the crowd yell in answer to each "WHY" asked flash the words on the TV displays]

Why??? Ignorance!
Why??? Fear!
Why??? Envy!
Why??? Jealousy!
Why??? Intolerance!
Why??? Stupidity!

Yet, I cast no stones

[Say at the end] Well I think we now know why. A lack of love is the answer.

"You're My Paradise"

You're my paradise
You're my passion too
You're my dream
You're my fantasy
Yes, it's true

You're my everything
You make my heart sing
All I want from you
Is that prenup and ring
[Pause] Prenup and ring
[Pause] Yeah, prenup and ring

I've been waiting for so long
I've kept my eyes upon you
I've been hoping for so long
I've kept on dreaming of you
I'm losing patience, not long now
I'm going to come for you
I'm tired of holding myself back
I'm telling you this simple truth

You're my paradise
You're my passion too
You're my dream
You're my fantasy
Yes, it's true
You're my everything
You make my heart sing
All I want from you
Is that prenup and ring
[Pause] Prenup and ring
[Pause] Yeah, prenup and ring

My heart's been moved by you
It beats faster looking upon you
When I hear your lovely voice
My heart rejoices, passionately for you
Let's together walk down the aisle

Let's together exchange vows and rings
Over and over, again and again
Over and over, again and again

You're my paradise
You're my passion too
You're my dream
You're my fantasy
Yes, it's true
You're my everything
You make my heart sing
All I want from you
Is that prenup and ring
[Pause] Prenup and ring
[Pause] Yeah, prenup and ring

A whole lot of unexpected urgency
Has come along, settling upon me
I've been alone for so long
My blond hair has gone gray
I've been silent for so long
I've lost my will to sing
All that I've asked from you
Has been love that's the truth
I've been imagining you'd come along
Over and over, and marry me.

You're my paradise
You're my passion too
You're my dream
You're my fantasy
Yes, it's true
You're my everything

You make my heart sing
All I want from you
Is that prenup and ring
[Pause] Prenup and ring
[Pause] Yeah, prenup and ring

"But I Won't Give That. . . "

And I have given away many things for love
But I'd give more from within my soul
All I ever wanted was my love returned
But all they wanted was my soul
But I'll never forget all the pain within my heart
Oh no. . . I can't
I could do anything with your love
But I won't give that
No, I won't give that
My soul for your love
Although I could do anything with your love
But I won't give that
No, I won't give that

All my days have not been easy
And this torture has no end
Some days seem not to end at all
True love is no game of pretend
And I have spent many nights alone
Without even a place to call home
Some nights repeat over and over
"Hey, I've seen this before!"
"Hey, I've done this again!"

I have been labelled crazy
My depression from my diagnosis
Is coming upon me again
I realize that my heart needs your love
No one else can save me, that's the truth
So long as my heart is beating
So long as the sun keeps burning
You're my living dream that has come alive!
I do admit it!
I have given away many things for love!
And I'll be there when the curtain falls
I have given away many things for love!
And all I can create for your prenup and ring
But I'll never be able to live with myself if you don't come my
way for life
I could do anything with your love
But I won't give that
No, I won't give that!

I can create anything with your love
I can encase you within a living play
Oh, I can create anything with your love
But I just won't give that...

I can create anything with your love
I can encase you within a living play
Oh, I can create anything with your love
But I just won't give that...

And many days and nights have I been alone
All I wanted was to save your soul
Sometimes I have prayed to God
When I see your face, I create once more

Yes, I am truly alone
Yes, I can create alone
But I don't ever want to
Without you, my heart's rose
So long as my heart is beating
So long as the sun keeps burning
You're my living dream that has come alive!
I do admit it!
I have given away many things for love!
And all I can create I'd give to you in return for that prenup
and ring
But I'll never forgive myself!
My heart refuses to turn the page!
It's now been many years . .
I have shed many tears. . .
I could do anything with your love
But I won't give that
No, I won't give that!

I can create anything with your love
I can encase you within a living play
Oh, I can create anything with your love
But I just won't give that. . .

I can create anything with your love
I can encase you within a living play
Oh, I can create anything with your love
But I just won't give that. . .

I can't ever stop dreaming of your love within my life
It's the absolute truth.

[Back to the top for another run-through]

"I'm Dreaming of a COVID-Free Christmas"

I'm dreaming of a COVID-free Christmas
Just like the ones we shared before
Where we could freely gather
Without the distance
And celebrate without masks upon our faces

I'm dreaming of a COVID-free Christmas
But sadly, there's not a vaccine in sight
May your health not waiver, that's right
And may your heart's joy burn bright

We shall again have a COVID-free Christmas
Times will revert once again back to the past
Where we could freely gather
With each other
And celebrate with smiles upon our faces

We're dreaming of a COVID-free Christmas
Finally, they announced a vaccine for our plight
May it work and not falter
May it freely be given
And may our freedoms again return

Yes, we shall indeed celebrate Christmas
It will again bring joy into our lives
As we stop for a moment
To cherish each other
And forgive others of their misdeeds

Please, let us all celebrate Christmas
If we can forgive, then we shall know peace
So stop all the hatred

And forgive each other
And our children will learn love

I'm dreaming of a COVID-free Christmas
Just like the ones we shared before
Where we could freely gather
Without the distance
And celebrate without masks upon our faces

I'm dreaming of a COVID-free Christmas
But sadly, there's not a vaccine in sight
May your health not waver, that's right
And may your heart's joy burn bright

We shall again have a COVID-free Christmas
Times will revert once again back to the past
Where we could freely gather
With each other
And celebrate with smiles upon our faces

We're dreaming of a COVID-free Christmas
Finally, they announced a vaccine for our plight
May it work and not falter
May it freely be given
And may our freedoms again return

Yes, we shall indeed celebrate Christmas
It will again bring joy into our lives
As we stop for a moment
To cherish each other
And forgive others of their misdeeds

Please, let us all celebrate Christmas
If we can forgive then we shall know peace

So stop all the hatred
And forgive each other
And our children will learn love

So let us get rid of COVID for this Christmas
So we can return to those we love
For now we must keep our distance
Wearing a mask and practicing cleanliness
And keep the faith within our hearts

We shall get rid of COVID for Christmas
With will unite humanity in the end
For by coming together
And eliminating differences
Common sense would once again reign
[Pause]

So, what are you thankful for this Christmas?

"We Can Dream of World Peace for Christmas"

We can dream of world peace for Christmas
But to do so, we must look the other way
For two wrongs cannot make things right
Forgiveness must be practiced all the time

We can dream of world peace for Christmas
Even though we cannot seem to agree
For so long as we are equals, that's right
There would no longer be any reason to fight

We can have world peace for Christmas
So long as we place value in our lives

Eliminate our differences, morning, noon and night
And we could have world peace for life

We can have world peace for Christmas
So long as we recognize everyone's point of view
Common rules, common laws, and justice would reign
If only we could begin, peace would reign

[Back to the top for another run-through]

"Beats from My Heart"

All this negativity
Takes a toll
All these melodies
Make me whole
I will try
Every single day
Come whatever
That truly may
Every single beats
From my heart
Along with every
Piece of art
Love's the glue
Between us all
Without love there's
Nothing at all
All the thunder
All the rain
All the wind
All the pain

All your lies
Hide the truth
Time does fly
I've got proof
All your negativity
Drives me insane
All my fears
Fall as rain
All the gold
In the world
Has no meaning
Without self-worth
All the rhythm
All the rhyme
All that happens
Time after time
All our insanity
All our prose
All shall frame
Our true rose

[Repeat]

"Encore"

Open up your mind
Followed by your heart
Dance to the rhythm
Shuffle to my rhyme
Open up your soul
Followed by your love

Dance to the rhythm
Shuffle to my rhyme

One, two, three, four
It's you I adore
You know the score
I want you more
Together upon the floor
Closer to the door

Open up your mind
Followed by your heart
Dance to the rhythm
Shuffle to my rhyme
Open up your soul
Followed by your love
Dance to the rhythm
Shuffle to my rhyme

One, two, three, four
It's you I adore
You know the score
I want you more
Together upon the floor
Closer to the door

More, more, more, encore. . .
More, more, more, encore. . .

Four, three, two, one
The countdown has begun
Together having some fun
Under the setting sun

There's nowhere to run
We've both truly won

"Beats Our Hearts"

[Refrain]
Thump. Thump. Thump.
Beats my heart
[Slight pause]
Thump. Thump. Thump.
Beats my heart
[Slight pause]
Thump. Thump. Thump.
It's steady rhythm
[Slight pause]
Thump. Thump. Thump.
Strengthens my art

[Main]
When I see her face
My heart begins to race
The pounding in my chest
I'm not able to rest
As she sings her art
She has stolen my heart

When I hear her voice
My heart begins to rejoice
She sends my heart racing
She's my future I'm facing
As her hand touched mine
Our eyes began to shine

Life is a joyful dance
Love defeats a bad romance
When two finally become one
That's when we finally won
The beats of our hearts
Inspired many works of art

Love's all that we need
This truth I do concede
In order to embrace life
A husband needs a wife

[Refrain]

Thump. Thump. Thump.
Beats our hearts
Thump. Thump. Thump.
Beats our hearts
Thump. Thump. Thump.
Their steady rhythms
Thump. Thump. Thump.
Inspires our art

"Just One. . . "

[Refrain]
You've thrown me for a loop. . .
One look from you, you, you. . .
You've thrown me for a loop. . .
One look from you, you, you. . .
As my heart beats
All I needs you, you, you. . .

[Main]
You have me
Tied in knots
One simple look
I'm outta place
My heart races
Then skips beats

Just one look
Just one touch
Just one smile
Just one kiss
Just one, one...
Taste

You have me
At a loss
Nowhere to turn
Nowhere to go
I'm craving you
Set my fire

Just one look
Just one touch
Just one smile
Just one kiss
Just one, one...
Taste

[Refrain]

I am yours
You are mine
We are one

Your my melody
I'm your beat
Together we're sweet

Just one look
Just one touch
Just one smile
Just one kiss
Just one, one. . .
Taste

Dancing in circles
You're my rhythm
I'm your treat
Together we're sweet
Nothing can beat
This sick beat

Just one look
Just one touch
Just one smile
Just one kiss
Just one, one
[Pause]
Taste

[Refrain]

[Back to the top for another run-through]

"Turn, Life, Live, Dance, Sing, Truth. . . "

Turn. . .
Sadness into gladness
Sorrow into joy
For there's only now
Live today for tomorrow. . .
Turn. . .
Bitterness into sweetness
Longing into triumph
For there's only moments
Why live with sorrow. . .

[Instrumental]

Life. . .
Live each moment
The time's now
Dwelling within one's sorrow
Drowns out one's tomorrow. . .
Life. . .
Swallowing bitter tears
Choking upon fears
Wasting all your years
Remember to live now. . .

[Instrumental]

Live. . .
Forget about tomorrow
Set aside sorrow
Celebrate every single triumph
Don't wait for tomorrow. . .
Live. . .

Cherish each moment
Yours and mine
Like a fine wine
It improves over time. . .

[Instrumental]

Dance. . .
To your song
It's never wrong
Follow one's own heart
Just begin and start. . .
Dance. . .
Let yourself go
Live life now
Chase after your dreams
Live to see tomorrow. . .

[Instrumental]

Sing. . .
A poetic song
Short or long
Strait from your heart
Live life through art. . .
Sing. . .
Heart felt truths
Sayings from youth
Wisdom shared for all
Give freely toward all. . .

[Instrumental]

Truth...
Hidden is lost
Let them go
Freedoms a precious gift
Embrace it for tomorrow ...
Truth...
Heals many lives
Defeats many lies
Embrace whom you love
Before you depart above...

"Homeless & Broken"

The smell of roses
Hung in the air
Everywhere that I looked
She was not there
Sadly... life is unfair

I was walking alone
Without a real home
I was crying inside
Looking for my bride
Sadly without any money
You get nowhere, honey

The smell of garbage
Hung in the air
Everywhere that I looked
It was sadly everywhere
Sadly... it's truly everywhere

I was sleeping little
Hiding in plain sight
Wandering around without hope
Crushed by invisible hands
Trying to simply exist
Trying to simply cope

Unable to simply change
Fate worn as clothes
I was being ignored
Everything that I tried
Sadly. . . was my fate

[Refrain]
Homeless. . .
Cast aside like a worn-out pair of dirty socks
Homeless. . .
People would always look past your red, tear-filled eyes
Broken. . .
Wandering aimlessly throughout each black, dark, death-
filled night
Broken. . .
Homeless and broken. . . Homeless and broken. . . Homeless and
broken. . .

"Mint"

Why must they truly print
Right direct from the mint!
To ease our markets volatility
And drive inflation our way

Why must there truly be
Debts between you and me?
Are we not truly equals
What's the difference between us?

Oh, our free market has gone to pot once again
Oh, our free market has gone down and up again
Oh, our blood pressure has risen quite suddenly once again
Oh, our blood boils when we fight and argue yet again

Why are we not equals?
What's the difference between us?
Why is our currency not equal to yours?
My life's of infinite worth!
The same truly as yours!

Why must we truly be
Trapped between cap and line!
What's the fixation on debt?
Redemption's truly a fine line

Oh, to be free from enslavement once again
Oh, to be free from debt collection once again
Oh, our lives are precious, worth saving once again
Oh, our lives are used time and time again

"From Each Moment On"

[Refrain]
From each moment
From our first glance
From every moment
That has come to pass

Our fires burning
So is our dance
From each moment,
On. . .
[Pause]

From each moment
From our first touch
From every moment
From our first kiss
Growing between us
So is our love
From each moment
On. . .
[Pause]

[Main]
I gave my love to you with all my heart
I gave it freely, right from the start
We came together and are now as one
We placed our hands within the others grasp
As we came together, our souls did touch
We then eventually confessed, yes each of us
Down the aisle we walked, under a rising sun
Bells were ringing, yet there was no sound
The preacher asked and we took our vows
You gave your love to me with all your heart
You gave it freely, right from the start
We came together and are now as one
My seed was planted within your fertile soil
Together life sprang forth, our name carries on

[Back to the top]

[Main 2]
We are both now old and our hair is gray
Our skin has withered; we've grown in many ways
[Smile and wink]
Wisdom given to our children, passing on what we know
Together we have built our precious young family
Soon it will be that we will go our separate ways
Our love shall linger, they shall carry on
Hopefully they too shall bring up their young
I wish that in truth we both could stay
But one by one, we shall walk away
God shall eventually call each of us away
Heaven or Hell He'll place us, so they say
Judgement shall indeed eventually come to pass
Perhaps we shall meet again under a rising sun
To again join the dance, becoming again one

[Refrain]
Yes, each moment shall linger, on. . .

"Oh, How Can I Avoid My Fate?"

I have my issues
Many I can name
I have my issues
Many I can blame
It's all on me
Life isn't a game

No, it's never been a game. . .

So I shall face
Each and every one
That I can name
Nowhere can I run
It's all on me
Life isn't a game

No, it's hard just the same...

I must try hard
To avoid these truths
I must try hard
To retain my youth
It's all upon me
No one to blame

No, nothing else can I say...

So I must face
These hard truths alone
So I must face
Truth's shall I own
It's all upon me
It drives me insane

Yes, I'm upon both my knees...

[Refrain]

Much time has past
I know the score
My mind does ponder
What's been done before
Trying to break free
So love can win

So our combined love can win. . .

Today is now gone
Still living life alone
Time has passed by
Lines within a song
I'm running on empty
This truth's set in

Yes, this truth has set in. . .

My blond is gray
My frame has grown
My skin has aged
My heart still roams
My dream is alive
My art hidden inside

Yes, my arts hidden deep inside. . .

I keep on dreaming
She will be along
I keep on dreaming
So please sing along
For love has meaning
It's our true treasure

Yes, life and love are my aim. . .

[Refrain]
Oh, how can I avoid my fate?
Oh, how can I avoid it?
Oh, how can I avoid my fate?
Oh, how can I avoid it?

Oh, I hope I'm not too late!
No, it's never too late. . .

I have my reasons
I have my fears
I have my dreams
I have my art
I have my heart

Oh, how can I avoid my fate?
Oh, how can I avoid it?
Oh, how can I avoid my fate?
Oh, how can I avoid it?
Oh, I hope I'm not too late!
No, it's never too late. . .

"Drinking. . . "

Drinking to try and ease my pain
Doesn't matter the reason again and again
Pour me some Jack then some wine
Followed by a tequila then a lime

Drinking to remember the good old days
Doesn't matter the reason again and again
Pour me some gin then some beer
Followed by a vodka then a juice

Drinking to try to forget my faults
Doesn't matter the reason again and again
Pour me a shot of something strong
Followed by a sangria then some stout

Drinking in order to keep me sane
Doesn't matter the reason again and again
Pour me some shots then something sweet
Followed by something served fast to eat

No matter the reasons, time or place
Drinking something helps the mood I face
Yeah. . .

[Dramatic pause]

Drinking something helps all my memories erase.

"Dreams Do Come True"

Some folks they say
Don't give up dreaming
But it's truly hard
Facing life living alone

Slowly does all our time flow
Like a river into the sea
Regardless of who we truly are
Some things happen simply in threes

We make our lives from luck
Betting it all upon our dreams
But the wheel turns in circles
Eventually we arrive upon our destiny

As age does eventually set in
We often forget were we've been

But still the cycle of life
Will end for you and me

Make time to dream
Some shall become reality
Open up your heart
Right from the start

So take a chance
Dreams do come true
So take a chance
I believe within you

Yes. . . I believe within you. . .

"Tears Will Fall Where They May"

Tears will fall where they may
Tears will dry and fade away
The sun will shine another day
Love's bound to come your way

Throughout the years
I've shed many tears
Waiting on you to
Come back around
Like a shooting star
Burning bright from afar
No trail to trace
Life alone I face

As time flows by
I think back why

You left me alone
Fending on my own
Swallowing my broken pride
Bitterness I can't hide
My smile's in place
Etched upon my face

My years have flown
My sins I own
Mistakes I have made
Cards I have played
The fix was in
They played to win
Money was their aim
Life is no game

My soul is free
Please let me be
I can't stand sin
Alone I will win
Like a sweet wine
Its taste is divine
My point's driven home
My heart beats alone

Like a drunken fool
Upon a broken stool
Falling upon the floor
Staggering out the door
My pride set aside
Heart still beating inside
Vision blurred by wine
Faking that I'm fine

Merlot fuels my dreams
Without love it seems
Yet silently I pray
For my wedding day
Outstretched arms open wide
Hiding my feelings inside
Waiting for my bride
My dream won't subside

Tears will fall where they may
Tears will dry and fade away
The sun will shine another day
Love's bound to come your way

Perhaps that day's today. . .

"We're Equals!"

Hey, we're equals. . . Can't they see it's true?
Come on, we're equals. . . What can I say it's true!
No matter where you are upon this earth
No matter the color of skin at birth
We're equals. . . It's a clear and simple truth

We have in this world those who hate!
We have currency differentials that stink of it
People want to be treated fair and with respect
Just because we're all different doesn't justify hate
Individualistic nationalism is another form of hate
Sealing entire cultures within the confines of their borders

Hey, we're equals. . . What I've said is true!
Come on, we're equals. . . We've done nothing unto you!

No matter how you look or what you say
No matter how you talk or what you do
We're equals. . . It's a clear and simple truth

We have in this world those that love!
We have dreams of a single currency and the one above
They try each day to extend their hand
Giving toward others their works from their hearts
Sending their money and goods near and far
Regardless of where you live or who you are

Hey, we're equals. . . I bleed the same as you!
Come on, we're equals. . . Yet sadly, we're enslaved by you!
No matter where we live or how we give
No matter where we lay or how we pray
We're equals. . . It's a clear and simple truth.

"Walking"

Laying alone in silence
Embracing my internal darkness
No end in sight
From my internal fight
So now I come unto you
With my open heart
Looking for your understanding
Looking for your love

Walking the earth alone
Walking without your hand
Walking. . . yes. . . I'm alone

Sitting upon my chair
Contemplating what has past
Although I found love
I've been set aside
So now I plead with you
With my open mind
Looking for your understanding
Looking for your love

Walking the earth alone
Walking without your love
Walking. . . yes. . . sad and alone

Carrying out daily tasks
In pursuit of nothing
For without my spark
Gold loses its meaning
Silver does not shine
Gems do not sparkle
Looking for your heart
Looking for true love

Walking alone in silence
Walking with nowhere to go
Walking. . . yes. . . broken and blue

The pursuit of money
For no real purpose
My destiny set aside
Filled with cold pain
Depression my true bane
Repeating this never-ending game

Looking for your trust
Looking for my home

Walking around on empty
Walking within my eternal night
Walking. . . yes. . . determined and true

My reasons are many
My sins are few
My soul is old
My heart is true
My purpose is new
My mind is focused
Looking for your heart
Looking for your desire

Walking about with purpose
Walking casting away my plight
Walking. . . yes. . . sadly, without you

Many years have passed
I've unearthed my stone
I've sharpened my reason
Though another person's hands
Taking ownership of nothing
Giving away my kingdom
Looking for a beginning
Looking beyond their greed

Walking knowing the reasons
Walking setting aside my hate
Walking. . . yes. . . determined and true.

"Can We Not Agree?"

[Refrain]
Cultural divisiveness
Individualistic nationalism
Currency differentials
Debt collections

We are all equals!
Enough!!!

[Main]
Can we not agree?
Isn't life most important?
Strapped to the wheel?
What's it all for?

Can we not agree?
Isn't life most important?
Working to get ahead?
Yet falling farther behind?

Can we not agree?
Isn't life most important?
What's yours is mine?
Wasting our precious time?

Can we not agree?
Isn't life most important?
Does life truly matter?
Strapped to the lines?

[Refrain]

Can we not agree?
Isn't life most important?
Why aren't we equal?
Why do we fight?

Can we not agree?
Isn't life most important?
Words of wisdom bind?
Why are we blind?

Can we not agree?
Isn't life most important?
One constitution for all?
Looking through broken glasses?

Can we not agree?
Isn't life most important?
Laws are always broken?
Words of truth spoken?

[Refrain]

We must create life
Pass on what's known
Leave behind a legacy
Built on simply love

We must promote life
In everything we do
In everything we say
Words must ring true.

[Refrain]

"Love, Wine, and Time."

Soon. . . I will begin to unwind. . .
After a long day, it's finally quitting time.
Upon arriving home I'll drink some wine.

Soon. . . I will once again return. . .
To continue my work until the end of my time.
We all need to earn and have purpose for our time.

Soon. . . I will have to rest. . .
In order to be ready for the next day.
I repeat this so often it's now more than a habit sad to say.

So. . . after having to much wine. . .
I had to stop drinking and sadly set it aside.
Depression is not an easy thing when you augment it with wine.

So. . . it's now been many years. . .
My health has improved through the passage of time.
With a doctor's help I'm now again one hundred percent fine.

So. . . I can count upon one hand. . .
The number of true friends still in my life.
Because perceptions change when you're not fine.

Perhaps. . . once again, I will dream. . .
Of a true love for my very own.
So that I can create life and pass along that which I know.

Perhaps. . . once again, I will sing. . .
Sharing my life wherever we may roam.
Spreading the joy of life with every tail that I know.

Perhaps. . . my love shall be returned. . .
For it is very hurtful when your filled with love yet are unknown.
So please come save me and accept my heart and love as your
very own.

Yes please accept my heart and love as your very own.

"Rage. . . Deep, Hate-Filled Eyes"

[Repeat twice] Olé. Olé. Olé. Olé. Olé. Olé.

Rage. . . deep hate-filled eyes. . .
Both have their points they wish to drive home.
Ancient. . . The dance between the bull and matador. . .
Who shall be the victor?
One shall knock upon Heaven's door. . .

Velour. . . red rose-laced cape. . .
All dressed in white awaiting for his foe.
Standing. . . in the center of the sand. . .
Waiting to put on their dance between the bull and matador.

Roses. . . flying through the air. . .
The victor shall return, to give the crowd some more.
It doesn't. . . matter who wins. . .
The crowd cheers the one who's left standing upon the blood-
soaked sand.

"Fishing. . . Reel, Spool, and Line. . . "

Fishing. . . reel, spool, and line. . .
Baiting a hook and casting. . .

In the hope of a catch, time after time.
Please. . . take the hook and feed me.
Oh, how I'd love to make you for dinner.
So come feed me. . .

Fishing. . . reel, spool, and line. . .
From many shores lines I've dreamed of your presence, on the
other end of my line.
Please. . . come and sustain me. . .
I need you in my life, so come feed me.

Fishing. . . reel, spool, and line. . .
Casting my net with the hope that you'd be mine.
Please. . . come dine with me. . .
You're the reason for my hunger, so come feed me.

Yes. You're the reason for my hunger, so come sustain me. . .

"Blue. . . Deep, Love-Filled Eyes. . . "

Blue. . . deep, love-filled eyes. . .
You keep on staring deep into mine.
Blue. . . deep, love-filled eyes. . .
You cannot hide what you feel inside.
Please. . . place trust in me. . .
Your reward of love's return shall set us free. . .

Years. . . many have flown by. . .
Your love has endured by my side.
Years. . . many have flown by. . .
Our love we share fills us both with pride.
Although we have weathered many storms
Nothing's changed between you and me.

Soon. . . we shall part our separate ways. . .
Sadly, we don't live life forever. . .
Soon. . . we shall part our separate ways. . .
In the end. . . we truly have no say. . .
Should I have to leave today. . .
I would wait for you. . . come whatever that may.

Blue. . . deep, love-filled eyes. . .
My true emotions I just can't hide.
Blue. . . deep, love-filled eyes. . .
Oh, how I've missed you by my side.
Please. . . come away with me. . .
Our reward of love's return shall set us free. . .
Our reward of love's return shall set us free. . .
Yes, our combined love shall set us free. . .

"All The World's Roses"

Roses, roses, all the world's roses
Pale in comparison to my love for you.
Roses, roses, all the world's roses
As they bloom, all remind me of you.

As the seasons tend to change.
My love grows as time passes along.
Many seasons have passed by.
Still my love grows for you.

No matter where I am each day.
No matter what comes my way.
No matter what I seem to do.
All the world's roses remind me of you.

Roses, roses, all the world's roses
Pale in comparison to my love for you.
Roses, roses, all the world's roses
As they bloom, all remind me of you.

Although the roses have their thorns
I would rather bleed than part from you.
Although the roses have their petals fall
In time, they come back in bloom.

Although the roses I've sent to you
They truly don't express how I feel for you.
Although the roses I've given to you
Your hands within mine are all I ask from you.

Roses, roses, all the world's roses
Pale in comparison to my love for you.
Roses, roses, all the world's roses
As they bloom, all remind me of you.

Many years have passed by your side.
No regrets exist because of your love.
Together we have given to all the world.
Our love, our art, and heart.

All that glitters turns to dust.
The pursuit of wealth, I've set aside.
I would rather be a penniless man
Than sacrifice my love for you.

Roses, roses, all the world's roses
Pale in comparison to my love for you.
Roses, roses, all the world's roses
As they bloom, all remind me of you.

All that glitters, all the greed
Makes me ill, I do concede.
When others place value in greed vs love.
Hell's what is then in store for them.
I have given much prose away.

In order for others to have my love.
I have rewritten many songs they sing.
In order to have your love mend my soul.
Roses, roses, all the world's roses

Pale in comparison to my love for you.
Roses, roses, all the world's roses
As they bloom, all remind me of you.

Yes. . .
Roses, roses, all the world's roses
With all their attributes pale to you.
Roses, roses, all throughout time.
Pale in comparison, to my love. . . for. . . you. . .

"The Call"

I say: "You don't know me." I say: "You got me wrong."
I say: "You gotta show me." I say: "You must move along."
What have you ever really given?
Oh, God! But I ain't coming back.

Although I say things lightly (Lightly), I am very seldom joking.
Oh, I've been wrong before (before), I face up to my faults.
Freedom, behind my many walls.
Oh, God! But I ain't looking back.
I'm staring into my future (Future).

Although I've twisted many words (Words), I have not truly lied.
Oh, I've forgotten my music (Music), I still write my beats.
I've been truly kind. I've given much away.
Love of life (This life), my soul (Soul).
God's been keeping me around.

I say: "You have heard me." I say: "I've played a clown."
I say: "I've got to rise." I say: "I've got to dream."
What have I ever given?
Oh God! They don't have a clue.

My heart is very heavy, I lost my true love.
My artistic gifts framed her, but she has stayed away.
It's complicated, I'm sad and don't feel appreciated.
Oh, God! She has sold her soul. Is there truly redemption?
Thank you for this life.

I've tried to be respectful.
I've tried to give for free.
I've been silently hurting.
I've been patiently waiting.
I've heard the call.

[Back to the top for second run-through]

Oh, God. . . I've answered your call.

"Twisted Love!"

Twisted love. . .
Oh, oh, oh, oh. . .
Twisted love!
Don't touch me please!

I just love it the way you tease!
I love you but you hurt me so,
So I walled up my art
And simply let you go. . .
Twisted love. . .
Oh, oh, oh, oh. . .
Twisted love!

Most times I feel
I've got to
Walk away
I've got to
Stop this play
I really can't give you any more from me
To make things right
I wanted your prenup and ring
And you think that love is simply just a game
But I'm sorry it don't work that way.

Once I came to you
From out of the blue
This bad romance you've given
I gave all this man could give you
You have my art, you have my heart
But that's not nearly all!
Twisted love. . .
Oh, twisted love!

Come find me please
I cannot walk this life in ease
I gave to you but you hurt me so
I simply packed up my art and heart!
Love me baby? Twisted love. . .

Love me baby? Twisted love. . .
Love me baby? Twisted love. . .
Love me baby? Twisted love. . .

Once I cam to you
From out of the blue
This bad romance you've given
I gave all this man could give you
You have my art, you have my heart!
But that's not nearly all!
Twisted love. . .
Oh, twisted love!

Trust in this, baby, it's a twisted love
Trust in this, baby, it's a twisted love
Trust in this, baby, it's a twisted love

"Darkness Falls upon the Doom of My Days"

No
No no
No no no
No no
No
No no
No no no
No no
No
No no
No no no
No no
No

No no
No no no
No no
No

There used to be love shining brightly alone in the sky
You were my light upon the dark side of my very soul
Love that drove me to give not for any cash
But did you know that the pain did grow
My heart burst forth and it encased you with art!

Baby, I have no other to compare you within my heart
Ooh, the less I got from you, the worse it became, yeah
Now that your career is in full bloom
A darkness falls upon the doom of my days

There's nothing more that I can give you, nothing else I can say
You remain my truth, my desire, my dream
Baby, to me, you're the pain from within my very soul
Won't you acknowledge me, is that right, baby?
But did you know that the pain did grow
My heart burst forth and it encased you with art!

Baby, I have no other to compare you within my heart
Ooh, the less I got from you, the worse it became, yeah
Now that your career is in full bloom
A darkness falls upon the doom of my days.

I'm determined to have you in my arms each day
I'm determined to have you in my arms each day
And if I should fail, my love simply won't go away!
My love is the light each and every day

There used to be love shining brightly alone in the sky
You were my light upon the dark side of very soul
Love that drove me to give not for any cash
But did you know that the pain did grow
My heart burst forth and it encased you with art!

Baby, I have no other to compare you within my heart
Ooh, the less I got from you, the worse it became, yeah
Now that your career is in full bloom
A darkness falls upon the doom of my days

There's nothing more that I can give you, nothing else I can say
You remain my truth, my desire, my dream
Baby, to me, you're the pain from within my very soul
Won't you acknowledge me, is that right, baby?
But did you know that the pain did grow
My heart burst forth and it encased you with art!

Baby, I have no other to compare you within my heart
Ooh, the less I got from you, the worse it became, yeah.
Now that your career is in full bloom
A darkness falls upon the doom of my days.

I'm determined to have you in my arms each day
I'm determined to have you in my arms each day
And if I should fail, my love simply won't go away!
My love is the light each and every day.

Baby, I gave you my art and my heart for free
Ooh, the more I gave, the farther you walked away
Now that your career is in full bloom
A darkness falls upon the doom of my days.

Yes I compare your absence to a festering wound
Ooh, the more I gave the farther you walked away
Now that your career is in full bloom
A darkness falls upon the doom of my days

Now that your career is in full bloom
A darkness falls upon the doom of my days

No
No no
No no no
No no
No
No no
No no no
No no
No
No no
No no no
No no
No
No no
No no no
No no
No

"COVID's Got Us All on the Ledge!"

Everyone in the world today is going quite insane. With COVID
upon their minds.
Everyone in the world I know is struggling to make ends meet,
take a number, and get in line.

COVID's got us all on the ledge!
All on the ledge! (You can't help the dead)
All on the ledge! (You can't help the dead)
All on the ledge!
Everyone in the world today is practicing aseptic techniques.
With COVID upon their minds.
Everyone in the world I know is struggling to make ends meet,
screw the bottom lines.
COVID's got us all on the ledge!
All on the ledge! (You can't help the dead)
All on the ledge! (You can't help the dead)
All on the ledge!
Austerity runs our world today and it drives me insane. With hate
upon their minds.
Austerity is our truth today, strapped to the wheel of life. It's time
to broaden their minds.
COVID's got us all on the ledge!
All on the ledge! (You can't help the dead)
All on the ledge! (You can't help the dead)
All on the ledge!
Tell us what you think of these
situations... aggravations... proclamations...
It blows my FN mind; is it getting to you?
Tell us what you think of these
situations... aggravations... proclamations...
It blows my FN mind; is it getting to you?
Over and over and over, and over again and again.

[Instrumental]

Tell us what you think of these
situations... aggravations... proclamations...
It blows my FN mind. Is it getting to you?

Tell us what you think of these
situations. . . aggravations. . . proclamations. . .
It blows my FN mind. Is it getting to you?
Over and over and over, and over again and again.
There's something right in our world today, filled with all our sins.
We still have time to right our world, so let us once again begin.
Love is sweeter than wine. COVID's got us all on the ledge!
All on the ledge! (You can't help the dead)
All on the ledge! (You can't help the dead)
All on the ledge!
Yeah, yeah, yeah, yeah, yeah, yeah. . .

[Alternate Lines]
Everyone in the world today is trying to stay inside. But from
COVID you can't hide.

"As He Plays His Guitar, He Quietly Dreams"

He looks upon his chores, seeing the mess sends him reeling
As he plays his guitar he quietly dreams
He looks upon his life and see the friends he's been keeping
Still he plays his guitar and quietly dreams
He doesn't know why nobody told him
How to face his truths and his life
He doesn't see that he matters
That the few in his life truly care
He looks upon his world and see the walls suddenly closing
As he plays his guitar he gently dreams
At every turn in his life he seems to have fallen
Still he plays his guitar and gently dreams
Well. . .

He doesn't realize that he does matter
It's the absolute truth
He doesn't realize that he has lots to offer
It's yet another simple truth
He's a good man and deserves a bit of cheering
As he plays his guitar he quietly dreams
He hopes that in his life he finds true love so he keeps dreaming
As he plays his guitar he quietly screams
He looks upon us all and sees the clock on the wall moving
Still he plays his guitar and he dreams
Oh how we want to cheer him
In order to make him see
Yeah. . .
Oh how we want to cure him
In order to make him hear
Yeah. . .
He looks upon his walls then suddenly gazes at his ceiling
As he plays his guitar he quietly screams
He has taken things to keep the pain masking his feelings
Still he plays his guitar and quietly screams
Oh how we want to cheer him
In order to make him see
Yeah. . .
Oh how we want to cure him
In order to make him hear
Yeah. . .
So he spoke of his life and all that is truly missing
While he plays his guitar he quietly screams
He has his issues but still he finds a way to be giving
Still he plays his guitar and quietly screams. . .

"The Game of Life"

Love is a pair with passion, so let us begin.
Throw down your hand, let our victory set in.

Love is a pair with passion, starting off with a glance.
Long lingering glances filled with a promising spark.
So why not now? Let me come in.

Our fate shall set in when two become one.
So with a winning hand, I let you walk on in.
My heart up my sleeve.

Although I see the trap set, sitting right in front of me,
There's really no chance for me. You with the sparkling eyes.
So I let you come right on in.

Love is a pair with passion, it's the game of life.
So let our game of chance truly begin.
Let our victory set in.

When all the cards fell upon the table,
Our victory was already within our eyes,
Hand after hand, little did we know.

It was only after our long, lingering embrace,
Passions began to truly flow,
Pulling us both to and fro.

Love is a game you must play to win!
So once again, let us begin. . .

"The Problems in This World"

The problems in this world.
Of multiple opposite opinions.
Is that every decision made,
Is unmade too.

The problems in this world,
Are so damn frightening.
There are too many people,
Too little food?

The problems in this world
Make it so uninviting.
Everything seems to be about
Funny paper bits.

The problems in this world
Make my head swirl.
Who's to be saved
Or perhaps not.

The problems in this world
Are based upon decisions.
Love must be used,
Not hate too.

The problems in this world
Make my blood boil.
Yet there is hope
From the faithful.

Oh the problems. . .
Oh the problems. . .

Oh, oh, oh problems. . .
Yet I do still love. . .

"A Secret of That Night"

It used to be alright to simply hook up.
Holding on so tight, not wishing to wake up.
Turning out the lights, making love that's true.
What was shared that night, between the two of us.
What was said that night, whispers between just us.
It would have been alright.
A secret of that night.
The secret in the night, two consenting people.
We both got off, yes that's right!
But sadly, it was just only on that night. . .

It was just the other day, our lonely paths had crossed.
Just our needs held sway; our hearts then joined as one.
It started out simply with a shared drink or two. . .
The day then turned to night; it was more than just love.
It truly would have been alright, a secret in the night.
The secret of that night, two consenting people.
We both got off, yes that's right!
But sadly, it was just only on that night. . .

[Instrumental]

Our regrets since that night, when we were together.
Silence held since that night, dreaming of forever.
But sadly, it was just only on that night. . .

[Instrumental]

Our regrets since that night, when we were together.
Silence held since that night, screaming out never.
But sadly, it was just only that one night. . .

[Instrumental]

Then we were simply through. A secret of that night. . .

"The Seeds of Love"

I gave you all my art.
Right from the start.
Without any of the strings.
Straight from my heart.
Greed got in the way.
My love's now cast away.
And I am living my life, alone.

What more must I give away?
What else must I give today?
For her to come my way?
For the Devil to stay away?
In order to sow the seeds of love.

I am truly a very. . . old soul.
Living life alone does take. . . a toll.
I fight off depression every day.
But my face gives nothing away.
As others play their games, with my heart.

My love simply has been. . . cast away.
Like a cool breeze upon an autumn day.

I'm a leaf. . . I'm a rose. . .
Color faded as the story goes.

Soon the autumn is. . . chased away.
Winter covers up all. . . the decay.
All is now white and cold. . .
Soon now I've become old. . .
And all of my love's. . . now gone.

For warmer days like spring. . . I do yearn.
Perhaps today's the day. . . you'll return.
Please help them find their way. . .
For we can't keep time. . . at bay. . .
By simply embracing my art, heart, and love. . .

"The Whispering Wind"

We are both in separate worlds.
Our paths have not yet crossed.
Both of us seeking the other.
With no road map from above.

It's by chance that we'll meet.
We shall trip over true love.
The fates shall have their say.
Through the gifts from God above.

We're both puppets within a play.
One encased within shades of darkness.
While the other's framed within light
And basks within the multitudes of love.

Light and love are both bound.
Yet my voice shall not sound.
My word given does bind me.
Yet my future's still my own!

[Refrain]
I shall be. . . the whispering winds.
I shall be. . . the North Star.
I shall carry. . . on within silence.
I shall keep dreaming, you'll be along.

[Back to the top for another run-through]

"A Dead Bed of Roses"

When will you be more than a friend?
When will you acknowledge my love?
Why do you carry me as a secret?
You've turned to me, and I fit like a glove!

When shall you want me, my friend?
To heal your wounds with my love.
Right now I'm just a dirty little secret!
Between you, me and the one above!

So, I have been living, my life alone. . .
No one to hold, for my own. . .
Although my heart is worn upon my sleeve!
You've never really acknowledged my love!

I gave you my art for free. . .
Hidden within was my love for you, set free. . .

But you've kept turning toward others!
So with a broken heart, I walked away...

I realized that you're not my friend...
I realized that my love was abused...
To you, I'm just your dirty little secret!
Tossed aside like a worn-out pair of gloves!

So I walled away my art and heart!
So I swallowed all of my pain!
I'll never let within my heart another!
For fear of this happening once again!

Dead am I truly toward you...
May you be happy, without love...
May whatever I gave toward you...
Frame you for life; my love...

I wish for you fame and success...
I wish for you to see me, now that I'm gone...
I never gave with any strings attached...
So you could simply know, true love...

I walk this earth within my silence...
I breathe air that's filled with love...
I have no need to replace you with another...
For I was called to you; by God above!

[Refrain]
So as a phantom, my love roams ...
Without anywhere to call truly home...
Alas, you're truly my broken dream!...
And my love's a dead bed of roses...

"Broken Dreams"

At my local cafe.
Sipping upon a coffee.
Sitting upon a chair.
Looking across the table.
Sadly, you're not there.
Tapping upon the table.
Hoping you would come.
Time keeps on going.
Yeah. . .
Gone are the dreams.
Living in the numbness.
Waiting for your number.
Yeah. . .
Broken dreams. Broken dreams.
Nothing is as it seems.
Yeah. . .
Broken dreams. . .

Suddenly, it's closing time.
Sadly, you're not mine.
Leaving, yeah, I'm leaving.
No longer looking back.
Stopping in a bar.
Sucking upon a lime.
Slugging back a tequila.
Not caring the time.
Yeah. . .
Gone are the dreams.
Living in the numbness.
Waiting for your number.

Yeah...
Broken dreams. Broken dreams.
Nothing is as it seems.
Yeah...
Broken dreams...

Lost within my sadness.
My love set aside.
Paper greed vs. love.
Lost within my silence.
Silence mistaken for defeat.
Prison of my design.
Encased within my heart.
Tomorrow is another day.
Yeah...
Gone are the dreams.
Living in the numbness.
Waiting for your number.
Yeah...
Broken dreams. Broken dreams.
Nothing is as it seems.
Yeah...
Broken dreams...

"Living within Circles"

And our world has stopped...
COLD!
Our memories have really gotten...
OLD!
Time flew out the window...

In the days
That entertainment was, sadly, set aside!

And our time has stopped. . .
COLD!
Our stories have really gotten. . .
OLD!
History does tend to repeat. . .
In the days
That truths were, sadly, set aside!

As they walk,
As they talk,
Nothing's ever complete!
As they lie,
As we die,
History does repeat!

[Sing softly]
Talking in circles,
Letting us down.
Living within circles,
Our ends are sadly bound.

And our world has stopped. . .
COLD!
Our memories have really gotten. . .
OLD!
Time flew out the window. . .
In the days
That entertainment was, sadly, set aside!

And our time has stopped. . .
COLD!

Our stories have really gotten. . .
OLD!
History does tend to repeat. . .
In the days
That truths were, sadly, set aside!

As they lied,
As they cheated,
Their fates, sadly, complete!
As they lived,
As we died,
Their fates tend to repeat!

[Sing softly]
Talking in circles,
Letting us down.
Living within circles,
Our ends are sadly bound.

And our world has stopped. . .
COLD!
Our memories have really gotten. . .
OLD!
Time flew out the window. . .
In the days
That entertainment was, sadly, set aside!

And our time has stopped. . .
COLD!
Our stories have really gotten. . .
OLD!
History does tend to repeat. . .

In the days
That truths were sadly, set aside!

In truths we're certain.
Our answers are found.
In truths we're certain.
Life does come around.

As they take,
As they steal,
Their fates are complete.
As we awake,
As we retake,
Yes, history does repeat.

[Sing softly]
Walking in circles,
Hidden truths in between the lies.
Talking in circles,
From this truth no one can hide.

And our world has stopped. . .
COLD!
Our memories have really gotten. . .
OLD!
Time flew out the window. . .
In the days
That entertainment was, sadly, set aside!

And our time has stopped. . .
COLD!
Our stories have really gotten. . .
OLD!
History does tend to repeat. . .

In the days
That truths were, sadly, set aside!

[Slight but loud instrumental that slowly fades]

[Sing softly, ending with a whisper]
Living within circles,
Death does come for us all.
Acting within circles,
The king was, sadly, set aside.

"Where's All the Love?"

When it began—
There's no way of knowing.
Everything seems to be going
WRONG!

When will it end?
There's no way of knowing.
Everything seems to still be going
WRONG!

Where's all the love?
We need it now that the market's down!
We need some love!
Where's our food going to come from?

The time is now;
This is when the strong keep going.
Even when they know that time keeps flowing
ON!

Life can't be replaced;
Everyone is truly worth knowing.
It's sad that so many are travelling
ON!

Where's all the love?
We need it now that many businesses are gone!
We need some love!
What is our purpose now that the money has gone?

How fragile life is!
There's really no way of knowing.
Where the wind is blowing
STRONG!

What need I say?
No one can say they're going.
So live life in each moment
STRONG!

We're reaching on out. . . with empty hands. . . but with hearts
filled with love. . .

Where's all the love?
People are dying and those left want to know!
Where's all the love?
God has enough angels up above!

We're reaching on out. . . with empty hands. . . but with hearts
filled with love. . .
Where's all the love?
People are dying and those left want to know!
Where's all the love?
God has enough angels up above!

The angels are all crying!
For there are too many dying!
Too many people are lying!
Things just got to stop going
WRONG!

"Lines, Lines, Everywhere Lines"

And the guy said, "Have you been sick recently? If so, we must
say goodbye."
So, I turned around, went to the back of the line, and I went
forward in order to ask him why
He said, "You can't be sick with a cold to enter here that's why!"
So, I shook my head, and said, "Imagine that. Huh, me coughing
upon you?!"
Whoa oh no!

Lines, lines everywhere lines
Blocking our admittance, it blows my mind
Start here, exit there, can't you see the line?

"What ever happened to the customer is always right?!"

And the guys said, "Anyone sick here can't enter for we don't
want to die."
So, I jumped out of line and yelled at the guys,
"Hey! What, don't we have rights?"
We put up with your lines; we put up with your rules! "Guys, give
me what's mine!"
They then say, "Sorry but you're way out of line!" Oh-ho-oh

Lines, lines everywhere lines
Blocking our admittance, it blows my mind
Start here, exit there, can't you see the lines?

"Talk through the glass and keep your distance. Clear?"
"Insert your card, enter your code upon the pad, so we can pull
up your file."
"Thank you for coming into our bank and here is your cash."
"Now have a fine day."
As you leave, another approaches the glass. "Minutes have turned
into hours!" Oh-ho-oh

And the guy said, "Everybody's welcome here. Bring us your
poor and sick they're welcome inside."
Whatever happened to the good old days? Nowadays, you can't
get inside a church!
Nowadays if you're ill, you're asked to stay home inside!

Lines, lines everywhere lines
Blocking our admittance, it blows my mind
Start here, exit there, can't you see the lines?

Lines!
Lines!
Everywhere lines!
Lines!
Lines!
Everywhere lines!
Lines!
Lines!
Everywhere lines!

[Scene]
A crowd in front of a bank acts out together as they stand in line.

All of them are either coughing, choking, gagging, wheezing, or sneezing while waiting to be served.

"Still My Heart Moves as He Sings"

I look at my cat, see the love, and hear him purring
While my heart moves as he sings
I look into his eyes with all his love asking for a feeding
Still my heart moves as he sings

I don't know why nobody held you
Nor why your love wasn't returned
I don't know how someone could abuse you
They didn't care for you

I looked into your world and I noticed it's turning
Because of the love I have given you
I look into your eyes with the love that you're needing
Still does my heart move as you sing

Well. . .

I don't know how you ended up with me
You're my little fur ball, true
I don't know how you put up with me
I'm just a pushover though; true

I look at my cat, see the love and hear him purring
While my heart strings skip a beat
I peak into his eyes, acknowledging the love he's giving
Still my heart skips a beat

Oh, how I'm thankful to have you
Oh, so thankful, so very thankful; true
I look upon my cat as he lay there gently sleeping
Wondering what tomorrow shall truly bring
Oh, how I am thankful to have you . . .

"We Want to Shake Your Hand"

We want to shake your hand.
We want to shake your hand.

And we shall think of something.
Like using a bag upon the hand.
And we, shall come up with something.
Of this, I do understand.

We want to shake your hand.
We want to shake your hand.

And we shall stop at nothing.
We've drawn a line in the sand.
And Masonry shall get matters,
Well simply back in hand.

We want to shake your hand.
We want to shake your hand.

Until then, we sit doing nothing.
Waiting for the cure to be on hand.
Until then, lodge sits empty and idle
By royal decree and command!

We want to shake your hand.
We want to shake your hand.

"COVID-19"

I can feel it coming
Nowhere to turn, nowhere to go
I can't see you coming
Yet you exist that I know
We're racing for the cure
Trying to save many, many lives

We can't stop your arrival
Nowhere to turn, nowhere to go
Everyone will eventually carry you
No matter what they do
We're racing for the cure
Trying to save many, many lives

We have a name for you
Nowhere to turn, nowhere to go
We must keep our distance
Trying to stop your spread
We're racing for the cure
Trying to save many, many lives

You seem to be everywhere
Everywhere we turn, everywhere we go
You're worse than the plague
You've taken too many lives
We're racing for the cure
Trying to save many, many lives

We have now identified you
Your death shall come in time
You're an utterly evil virus
Praying upon us, your host
We're racing for the cure
Trying to save many, many lives

What will we all do?
When we're finally rid of you
We'll celebrate your departure with wine
What will we all do?
When we're finally rid of you
We'll commemorate your departure in time

Oh, to be able to turn back time and bring back our dead.
Oh, to be able to turn back time and bring back our dead.
Oh, how we'll celebrate and commemorate your death.
Oh, how we'll celebrate and commemorate your death.
Oh, to be able to turn back time and bring back our dead.
Oh, how we'll celebrate and commemorate your death.

"How About Now?"

[Refrain]
I'm sorry for loving you
For everything that I thought to do
I'm hurting for loving you
For everything that I made it's true

Within my humble art
Is my beating heart
My life fell apart

Where I hit restart
I paid the price
Just by being nice
I live in isolation
Without love as consolation
You're my guiding light
Hidden from my sight
I've been set aside
Hurting this lion's pride

[Bridge]
You're the light against my darkness
You're the treasure of my dreams
You're the truth against their lies
You're the love against their hate
You're the balm against my hurt

Soft spoken part:
Do you get the picture now? Now? How about now?

Back to the top for another run-through.

"The Love Is Gone"

[Refrain]
The love is gone; no turning back time.
The love is gone; bring me more wine.
The love is gone, hiding within my pain.
The love is gone; I'm now alone again.

[Main]
Seems like it was just the other day
That you smiled at me and came my way.

If only I knew the future, I would have changed my ways. . .
Ooh, ooh

I'm sorry for what I said and didn't do.
I just couldn't help myself is the utter sad truth.
You inspired my art and fueled my dreams. . .
Ooh, ooh

I'd take back the words that I sadly said.
I'd try to erase all the pain and sow love instead.
Now I face life alone, which I utterly dread. . .
Ooh, ooh

I would wipe away all your tears,
I would share life through all my years.
I would simply hold you and erase your fears. . .
Ooh, ooh

My reflection hides many broken dreams.
The pain inside I wear upon my sleeves.
I've given much away to the extent that you'd never believe. . .
Ooh, ooh

There comes a time when you must face truths.
No memories of love shall pull me through.
There's not much else that I can say or do. . .
Ooh, ooh.

"Can Somebody Save Me and My Precious Love?"

Can somebody save me. . . and my precious love?

Each moment I live I die a little
Roses lay strewn at my feet

[Look within a mirror sadly]

I've stepped back from the brink and cried
Look at what God has done to me
I've spent all my years in service to you
Working for absolutely free, oh. . .
Anybody, anybody!
Can somebody save me. . . with their precious love?

I've tried hard (He's trying hard) each moment in life
There's nothing in it for me
At the end (At the end of my days)
Sometimes sleep doesn't come for me
I wear a mask (Mask) I'm crying inside (Inside)
My frustration keeps me silent
As my blond hair has turned gray
(Please) Can you guess whom it is that I do love?

(He does not yield)
Everyday (Everyday) I've given much of what I can say away
But nobody wants to lend me a hand
They have me on meds to keep depression at bay
They say you can't choose whom to love
God knows that's not true (That's untrue!)
I can't give up in my true love

Heaven knows (Heaven knows) I've prayed and I've prayed and
I've prayed
Can anyone guess who it is. . . that I love?
Can somebody save me. . . with their precious love?

I always feel with the rhythms of my heart
It never has skipped (Lost) its beat
You have no idea the pain that I hide
Working for absolutely free
It's okay; it's alright (He's the KING; he's our KING!)
I will not succumb to defeat

I just got to get on with my life
One day (Someday) She'll come for me oh. . .
GOD!!!!!
Can somebody save me. . . with their precious love?

Send into my life her love
Send into my life her love
Send into my life her love
Send into my life her love

Send into her life my love
Send into her life my love
Send into her life my love
Send to her, send to her my love, my love, my love
Send into my life her love
Send into my life her love
My dream, my dream, my dream
My dreams shall come for me with love
Can somebody save me. . . with their precious love?

I've encased my dreams with much of my art
Given to set her free (Set her free)
I look into the mirror and cry
Her association is hidden from me
I've always given to help others

So when shall she come for me... oh...
And my precious love?

Oh, she lives a life filled with lies
Roses do tend to have thorns
I have bleed, I have bleed (He's been pricked)
Our KING of old reborn...
Nobody shall ever keep me down!
Eventually I'm gonna bust free... oh...

Send into my life her love
Send into my life her love
I exist although I tend to hide
Within my modest life (Modest life)

I've given away much of what I had to say
Others sing what I have said (What I've said)
So come unto me, come unto me
My true love, love, love!
Come unto me, come unto me
My true love, love, love!

"Hurt!"

I hurt within today
The same as yesterday
I embrace my pain
Trusting in my heart
Their absence is my wound
The old familiar thing
Trying to give it, everyday
But sadly they've left, sad to say

What have I done?
Why am I last?
All of my passion and love
Goes to her in the end
And she will take it all
All my pain and hurt
Even after I'm gone
My soul shall carry on through hurt

I am the king of old
Sitting in my plain old chair
Full of love-filled dreams
That have escaped my care
Beneath the strains of loss
The feelings ebb and flow
You're with someone else
I am still right here

What have I done?
Why am I last?
All of my passion and love
Go to her in the end
And she will take it all
All my pain and hurt
Even after I'm gone
My soul shall carry on through hurt

If I could start again
Right here is where I'd be
I'm not going to risk myself
My soul is mine today

"The Die's Been Cast"

Oh ah oh ah
Oh ah oh ah
Oh ah oh ah
Oh ah oh ah
I've been simply waiting
For things to unfold
I've been born anew
This king of old
Oh ah oh ah
Oh ah oh ah
Oh ah oh ah
Oh ah oh ah

Sitting here all alone
Doing nothing here at home, yeah. . .
Waiting for the future
Born from my humble past, yeah. . .

Oh ah oh ah
Oh ah oh ah
Oh ah oh ah
Oh ah oh ah
Sad I am sad
Mad I am mad
Glad I am glad
I have been had
Oh ah oh ah
Oh ah oh ah
Oh ah oh ah
Oh ah oh ah

Sealed is my doom
I'm great at the loom, yeah. . .
Healed is my heart
By the power of art, yeah. . .

Oh ah oh ah
Oh ah oh ah
Oh ah oh ah
Oh ah oh ah
Wisdom from ages past
Helping others' futures last
The die's been cast
I'm alone and last
Oh ah oh ah
Oh ah oh ah
Oh ah oh ah
Oh ah oh ah

[Back to the top; run through three times]

"Playing Our Game of Love"

[Speaking into a cell phone]
What? What did I say?
What? What did I do?
Hello? Hello?
God knows I try!
What?
What did you say? What did you do?
I'm done; we're through!
[Hang up abruptly]

[Refrain]
Our life's lived in circles
We both share the blame
Our pain shared with others
Just to simply get through
We both blame each other

[Pause]

Oh, the darkness, the pain

[Pause]

Walking around on empty
Carrying on without joy
Looking for some understanding
Waiting around on empty
Carrying on without love
Looking beyond our frustration

[Main]
Our paths crossed each other's
Nothing's truly by utter chance
Our hope rose and fell
Playing our game of love
Living within our own Hell

Our desire's burned up brightly
Star crossed by God's will
Our prayers had been answered
Playing our game of love
Living within our own Hell

Our actions often define us
God does use us all

We'll both keep on searching
Playing our game of love
Living within our own Hell

Our gifts shall remain behind
Everything happens for a reason
Our hopes rose and fell
Playing our game of love
Living within our own Hell

"Without Love"

I live alone, encased within my silence
I live alone, trapped without my true love
I'm bringing this to all of you paying attention
That my soul cries out loud
That my tears fall like rain
But I am carrying on, without love
Without love.
[Pause]
I'm all flustered when I see her
As she sings my prose out loud
I always stop to listen to her voice
Sharing my love through my art
Sends shivers. . .
Down [Pause], down my spine
Down my spine.

[Sad instrumental]

I live alone, encased within my silence
I live alone, trapped without my true love

I'm bringing this to all of you paying attention
That my soul cries out loud
That my tears fall like rain
But I am carrying on, without love
Without love.
[Pause]
I'm caught within a web so fine
Born from out of my heart and soul
Working for free has truly cost me
My true love for all time
Sends tears . . .
Down [Pause], down my face
Down my face.

[Sad instrumental]

I live alone, encased within my silence
I live alone, trapped without my true love
I'm bringing this to all of you paying attention
That my soul cries out loud
That my tears fall like rain
But I am carrying on, without love
Without love.
[Pause]
I carry on in life without her
Living a life without her love at all
But my soul keeps longing for her
My true love has my heart
Encased within my words and actions
Sends sadness . . .
Through [Pause] through my mind
Through my mind.

[Sad instrumental]

I live alone, encased within my silence
I live alone, trapped without my true love
I'm bringing this to all of you paying attention
That my soul cries out loud
That my tears fall like rain
But I am carrying on, without love
Without love.
[Pause]
Although I lead a saintly life
Without my wife, love, and dream
She's still at the very center
Of my heart for all time
Like a fine wine, improving with [Pause] with age
With age.

[Sad instrumental]

[Sing in a soft voice denoting sadness]
I live alone, encased within my silence
I live alone, trapped without my true love
I'm bringing this to all of you paying attention
That my soul cries out loud
That my tears fall like rain
But I am carrying on, without love
Without love.

"She's My Angel"

[Main]
I've given away

Love and art
For her to come my way
For her to grant me love
For her to make me whole
[Pause]
My dream is
Alive and well
Showcased with fame built from love
Showcased with words sent from above
Showcased with art from my heart
[Pause]
Every heartbeat
My pulse quickens
At the mention of her name
At the sound of her voice
At her looks from the air
[Pause]
From her nails
To her hair
She's an angel in true disguise
She's an artist that can mesmerise
She's not capable of living lies
[Pause]

[Refrain]
Who's the angel. . . of my song?
Who's my angel. . . in my heart?
Who's my only. . . on my mind?
She's my rose. She's my rose.
[Pause] [Spoken softly:] Can you guess?

"We've Simply Not Crossed Paths Yet"

With mock surprise
I suddenly realize
Working for free has captured my love for all of eternity!
I walked in
I walked myself out
I'm truly all messed up then I simply cut out
Oh, I tried hard as KING not to hurt
I tried so hard to give my love away
They came upon me with their hate
They wish to justify hate through war
I realize that someday you'll be in my life
That prenup and rose ring from you are more than enough
I promise you, woman, that I'll work for free just for the sake
of love
Sad we've not crossed paths yet. Oh, sad, sad, sad. . .
Oh, I will have to wait
You're my beating heart
They say that we don't choose whom we're to love
Wherever you are
Wherever you go
You'll find that my love is always with you
And I know that together we're truly so amazing
My love for you has forever changed me
Although the TRUST has kept you from me, yyyaaa. . .
And somehow I know you'll finally turn up
And you'll take me at my word and that it will all work out
And I promise you woman that I'll work for free just for the sake
of love, yeah. . .
We simply haven't crossed paths yet
I know they're unfair

Hate won versus love
But they're unable to truly break me
We'll get along alone all right
Our souls touched
And together in this world we'll be so amazing
Being your husband isn't going to change me
Come for me and set our love free, yeah. . .
Someday you and I shall truly be one
The TRUST will work it all out!
Promise you, woman, I give more than I take!
Then I take! Then I take! Then I take!
Oh, you know that I'm the real deal!
And our prenup and rose rings shall unite us as one
And I promise you, woman, that I'll work for free just for the sake
of love, yeah. . .
But sadly you've not come for me yet!
Oh, we just haven't met up yet
Yeah, our paths haven't crossed yet
And I promise you, woman, I give so much more than I take
(I cry out LOVE, LOVE LOVE, LOVE)
(LOVE, LOVE, LOVE, LOVE)
We simply haven't met up yet (LOVE, LOVE, LOVE, LOVE)
Someday day ay ay ay ay ay, yeah (LOVE, LOVE, LOVE, LOVE)
We've simply not crossed paths yet

"I Still Try"

Can you imagine our future
If you and I engage in war?
Trying to justify our hatred
When we're all equals. . .

Can't we get along?
Dreaming of a positive bright future
With multitudes of flowers in bloom
Statues in various poses
Basking in the light
The light between you and me
Why must we go on with pretending?
In our pursuit of money and fame! (And fame)
As KING all I asked for
Was for love in return for my all. . .
Healing the rift between opposite opinions
Sadly I failed (Sadly I failed)
Why must we try to rule over another?
We all sin against each other. . .
Because of pride
Try to touch the lives of others
Through kindness and acts of love
My heart beats for all of you
Even though I've been set aside
How can we just keep on pretending?
Forsaking our world with our greed! (Greed)
Maybe we are both too demanding
Maybe we need to take a step back (Step back)
Why do we fight with each other?
This is what my mind's like
I did try. . .
How can we just keep on pretending?
Forsaking our world with our greed! (Our world with our greed)
Maybe we are both too rigid (Maybe, maybe just like our beliefs)
So I've prayed to our heavenly father simply told (Ya know this issue is old)
Maybe we all are too demanding (Maybe you're just like me)

We're never satisfied (We're never ever satisfied)
Why do we lie to each other (Why do we fight, why)
This is what my mind's like
I did try . . .
I did try (Did try, did try)
I did try (Did try, did try)
I still try (Still try)
I still try
I still try
I still try
I still try (Still try, still try, still try)
Still try
I won't lie
Won't lie
Won't lie
I still try. . .

"L. . . O. . . V. . . E"

L. . . O. . . V. . . E
Come back to me
L . . . O. . . V. . . E
Set my art free

Burning embers of desire
Rapture taking us higher
Emotional attachments gone haywire

Two hearts on fire
Two now actually one
Back and forth fun

Under the setting sun
Baby, we're never done

A husband and wife
Through hardship and strife
The creation of life
Building a home fyfe

Age does set in
Wherever you've ever been
Children singing a vibrant hymn
Teach about avoiding sin

Soon they are grown
Moving on their own
Facing their own unknown
Regular calls at home

L. . . O. . . V. . . E
Come back to me
L. . . O. . . V. . . E
Set my art free.

"Give Me the Money"

[Refrain]
Give me the money. . .
Give me the money. . .
Give me the money. . .
Crisp, clean, freshly minted. [Slight pause]
Yeah. . . money. . .
Yeah. . . money. . . [Slight pause]
Give me the money. . .

Give me the money. . .
Give me the money. . .
Crisp, clean, freshly minted. [Slight pause]
Yeah. . . money. . .
Yeah. . . money. . . [Slight pause]
Give to me, yeah. . .
Give me your money!
Give to me, yeah. . .
Give me your money!

[Main]
Look at me. . .
Sexy clothes
Confident walk
New rolls
New home
Look at me, yeah. . .
Warm stare
Smooth talk
Unlimited cash
Unlimited bling
Look at me, yeah. . .

[Refrain]

Look at me. . .
Dazzling smile
Confident air
New identity
New friends
Look at me, yeah. . .
Strong hands
Manicured nails

Fresh cologne
Your KING
Look at me, yeah. . .

[Refrain]

Money language. . .
Money language. . .
Money language. . .
Money language. . .

[Back to the top for another run-through]

[End with refrain repeating]

"Oh, Make Believe"

[Refrain]
Ohhh. . . make believe
Ohhh. . . make believe
Fantasy-altered reality
It's what the
World needs now
Something to ease
And counter hate
Ohhh. . . make believe
Ohhh. . . make believe

[Softly yet firmly spoken]
Where's the love?
The people crave?

[Main]
We can have
Eden upon earth.
We can have
Peace between us.
We can have
Cures for everything.
We can have
Rules to govern
We can have
Money to motivate
We can have. . . yes, we can have.

[Refrain]

We can give
From our hearts.
We can give
Hope toward all.
We can give
Peace a chance.
We can give
Faith a chance.
We can give
Toward each other.
We can give. . . yes, we can give.

[Refrain]

"Have You Ever?"

[Refrain]
Have you ever. . . peered through broken windows? Tripped upon some truth? Watched as others lied?
Have you ever. . . worked utterly for free? Hurt because you're unknown? Held in silent agony?
Have you ever. . .

[Main]
I'm truly
Very tired
I've given
Much away
Within our
Cosmic play
In order
To return
The love
Deep inside.
I'm truly
Very thankful
For the
Time given
So I
Can give.
Being a
Benevolent phantom
I kept
All within
My mind
And soul

Trying to
Give back
So not
To offend.
I am
Very unselfish
Sacrifice is
My aim.
A healer
Of sorts
Trying to
Restore balance
Through love
For life
To flourish
All around.

[Refrain x 2] (Spoken softly) Have you ever?

"Swallow the Medicine Doåwn!"

[Refrain]
Swallow the medicine down!
Swallow the medicine down!
They will help you—
Right!
Swallow the medicine down!
[Slight pause]
Swallow the medicine down!
Swallow the medicine down!
They will restore balance—

Yeah!
Swallow the medicine down!

[Main]
They brought me back
From my personal Hell
So I may live
To confront my love
I am the KING
Reborn from total darkness
Thankful for my life
So I work freely
To re-establish some TRUST
Within our beautiful world

[Refrain]
I was in limbo
Like Richard of Old
An utterly blank vessel
Filled with eternal darkness
Living within a hospital
Without my personal freedom
Due to my condition
With a definite description
I'm a chronic manic
Living with being bipolar

[Refrain x 2]

"Love"

Love...
Don't walk alone
Share the ride
Through true love
To become whole
Love...
Light the fire
Burn with desire
Never ever surrender
To any pretender
I've been listening
To many songs
To piece together
My broken heart
With many melodies
My stitches heal
You've touched me
All I need is

Love...
Don't waste time
Open your heart
Embrace your art
Confront your future
Love...
Light the fire
Burn with desire
Never ever surrender
To any pretender
I have found

My special one
With God's help
I was called
Courting with love
All who came
You've healed me
All I want is
Love...

[Back to the top for another run-through]

"Treasure My Love"

[Soft whisper] Treasure...
Looking for your love
To mend my heart
[Soft whisper] Treasure...
This better be love
Give me another chance
[Soft whisper] Treasure...
I'm looking for you
To embrace my art
[Soft whisper] Treasure...
I played by the rules
Made my share of mistakes
Yet you're too busy drinking
Partying and having your fun!
[Soft whisper] My love...
Life is not a game
I suffer now in silence
My mask made of darkness

Absorbs the light of truth!
[Soft whisper] My love. . .
I've paid for your success
With my determination and pain
You just don't really care
My gifts are set aside!
[Soft whisper] My love. . .
Like many jagged glass shards
Protruding from a broken mirror
Reflecting imperfectly your singular perfection
Darkness does cover all eventually!
[Soft whisper] My love. . .
I'm waiting to be acknowledged
Will it finally truly happen
That you would rescue me
From this box I'm within?
[Soft whisper] My love. . .

Yes. . .
Treasure my love!

"Lost"

They go down so easy.
The drugs they give you.
Keeping you sane and sober.
Starting life as if anew.
They've got medicine for everything.
Keeping you hooked, nothing's new.
You pay through conscious efforts.
As your employer pays you.

Nothing is really ever easy.
What did you give away?
Sanity coated with my Prozac.
Fluoxetine helps keep you calm.
The ability enhances their effects.
Together to help my mind.
They say that I'm manic.
Diagnosed bipolar one and two.
Prior to getting my medicine.
I lost myself, that's true.
This is my real story.
That I'm singing to you.

Lost are my dreams from yesterday
Lost are memories which faded away
Lost are many faces and things
Lost. . . Such is what's been paid.

"Heaven or Hell . . . "

[Refrain]
Syringes and needles
Band Aids and promises
What's your direction?
What's your life?

[Soft whiser] Heaven or Hell?

Chasing your addictions
Life's simple fixes
What's your reason?
What's the use?

[Soft whisper] Heaven or Hell?

[Main]
Lies and truths
Land of opposites
Reality is perception
Clouded by actions
Hidden by greed

The touch is upon you
A pawn you've now become
Dancing to a hidden tune
Pulse quickens before the fall
Adrenaline pumping through your veins

Will you become
A wasted sacrifice
Simply cast aside
By invisible hands
Hidden by circumstance?

The crows feast upon you
A corpse you've now become
Rotting within your own death
Another will take your place
The house always does win

Will they become
A wasted sacrifice
Simply cast aside
By invisible hands
Hidden by circumstance?

"Greed and Paper vs. Love"

Just like all the stories,
Alternate realities from long ago,
I just wished upon you,
My messed up pure love
With nothing to go on
Except art within my heart.

It took me to believe,
Star crossed from the start.
I gave away many things,
For your career and dreams.
But they kept you away,
Greed and paper versus love.

I gave you my prose,
All for free without strings.
Yet others have taken credit,
For my deeds of love.
I have no real reality,
Except my love filled dreams.

I've suffered with living homeless,
Yet I still find ways.
I've suffered without your love,
Yet I am still here.
I've walked the path rightly,
Yet I am still alone.

I'm married to my dreams,
My heart was given within.
I can rule the world,
But there's nothing for me.

If I can't have you,
Nobody else will ever do.

I wore you down,
I lifted you up.
I tore them down,
I lifted them up.
To all with love,
Ya. . . love.
My pain is within,
Every breath I take.
My arms are empty,
Yet my heart's full!
To all with love,
Ya. . . love.

"A Taste of Money"

A taste of money
Chasing money all the time

I dream of your cherished presence
And then I count upon you my friend

A taste of money
Chasing money all the time

I will spend, yes, I will spend
Helping others with the money and you

Yours was the gift that freed my art
That lingers still, long after I part

A taste of money
Chasing money all the time

Oh I will return, yes, I will return
I will come back, that's the truth
For my art, for the money, and you

"Dancing around the Christmas Tree"

Dancing around the Christmas tree,
Decorating it for the first time!
Holly and lights making us sing,
Well late into the night.
Dancing around the Christmas tree,
The spirit of the season sets in!
Later we'll have some special treats,
The jolly Old Elf shall soon bring!
As time slowly marches on,
We'll reminisce upon memories from before.
Raising our voices in song and cheer,
We'll belt out our festive songs!
Raise your voices, raise your glasses,
Give each other a wonderful smile!
Suddenly the gifts have appeared,
All around the Christmas tree.
With thankful smiles throughout the house,
Making memories to reminisce and sing!
Dancing around with the mistletoe,
Kissing everyone upon their cheeks!
As time passes and memories fade,
You will carry about Christmas inside.

As the secrets of the season are known,
Your joy you'll be unable to hide.
So remember, the jolly Old Elf's watching!
Remember not to really misbehave.

"Hidden"

[Whisper softly] Hidden

[Scene opens with this message playing through the speaker upon a red answering machine. Gaga sits in a white velour, triangular chair, silently listening and sipping merlot with a triangular glass trash recepticle full of prose and roses adjacent (left side of chair).]

[Speaking part] Didn't you. . . get my messages? Didn't you. . . get my prose? Didn't you. . . see my rose?

[*Click* of the receiver hanging up and a dial tone can then be heard. "Thirty-three" is the number on the machine's display. Gaga puts down the empty triangular glass of merlot next to a three-quarter-full bottle of any expensive Brunello brand, situated near the answering machine, resting upon a small triangular glass table.]

[Refrain]
Hidden by inaction,
For all and none to see.
For you must simply find me.
Gifts without any of the strings.
True love hiding in the wings.
[Whisper softly] Hidden

[Main] [Sing song with a sad yet determined voice]
Although I've got many issues,
I'm giving and I'm kind.
Looking for that special man,
Known as simply Mr. Right!
I've been framed by art,
For everyone to truly see.
But because I have money,
Mr. Right has avoided me!

[Refrain]
Although I've got my fame,
I need that special flame!
Looking for that special man,
Known as simply Mr. Right!
I've been framed by heart,
For everyone to truly see.
But because I am driven,
Mr. Right has eluded me!

[Refrain]

[Back to the top and repeat]

[Gaga throughout the video rejects passes from many men (turn lots of corners) and settles back in her chair pouring another glass of merlot from a triangular decanter, shaking her head with sad determination upon her face. Film at night.]

"Hollow"

[Scene]
Fog upon the floor, an empty bedroom with a film projector

running candles (lighting dim) and a mirror from the *Phantom of the Opera* with multitudes of roses all over the place in vases. Red velour drapes frame the single window (film at night) bed is also in red velour with white pillows.

The camera focuses upon a picture of a man in a full tuxedo and mask, framed within a red broken heart frame, made into a puzzle with a few pieces missing next to a Masonic apron and Shrine fez upon a candle lit night stand that's to the right of the window, left side of the bed.

All the magazines from over the years with Gaga on the covers cover the floor next to an empty closet, left of the window. A single ticket—next to Sony's seats from Radio City Music hall with an unfulfilled meet and greet invitation—left upon the bed.

I need you
That's the truth
I'm falling apart
Without my dream
It's no fun
Giving for free
Nothing's for me
Love set free

I need you
Need to repair
Patch my heart
Walking in silence
It's no fun
From my view
Sadly no pre-nup
A familiar ring

Refrain:
Hollow... Hollow...
Polaroid framed dreams,
From Hollywood magazines.
Hard thing to swallow...
Hollow... Hollow...
Polaroid framed dreams,
From Hollywood magazines.
Hard thing to swallow...

[Scene]
Pictures of Gaga: scenes from out of magazines, on film being
shown against a sterile white wall within a nearly empty room.
A single table to the right with an unsigned pre-nup, ring, and
a single red rose with white lace on its stem on it; lit by the film
projector's light and a single white chair with her teacup upon it.

Final scene fades with the song "Bad Romance" playing.

"A Saint without Wings"

Ahh, ohh, ahh, ohh, ahh
Ohh, ahh, ohh, ahh, ohh

I've walk many miles,
I've given many smiles.
Hiding my pain inside,
Looking for my bride.
I've given many things,
A saint without wings.
When will it be,
You'll be with me?

Ahh, ohh, ahh, ohh, ahh
Ohh, ahh, ohh, ahh, ohh

Your love is priceless,
My love is limitless.
Puting forth a smile,
Dreaming all the while.
I've proven many things,
I've taken away nothing!
When will it be,
You'll be with me?

Ahh, ohh, ahh, ohh, ahh
Ohh, ahh, ohh, ahh, ohh

I work to live,
I work to give.
I'll say it plain,
You're worth the pain.
I work for charity,
Seeing with utter clarity!
When will it be,
You'll be with me?

Ahh, ohh, ahh, ohh, ahh
Ohh, ahh, ohh, ahh, ohh

Today is the day,
You're coming my way!
My prenup and ring,
Not a simple thing!
I can't really hide,
What going on inside!

So, when will it be,
You'll be with me?

[Back to the top for another run-through.]

"On With the Show!"

[Intro by announcer speaking part]
The wheel of many fortunes! The price is never right! Try to make a deal!
Come on down!
You're the next contestant on my show, that's right!
Welcome to the life and styles for the poor and nameless!
And your name is. . . ? It doesn't matter what your name is!
On with the show!

[Crowd shouts] Take a chance!. . . Go for broke!. . . Take the rose!. . . Accept his ring! . . .

[Main]
Greed is truly a funny thing, it leaves you with
absolutely nothing.
No matter the game you play, you're another sucker on display.
Some things you're better off keeping, some you're better of walking away.
All you have is the moment, the next moment may never come.

Take a chance! Go for broke! Take the rose! Accept his ring!
Take a chance? Go for broke? Take the rose? Accept his ring?

Morality is truly a funny thing; once lost, you are left
with nothing.
No matter the angle you play, you're another sucker in a play.

Some things you're better at loosing. Some can't be replaced
once gone.
Life is not a television game; your soul once lost you're done!

Take a chance! Go for broke! Take the rose! Accept his ring!
Take a chance? Go for broke? Take the rose? Accept his ring?

[Back to the top for another run-through.]

"We Must Try!"

Think, if you will, on our future,
You and I engaged in war.
We are all supposed to be equal,
Life is too precious!

Can't we make peace?
Together we can build a future
Of love between you and me.
Why must we keep on pretending?

Neither side shall be the victor,
With hostility between both you and me.
How can we keep on pretending?
In this world our conflict is old. (So old!)

Aren't you sick of this story?
Aren't you sick of all this BS?
Truthfully we're just like each other,
We're never satisfied. . . (We're never satisfied!)
Why can't we have peace with each other?
Eden is what we'll have,

If we try.
I'm sick to my stomach

Of all our sins and lies!
My stomach turns with our politics all tied up.
We all now can see very clearly.
We are sick of the lies!

How can we keep on pretending?
In this world our conflict is old. (So old!)
Aren't you sick of this story?
Aren't you sick of all this BS?
Truthfully, we're just like each other,
We're never satisfied. . . (We're never satisfied!)
Why can't we have peace with each other?
Eden is what we'll have,
If we try.

How can we keep on pretending?
In this world our conflict is old. (So old!)
Aren't you sick of this story?
Aren't you sick of all this BS?
Truthfully, we're just like each other,
We're never satisfied. . . (We're never satisfied!)
Why can't we have peace with each other?
Eden is what we'll have,
If we try. (We MUST try)

Why must we fight with each other? (Why must we lie, why?)
Eden is what we'll have
If we try. (We MUST try)
If we try
If we try

If we try (We MUST try)
Must try,
MUST TRY!
If we don't,
We'll die. . .
We'll die. . .
WE MUST TRY

"Set Us Free!"

When our world plummets into darkness,
Heavenly Father what say thee?
Praying to you for direction, set us free.
I'm living in the light you give,
But I'm clueless to where I can find thee!
Praying to you for direction, come save me.

Come save me, come save me. . .
Come save me, come save me. . .
Praying to you for direction, set us free.

The people need love, that's right
It's simple for us all to see,
We must stand to question, "Why punish me?"
For although we are imperfect,
There is still a chance for God to see. . .
Praying to you for direction, set us free.

Come save me, come save me. . .
Come save me, come save me. . .
Yes, God, you need to answer; come save me.
Come save me, come save me. . .

Come save me, come save me. . .
Praying to you for direction, set us free.

Come save me, come save me. . .
We pray to thee, oh pray to thee
Praying to you for direction, set us free.

And when the sun goes down at night
You still light the way for us to see
Shine on and release us tomorrow, come save me.
We humbly ask for love from thee
Heavenly Father, what say thee?
Praying to you for direction, set us free.

Set us free, set us free. . .
Set us free, set us free. . .
Yes, God, you need to answer; come save me.
Set us free, set us free. . .
Set us free, set us free. . .
Praying to you for direction; come save me.

"Halloween"

Halloween. . .

Dare to make a scene,
Dress to make a scream!

Let the real night fall,
Can you feel the call?

Designs that give a scare,
Claws up in the air!

Give your partner a fright,
Have a great time tonight!

Embrace the imagery, that's right.
Remember the magic of night!

Remember those who passed beyond,
So share our magic bond!

So let's have ghoulish fun,
Pull a prank on someone!

Halloween...

Let's go on a limb,
Let the midnight hour begin!

Monsters embrace your inner passions,
Show off those awesome fashions!

Artistic pageantry on eternal display,
Mama Monster has come to play!

Haus of Gaga is back,
So cut me some slack!

Let's wear our love tonight,
Our future together is bright!

What more need I say,
I'm on top to stay!

Let's start our own cosplay,
You're dressed for it anyway! [Laugh]

Halloween...

[Back to the top for another run-through.]

"Oblivion"

I was homeless...
I was jobless ..
I was lost...
Nowhere to be...
Nowhere to go...
Living on empty.

[Sing softly] Oblivion

Take a match,
To your past...
Take a match,
To your future...
Take a match,
To your dreams...
Take a match,
To your money...

Ashes and dust...
All that's left,
Ashes and dust...

I was homeless...
I was jobless...
I was lost...
Nowhere to be...

Nowhere to go. . .
Living on empty.

[Sing softly] Oblivion

Take a match,
To your lies. . .
Take a match,
To your words. . .
Take a match,
To your actions. . .
Take a match,
To your things. . .

Ashes and dust. . .
All that's left,
Ashes and dust. . .

"Circles"

I'm stuck in one place
You laughed in my face
I'm caught in this race
Stuck reversing in last place
Driving with my rearview
Not knowing what to do
I'm hurting deep inside
Pain I can't truly hide
I've given you my art
No strings, from the heart
I'm stuck in my place
Empty future I now face

Stuck in a silent scream
Chasing my only real dream

You're my center
You're my muse
You're my rhythm
You're my blues
[Sing with sad frustration] CIRCLES

You're my puppet
You're my fire
You're my dream
You're my soul
[Sing with sad frustration] CIRCLES

You're my reason
You're my sanity
You're my desire
You're my angel
[Sing with sad frustration] CIRCLES

You're my devil
You're my heart
You're my life
You're my fantasy
[Sing with sad frustration] CIRCLES

[Back to the top for another run-through.]

"Sacrifice"

[Refrain]
It has been too many years

Without you I spin in tears
[Whisper] Sacrifice

I have given too much away
For you to have your day
[Whisper] Sacrifice

[Main]
I have fallen
You have risen
I have risen
You have fallen

I have lost
You have won
I have won
You have lost

I have given
You have taken
I have taken
You have given

I have died
You have lived
I have lived
You have died

I have laughed
You have cried
I Have cried
You have laughed

[Back to the top for one more run-through]

"Pretender!"

I gave. . .
My loving heart.
I sacrificed. . .
My written art.
Some things. . .
Just never end,
While others. . .
Simply play pretend.
Pretender. . .
Some things. . .
Happen well before,
While others. . .
Never happened before
Pretender. . .
Some things. . .
Are worthwhile,
While others. . .
Aren't worthwhile
Pretender. . .
Everything. . .
That you did,
Everything. . .
That you said,
Pretender. . .

[Spoken sadly with hurt upon face shaking your head and pointing to the exits] Pretender. . . use the door. . .

Why did you. . . lie to me?
Why did you. . . turn on me?
[Whisper] Pretender. . .

Why did you. . . say those things?
Why did you. . . lie and run?
[Whisper] Pretender. . .

I gave. . .
My loving heart.
I sacrificed. . .
My written art.
Some things. . .
Happen in three,
While others. . .
Set you free
Pretender. . .
Some things. . .
Bend your will,
While others . . .
Fortify your will
Pretender. . .
Some things. . .
You throw away,
While others. . .
You cherish anyway
Pretender. . .
Everything. . .
That you did,
Everything. . .
That you said,
Pretender. . .

[Spoken sadly with hurt upon face shaking your head and
pointing to the exits] Pretender. . . use the door!

Why did you. . . lie to me?
Why did you. . . turn on me?
[Whisper] Pretender. . .
Why did you. . . say those things?
Why did you. . . lie and run?
[Whisper] Pretender. . .

[Sing with anger and hurt] Welcome to show business!

"Wounded Love"

I have had to give away,
Much of what I had to say!
Others now sing and act today,
From what I have said yesterday!

Not only giving a helping hand,
I have made a love-filled stand!
I've become a one-man band,
Love returned is my only true demand!

By my living a humble way,
I am able to hold true sway!
By building a tomorrow on yesterday,
Love is here in truth to stay!

I have had to stand aside,
As my love was sadly set aside!
A wound which festers deep inside,
My pain I can no longer hide!

Many things that I have done,
My gifts hidden by the setting sun!

I have already in truth won,
But others profit by what I've done!

[Refrain]
What else must I give away,
For her to finally come my way?
What else must I really say,
My romantic old soul does hold sway!

[Repeat from the top once through.]

"Love!"

Engines are roaring
And tires burn
All are waiting
For their turn
Engines are roaring
And tires burn
All are waiting
For their turn

Driving in circles
All for show
Waiting their turn
Nowhere to go
Driving in circles
All for show
Waiting their turn
Nowhere to go

[Announcer shouts] Let the race begin!

The flag drops
Cars in place
Suddenly they move
Vying to place
The flag drops
Cars in place
Suddenly they move
Vying to place

Pace is set
Now to race
Lap after lap
They change pace
Pace is set
Now to race
Lap after lap
They change pace

[Announcer shouts] A caution is thrown!

They start over
Ready to go
The track clears
Ready, set, go!
They start over
Ready to go
The track clears
Ready, set, go!

Not all finish
What they begin
Some must pit
One will win!

Not all finish
What they begin
Some must pit
One will win!

[Back to the top, repeat once]

[Announcer shouts] Ragan has just won!

[Insert video clip of Ragan celebrating with a Shriners child!]

Looking at highlights
Moments in time
Captured in glory
Our hero's won!
Looking at highlights
Moments in time
Captured in glory
Our hero's won!

[Insert video clip of Ragan walking holding hands with a
Shriner's child!]

[Announcer shouts] LOVE TO THE RESCUE!

"Johnny, a Twisted Soul!"

There once was a man named Johnny
A twisted soul had he
He danced to the tunes of his own
And lived in poverty

Although he had been named a king
He gave his work for free

And he'd be a wealthy fellow
If he sinned in perpetuity

Now as you guessed I'm that man
A puppet with many strings
I've been caught up within a fable
And clearly I do truly see

The morals born out of my story
Are set forth where none can see
For I bear a lack of associations
Thereby I now live in obscurity

The world is full of opposites
Just like you and me
I'm caught in a web that's so fine
It doesn't exist within reality.

"Queen of My Heart"

So don't you have need of me?
I gave to you my art, heart, and imagery.

Framed with looks for a rising star.
Queen of my heart is truly, who you are!

I walk in silence, and I'm alone.
[Softly sing] I'm waiting to call your love, my very own. . .

So when will you come for me?
I silently wait for only you, ever so patiently.

I've given my word, which binds me!
In the hope that your heart would find me.

Never have I taken things from you!
[Softly sing] I've been waiting patiently since, for only you...

So I've been waiting, not so patiently.
With an open mind and heart, filled with sincerity!

For only you can set me free.
[Softly sing] All that I need, is your love...

[Instrumental]

[Back to the top for one more run-through]

"I'm a Friend!"

[Refrain]
I've had much success,
At every single thing!
Yet I am alone,
Life with no dreams!
No pre-nup and ring,
Not a simple thing...
Yes, I've had success,
At every single thing!
Yet I am alone,
Life with no dreams!
No prenup and ring,
Not a simple thing...

[Main]
Oh, I'm a friend...
So long as I
Do what they want!

Why must I compromise?
Why must I give?
I need to live!

Oh, I'm a friend. . .
So long as I
Give away my art!
Why must I compromise?
Why must I give?
I need to live!

Oh, I've had friends. . .
With money and fame,
We worked in unison!
Through merlot and games,
Helping others for charity,
Riding upon their names!

Oh, I'm now alone. . .
With very few friends,
My money's now gone!
Spent upon my dreams.
My art takes wing!
Not a simple thing. . .

Oh, I'm a friend. . .
So long as I
Did what they wanted!
Why must I compromise?
Why must I give?
I need to live!

Oh, I'm a friend. . .
So long as I

Gave away my art!
Why must I compromise?
Why must I give?
I need to live!

Oh, I've had friends. . .
With money and fame,
We worked in unison!
Through merlot and games,
Helping others for charity!
Riding upon their names. . .

Oh, I'm now alone. . .
With very few friends,
My money's now gone!
Spent chasing my dreams.
My art takes wing!
Not a simple thing. . .

[Back to the top for one more run-through]

"Just One"

Perception within a reflection
Beauty is captured within
Actions facing their opposites
Perception the grand design
Clarity of my mind
She is my dream
More than she seems
Queen of my heart. . .

Just one glance
Just one touch
Just one smile
Just one word
Just. . . one. . .
Just. . . one. . .
Just. . . one. . .
Just. . . one. . .

Tears held back within
My soul of lava
Stone cold to touch
I want her badly
Along with everyone's love
Clarity of my mind
These are my dreams
More than they seem
This is my heart

Just one glance
Just one touch
Just one smile
Just one word
Just. . . one. . .
Just. . . one. . .
Just. . . one. . .
Just. . . one. . .

Years have now passed
No change of heart
Burning brightly in silence
Perceptions a funny thing
I've given much away

For everyone else's love
This makes me smile
While embracing my silence
More than I seem
These are my actions. . .

Just one glance
Just one touch
Just one smile
Just one word
Just. . . one. . .
Just. . . one. . .
Just. . . one. . .
Just. . . one. . .

"Baby, Yeah, Yeah . . . "

I dream of you constantly
Baby
I wish you were mine
Baby
Bring your love on over
Yeah, yeah
Let's roll in the clover
Yeah, yeah
I'm waiting for my chance
Baby
Some day you will arrive
Baby
Bring your love on over
Yeah, yeah

Let's roll in the clover
Yeah, yeah
I need all your love
Baby
We fit like a glove
Baby
Bring your love on over
Yeah, yeah
Let's roll in the clover
Yeah, yeah
I'm still out here waiting
Baby
I'm hung up on you
Baby
Bring your love on over
Yeah, yeah
Let's roll in the clover
Yeah, yeah
I've asked for your number
Baby
But you don't see me
Baby
Bring your love on over
Yeah, yeah
Let's roll in the clover
Yeah, yeah

[Back to the top, repeat second time through]

Don't give me your shoulder
No, no
Don't give me your shoulder
No, no

Don't give me your shoulder
No, no
Bring your love on over
Yeah, yeah
Let's roll in the clover
Yeah, yeah
Don't give me your shoulder
No, no
Don't give me your shoulder
No, no
Don't give me your shoulder
No, no

No. . .

"Waiting on Love's Return"

Can't they see?
That you're my life,
And my love?

All I want
Is to live life,
Giving away love!

My heart bleeds!
My soul cries!
My mind races!
My time flies!

Waiting. . .
On. . .

Love's. . .
Return. . .

[Insert music melody without voice and use as the refrain]

And further more,
I knew the score,
Took the door!

That being said,
You're worth the wait;
Let's not pretend!

When life's gray
Making me feel blue,
I call you!

My heart bleeds. . .
My soul cries. . .
My mind races. . .
My time flies. . .

Waiting. . .
On. . .
Love's. . .
Return. . .

"You're Worth It!"

I gave away
Much of my written art.
Hidden deep inside
Was my big, beating heart.

No strings attached
So as not to offend!
A silent partner,
I hurt all the time.

You're worth it;
All of my soul's pain, ya!

I was searchin'
For most of my life.
For true love.
To finally come my way!
So when is
My lucky love filled day?

You're worth it;
All of my soul's pain, ya!

All I want
Is my prenup and ring.
A simple request
From my love-filled heart.
You can have
All my skillfully written art.

You're worth it;
All of my soul's pain, ya!

I am waiting,
Knowing the truth's deep within.
You're my one;
I can't let you go!
I am lost
Without my soul's better half.

You're worth it;
All of my soul's pain, ya!

You're worth it;
I'd do it all again, ya!
You're worth it;
Love is not a game. No!
I found you,
Seems like the other day!

You're worth it;
All of my soul's pain, ya!

"Can't You Tell?"

[Refrain]
Can't you tell. . . that the world. . . spins us around?
Can't you tell. . . that the sun. . . rises each day?
Can't you tell? Can't you tell? Can't you tell?

[Main]
We are truly. . .
All of us
Wearing the blame!
Ruining the earth. . .
Pursuing our dreams
Every single day!
We are truly. . .
All of us;
Hiding our pain!
Chasing after money. . .
Sacrificing our morality

Every single way!
We are truly. . .
All of us
Lying to ourselves!
War solves nothing. . .
Few over many
Playing their games!
We are truly. . .
All of us
Tested every day!
Working away endlessly
Until retirement day!

[Refrain]

"Nothing's Written"

It was a cold winter morning.
With nothing but white to see.
It was a time for reflection.
I had nothing except my creativity.
So armed with pen and paper.
I started to confront my destiny.

Too often in life we ignore.
Those few who mean us well.
Many times we simply turn away.
Ending up within our own Hell.
The process is slow, nothings written.
So I started. The strokes fell.

After I wrote a few letters.
The words just started to flow.
I suddenly was thinking of you.
Finally my heart was letting go.
Of what I held deep within.
I will now share what's known.

[Speaking part]
"The River Still Flows"
Solitudes are like thoughts without sleep. No one is at peace,
since none shall capture nor keep.
Light rises with the dawn off into the distance. Perception
misperceptions hear the carrion call.
Since my death at twelve I have been reborn. Dear lady, dear lady,
I have heard your call.
I am here, I am near, "The River Still Flows." I am as the rain
saturating your soil.
In time your seeds shall grow. "We die more than once in life. I
have done so more often than most."

I was healing now very slowly.
Sharing what I concealed in past.
This piece does indeed mark you.
But the die had been cast.
You're in the arms of another.
I truly ended up finishing last.

"Sinning All over Again!"

Love some say
Is the reason
For all our sins.

But we can't help sinning all over again.
Shall we pray?
Could it be factored in?
For we can't help sinning all over again.

Time does always flow, forward for you and me.
So this truth goes, some things aren't meant to be.

Take God's love
Take it to your hearts
For God can't help his love for you.

Time does always flow, forward for you and me.
So this truth goes, some things aren't meant to be.

Take God's love
Take it to your hearts
For God can't help his love for you
For God can't help his love for you.

"Benevolence"

I gave away my art
To conceal who I am
I focus on their needs
Our combined love is real
Their absence wears me down
The feeling of being alone
Their love is my addiction
But I remember some things

Who have I become?
My perspective's bent!

Everyone I love goes away
In the end
They can have it all!
My memories of sorrow and hurt!
I will let them go!
When they encase me in dirt.

I wear no crown of gold
Upon my troubled brow
Full of broken dreams
I can't reconcile
Will I be remembered?
I hide in plain sight!
My gifts and deeds unknown!
So as not to offend!

Who have I become?
My perspectives bent!
Everyone I love goes away
In the end
They can have it all!
My memories of sorrow and hurt
I will let them go
When they encase me in dirt
If I could do it again
I wouldn't know where to begin
I would remain as I am
I would find a way!

"Who, What, Where, When, Why"

Who, what, where, when, why?
Who, what, where, when, why?

Many truths are hiding lies!
Freedom costs us our lives!
The victors dictate our rules!
They think we're all fools!
Playing games to govern life!
Giving us calamities and strife!

Many phrases are simple truths!
Simply stated delivered in youth!
Perceptions can free ones soul!
Such as knowing your roll!
Pendulums swing in both ways!
Proper timing does hold sway!

Who, what, where, when, why?
Who, what, where, when, why?

"Nothing Is as It Was Before"

Where did our youth go?
Time flew out the window!
Our souls fill with sorrow.
Each day leads into tomorrow.
Where did our youth go?

"Nothing is as it was, before."

Where did the time go?
Youth flew out the window!
Our lives spent chasing money.
Strapped to the production wheel.
Where did the time go?

"Nothing is as it was, before"

Where did our freedom go?
Choice flew out the window!
Our dreams spent upon reality.
Each end is a beginning.
Where did our freedom go?

"Nothing is as it was, before."

Where did the love go?
Wisdom flew out the window!
Our wills spent paying debt.
Enslaved to their hates agenda.
Where did the love go?

"Nothing is as it was, before."

Where did our hope go?
Lives thrown out the window!
Our time has finally come.
War used for population control.
Where did our hope go?

"Nothing is as it was, before."

Where did the balance go?
Love and hate at war!
Our efforts spent in circles.

Neither side forgives the past.
Where did the balance go?

"Nothing is as it was, before."

"Nothing Is Free!"

Don't you see that you're mine.
All I've given, time after time.
Working for free, nothings for me.
Doing what's right, from my heart.

Healing your hearts with my giving.
Encasing you within all my art.
I've truly erased my very existence.
To show you what loves about.

Can't you see I've worked freely.
That I deserve love not hate.
Life is precious, truly worth living.
My true love's trapped by fate.

Nothing in life is truly free.
I have failed, yet I've won.
Through our love, yours and mine.
As a focus, sent from above.

[Refrain]
Will you return it to me?
Don't you see, you've hurt me.
Nothing in life is truly free.
Will you come back to me?
Will you turn away from me?

My love's priceless, can't you see?
Will you give back to me?

[After the second run-through, the refrain changes a bit,
as follows]
Will it return, back to me?
Don't they see, they've hurt me?
They say that I'm now free.
From both the Shrine and Masonry.
My love's priceless, can't they see?
Will they give back to me?

"When"

How many times must we repeat the same things
When we know it's wrong?
How many ways must we try the same things
Just to prove we're wrong?
When you fall don't you get back up?
I know you did!
When you stumble, don't you catch yourself?
Yeah, I know that's right!
When you err, don't you make amends?
Or do you move along?
When you fail, don't you try again?
I know I do!
When we lie to avoid the truth
We also lie to ourselves!
When something works, why must we mess with things?
Leave it well enough alone!
When you give, don't you feel really good?

I know I do!
When our time comes, we'll simply move along
Back whence we came!
When has it been proven that we come back
Simply to live again?
All we have is the here and now
That's the simple truth!
Embrace your time, for it's now
Before your end comes for you!

"Even God Lies?"

[Refrain]
Can you imagine,
Good versus evil?
We have to
Love each other?

[Spoken softly]
If you build something upon a lie,
Will it stand the test of time?

[Main]
Do we have
Too many problems?
Not enough solutions?
Not enough resolutions?
We make pollution?
We cause extinctions?
Chasing bottom lines?

We're fed up!
We're all equal!
Drives me crazy!
Knocks me out!

They can see!
Feed the needy!
House the homeless!
Wipe out debts!
Giving not taking!
Capping the treasury!
War over nothing!

We're fed up!
We're all equal!
Drives me crazy!
Knocks me out!

Can we see?
Talking in circles?
Even God lies?
Is this Heaven?
Is this Hell?
We have balance?

We're fed up!
We're all equal!
Drives me crazy!
Knocks me out!

Are we forgiven?
Are we forsaken?
Is there redemption?
Is morality defined?

Law versus politics?
Masonry versus Shrine?

We're fed up!
We're all equal!
Drives me crazy!
Knocks me out!

[Refrain]

"Can Someone Spare Some Time?"

Can you truly imagine?
You're unable to speak.
Stuck in a chair,
Each and every week.
Trapped within your mind.
Your future is bleak.
Reaching out from within.
Fighting for every moment.
Under our blooming sun.
Waiting for your end.

[Soft whisper] Has it truly come?

Emotionally compromised.
Physically immobilized.
Spiritually demoralized.
Why God?
Why?

[Soft whisper] We need each other. Can someone spare
some time?

Can you truly imagine?
You're crying deep inside.
Everyone is busy living,
Chasing their own dreams.
Too busy for hello,
As they walk by.
Wearing a false smile,
Holding back your tears.
Swallowing all your pride,
As life passes by.

[Soft whisper] Has it truly come?

Emotionally compromised.
Physically immobilized.
Spiritually demoralized.
Why God?
Why?

[Soft whisper] We need each other. Can someone spare
some time?

Can you truly imagine?
Taking pills for everything.
Unable to return home,
Having to sell everything.
Still he does smile,
Greets everyone passing by.
Gives his food away,
Overcome by almost everything.
Kind as the wind,
Unable to convey sadness.

[Soft whisper] Has it truly come?

Emotionally compromised.
Physically immobilized.
Spiritually demoralized.
Why God?
Why?

[Soft whisper] We need each other. Can someone spare
some time?

"Yes, Love. Without It, We're Not Whole"

Yes
When I get where I belong
Within her warm, loving, tender arms
I will shed many, many tears
To release both pain and joy.

Yes
For I've been waiting many years
For her to enter my life.
I have her still within my heart
This truth I simply can't hide.

Yes
I've given away many precious things
For her to come my way.
She's the beat of my heart.
What more must I truly say.

Yes
Others have tried by her side
To be where I truly belong

That is why I walked away
And am writing her this song.

Yes
Others want me to throw away
My precious soul along the way
In this exchange, I would receive
Fame, fortune to come my way.

Yes
I do truly love them all.
They're my family within my heart.
They need me running this place.
That's where I, in truth, belong.

[Back to the top for one more run-through]

Yes
Without love within someone's life
Your moods turn black and blue.
So have you seen her, yes, my wife?
She's standing right next to you!

[Pause for dramatic effect] Laugh!

Love
This is the reason for everything!
Good or bad within this world.
We are all searching for someone.
Without them, we are not whole.

"We've Been Down This Road"

[Scene of drinking; a wine glass hits the floor, breaking]

Early in the morning,
Not sure where you've been.
Drinking yourself to oblivion
To forget the pain within.
It's a rough road
When your love goes cold.
No use in pretending
This story is old.

We've been down, down, down, down. . .
We've been down this road.

Every night you're drinking,
Hoping to forget your plight,
Holding onto good times,
Trying to make things right.
But in the end,
You both have no one,
Nothing to hold onto.
Nothing turns out right.

We've been down, down, down, down. . .
We've been down this road.

[Refrain]
Down this road,
Nothing's right!
Love's gone cold,
Another sleepless night!
Why must we fight?

This story's old!
Come on, let go.
This story's quite old.

Twenty-nine years ago
We both turned the page.
By us both leaving,
We both learned with age.
We grew to admire
What we both left behind.
The light had dawned.
This story's quite old.

We've been down, down, down, down. . .
We've been down this road.

[Refrain]

We've been down, down, down, down. . .
We've been down this road.

"Try Again!"

There comes a time
In everyone's life
When you're down
With no way out
What do you do?
Do you give up?
Oh, no. . .
No. . .
You get back up
After every fall

Battered and bruised
But to give it your all
You try again
You try again!
Oh. . .
I've cried real hard
When I hurt inside
Some of your pain
You just can't hide
What do you do?
With no way out?
Do you give up?
Oh, no,
No. . .
You dry your eyes!
Swallow your pride!
You get back up
Pushing failure aside
You try again
You try agan!
Yeah,
You try again!
Success is a pattern
In one's life
When you're up
All seems all right
What do you do?
When you have it all?
You give someone else
A helping hand
Oh yeah. . .
Yeah. . .

You help them up
After every fall
Battered and bruised
They will give you their all
They try again
They try again!
Yeah,
They try again!
You've earned a friend!!

"Oh, My Gaga"

I've been chasing you since I don't know when.
I've been waiting for you; this game has no end.
Get me now? I will never learn!
I don't know how, but my heart's in control.
There's a need to heal my soul.
Your many looks make my heart sing!
I'd write for you for a prenup and ring!
Oh,
Oh, my Gaga, here we are again!
This is no game of pretend!
Oh, my Gaga, here we go again!
Will this distance ever end?
Yes, I've been down-hearted,
Sad since the time this started.
Why not come into my life?
Oh, my Gaga, here we go again!
This is no game of pretend!

I am glad your dreams came true.
Just so you know, you're mine, truth.
Wherever you roam, I will wait for you!
How did you know? That I lost control.
One look at you, long ago!
Your many looks make my heart sing!
I'd write for you for a pre-nup and ring!
Oh,
Oh, my Gaga, here we go again!
This is no game of pretend!
Oh, my Gaga, here we are again!
Will this distance ever end?
Yes, I've been down-hearted,
Sad since the time this started.
Why not come into my life?
Oh, my Gaga, here we go again!
This is no game of pretend!
Oh, my Gaga, this is not a game.
A ring means forever!
Oh, my Gaga, here we go again!
My life is to make you happy.
Oh, my Gaga, what must I do?
To have you enter my life?
Yes, I've been down-hearted,
Sad since the time this started.
Why not come into my life?
Oh, my Gaga, I really know.
Once I have you, I'd never let you go!

"Living Life Alone"

[Refrain]
I am so lonely,
Sitting here at home.
No one to turn to.
Nowhere to go.
Captured,
In this moment forever.
My frustration.
Living life,
Alone.

[Main]
I've chased my dreams.
A specific woman to love.
Encased her with my art.
Looking for a start.
Sadly, fates took a turn
Away from my directions.
Who can say when.
If we will meet again.

My writing's from the heart.
About my bad romances.
They were all one direction.
And they reached their conclusions.
So I am all alone.
Staring sadly at my telephone.
A life lacking motivation,
And opportunities for participation.

I've given much away.
To direct true love my way.
To fuel my burning embers.
That my soul remembers.
Just trying to heal inside.
From life's many losses.
That I no longer hide.
Even if I were to try.

[Refrain]

"Battered, Bruised, and Broken"

[Refrain]
I'm battered, bruised, and broken,
Living life like the movie *Groundhog Day*!
It seems to keep repeating,
What's in my heart; what can I say?

[Main]
I've put myself back together,
By taking medicine and living off my EIA.

Living life without a spark.
I've given away most of my lyrical art.

[Refrain]

Yin and yang are united,
Although they are different like night and day.

I've died in many ways.
Giving so that others could have their way.

[Refrain]

I truly love them all,
But they have warned me not to care.

How can it truly be,
That a king's sacrifices are not to be?

[Refrain]

[Whisper softly]
I'm wounded, nowhere to go.
Trying to heal myself without my true love.

[Back to the top and repeat for a second run-through]

"Beat of My Heart"

[Refrain]
Don't you hear what I hear?
Can you truly feel the rhythm?
It's the beat of my heart!
Can you see what I see?
Don't you see into my eyes?
They are windows into my soul!

[Main]
I've been truly waiting
For someone that's you
To enter my life
And make me whole

For years I've waited
Giving toward other people

And their collective dreams
Trying to actually heal

We are all equal
No one is perfect
But we keep trying
Looking for our equal

My other half exists
I heard her call
My angel to love
Patience is a virtue

I wish to exist
But on my terms
My soul's my own
It's not for sale

Life is a circle
Patterns tend to repeat
A map toward heaven
Written within the stars

Art given as payment
Seeking understanding and love
I am the light
She is my night

[Refrain]

"Fables Filled with Lies"

"What would you give?
What is your price?
What can one believe?
What can one perceive?
Fables filled with lies?!
What one will believe!
What one will perceive!
Fables filled with lies?!"

Times from long ago,
Echo within our days.
Patterns do often repeat.
Methods from the past.
Repeated time after time.
Looking for our king.
To find his place.
As sacrifice for sins.

Years spent in Hell.
Years spent in Heaven.
Living in our darkness.
Searching for the light.
God must truly return.
To set things right.
Mysteries of the mind.
Twists in one's heart.

Sometimes we are wrong
Sometimes we are right.
We are all equal!
Why must we fight?

Just as there's day,
We have our nights.
You decide your direction.
What is your price?

"Baby, Ya, Oh, Ya!"

I want no one but you, baby.
I need no one but you, baby.
Every woman reminds me of you, baby.
I want no one but you, baby.
I need no one but you, baby.

Ya. Oh. Ya.
Ya. Oh. Ya.

Much time has now passed by, baby.
My needs are the same now, baby.
I bring you flowers now daily, baby.
I need you in my life, baby.
I want you as my wife, baby.

Ya. Oh. Ya.
Ya. Oh. Ya.

It's now two thousand and seventeen, baby.
I've been chasing you for years, baby.
You're truly my broken dream now, baby.
I'm done working remotely for free, baby.
Enjoy your fame and the fortune, baby.

Ya. Oh. Ya.
Ya. Oh. Ya.

I was never after the money, baby.
But they had wanted my life, baby.
Just because I truly love you, baby.
My soul is "NOT FOR SALE," baby.
My art has framed you forever, baby.

Ya. Oh. Ya.
Ya. Oh. Ya.

Know that it's not your fault, baby.
I've given you my imagery forever, baby.
Know that its you I wanted happy, baby.
I've done what I was allowed, baby.
The devil has been the details, baby.

Ya. Oh. Ya.
Ya. Oh. Ya.

I wanted no one but you, baby.
I needed no one but you, baby.
Every woman reminds me of you, baby.
I wanted no one but you, baby.
I needed no one but you, baby.

Ya. Oh. Ya.
Ya. Oh. Ya.

"Come Dance with Me"

I truly don't remember
What they had said
Just looking upon you
Had captured me instead

Your eyes caught mine
A gift from above
My heart beat faster
Caught by true love

No words were spoken
Your hand grasped mine
My mind spun swimming
Music started to whine

"Come closer now, baby
You're now with me
Your search is over
Come dance with me"

"Come closer now, baby
You're now with me
Your search is over
Come dance with me"

As if from memory
From a distant past
Fate put us together
Love which would last

I truly don't remember
What they had said
Just looking upon you
Had captured me instead

Your eyes caught mine
A gift from above
My heart beat faster
Caught by true love

No words were spoken
Your hand grasped mine
My mind spun swimming
Music started to whine

"Come closer now, baby
You're now with me
Your search is over
come dance with me."

"Come closer now, baby
You're now with me
Your search is over
come dance with me."

As if from memory
From a distant past
Fate put us together
Love which would last.

"I Never Said Goodbye"

Father,
We cried for you
When God took you
We all died too
When we lost you
Oh
We're deeply sorry for
Our loss that's true
We had each other
To rely on, true.

[Whisper softly]
We never said goodbye
To you, it's true

It's now been many yesterdays
Our tears have now dried away
Many memories lost sad to say
Many walls held within my way
Are you looking down upon us?
I'm sorry for our loosing you!
For all that you suffered too.

Father,
I tried to do
Since I lost you
Nothing has come easy
That's the simple truth
Oh
I've given much away
To hide my pain
Encased others with art
But nothing replaces you.

[Whisper softly]
I never said goodbye
To you, it's true.

It's now been many yesterdays
Our tears have now dried away
Many memories lost sad to say
Many walls held within my way
Are you looking down upon us?

I'm sorry for loosing you!
For all that you suffered too.

Father,
No matter where I go
No matter what I do
No matter who I become
It's mainly because of you
Oh

[Softly whispered] I'm hurting, missing you.

"Easy Come, Easy Go"

Easy come and easy go.
Try to play to win.
It doesn't matter, any game.
Odds are low to win.

Easy come and easy go.
Try to pray, not sin.
It matters; life's no game.
Yet the fix is in.

Easy come and easy go.
Try to give, not take.
Set aside your personal matters.
Death always collects the spoils.

Easy come and easy go.
Try to live, not die.
It matters; take few risks.
Unless you know you'll win.

Easy come and easy go.
Try to love, not hate.
It matters; we're all equal.
Regardless the color of skin.

Easy come and easy go.
Try to govern, not enslave.
The devil's in the details.
Break no laws to win.

Easy come and easy go.
Try to serve for free.
Both Masonry and the Shrine.
Life and unity MUST win.

"You're My Living Dream"

Oh, how my heart's
So raw and tender.
It's hard to leave,
Each moments forever.

My world, it's you,
You're my living dream.
Each and every way,
So Happy Valentine's Day.

Oh, how our heart's
Two halves now whole.
As we make love,
The bells do toll.

My world, it's you,
You're my living dream.
Each and every way,
So Happy Valentine's Day.

Even though we're apart,
You complete my heart.
I'll return that's true,
My love, that's you.

My world, it's you,
You're my living dream.
Each and every way,
So Happy Valentine's Day.

"What Do You Want from Me?"

Just because I believe you,
Doesn't mean I need you!
Oh just get out of here. . .
Oh just get out of here. . .
Just get out of here!
Just because we made love,
Doesn't mean we are one!
Oh let me out of here. . .
Oh let me out of here. . .
Let me out of here!

[Speaking voice]
Please just leave me. . .
Please just leave me. . .

What do you want from me?
What do you want from me?

Oh, I've fanned your fire. . .
Passions lit, filled with desire.
We combined, two into one. . .
Don't mistake love for fun!

What do you want from me?
What do you want from me?

Just because I believe you,
Doesn't mean I need you!
Oh just get out of here. . .
Oh just get out of here. . .
Just get out of here!
Just because we made love,
Doesn't mean we are one!
Oh, let me out of here. . .
Oh, let me out of here. . .
Let me out of here!

[Speaking voice]
Please, just leave me. . .
Please, just leave me. . .
What do you want from me?
What do you want from me?
Oh, I've fanned your fire. . .
Passions lit, filled with desire.
We combined, two into one. . .
Don't mistake love for fun!

What do you want from me?
What do you want from me?

"You've Captured My Heart"

You've captured my heart. I don't know what to say. I didn't expect it to happen this way.
Your smile touches me in such a way.
I long for your company, spending time together, being your friend, & being there for you.
Now as time passes, I hope you'll feel about me like I feel about you.
Oh, yes, I hope. [Pause] You've captured my heart.

You frightened me this summer when you asked me if I loved you.
I was scared of the truth and tried everything I could think of to push you away from me.
Hiding behind my age, job, & whatever else came to mind at that moment.
The hardest thing I had to endure was seeing you with another. I died that day.
I must make amends for my weakness, my lack of faith and trust.

Now sometime has past & I hope you'll feel about me like I feel about you.
Oh, yes, I hope. [Pause] You've captured my heart.

Now much time has passed. My feelings remain unspoken, buried deep within my chest.
I have long enjoyed your company. The times spent together, being your friend & being there for you.
Over time, you've brought much joy into my life. Your charm, thoughtfulness & the warmth of your smile.
I must convey what my heart wishes to say. You're the one I want in my life.

I hope you feel about me like I feel about you. Lord, please give me the strength I need today.
Oh, yes, [Pause] I hope. [Pause] You've captured my heart.

As fate would have it, this blessed day has come. To offer her my hand in the hope that she would lend me her strength, to be as one.
I have taken my time, denied myself my dreams, and sacrificed my inner self for reasons that are still unclear.
I have come down this long road, realized my life was without the meaning a woman's love would provide.
You are the one, you are my life, and, please, Lord, grant me one wish that she'd consent to being my wife.
Oh, yes, I hope. . . You've captured my heart.

"4 Plus 4, Dance Some More"

[In a sultry, seductive voice]
Inspirations, infatuations, perspiration, respiration. Let yourself free.
Move your body. . . that's right, baby. . . in the throes of ecstasy.

Live the moment. . . love to live in time. . .
Mix fiction with fantasy. . . that's right, baby. . .
Become one with me. . . it's time. . .
I'm going to make these four minutes move romantically
[Sultry voice]

As we approach. . . down on the floor. . .
The rhythm of the music. . . increases tempo. . .
That's right, baby. . . grind your body into mine some more. . .
Come dance with me [Sultry voice]

Release your inhibitions. . . forget your rigid self. . .
Finish off your liquid confidence. . . and come shake yourself. . .
We only have three minutes left. . .
Hurry up. . . come here to me. . . [Sultry voice]

Forget all your troubles. . . lose yourself in time. . .
That's right, baby, come over. . .
I have these two minutes. . . so get into this rhythm. . .
Soon you'll be mine [Sultry voice]

As the tempo slows. . . we have a minute to go. . .
Come on, hold her closer now. . . move around as one. . .
This song may be over. . . but the next is soon to come
[Sultry voice]

Perhaps they are the ones. . . you've been looking for. . .
To take home to your mom. . . .
HaHaHa . . . OH____HHH!

[Back to the top and repeat]

"End Begins"

[Spoken into receiver with passion]
Please don't leave me,
I will change. . . promise.
[Pause]
Why do you say this when you mean that?
[The phone is hung up]
"An end is another beginning. Any beginning has another end."

Life is a string of choices made
Some find happiness while others are played

Looking for love to come my way
Alas, just another country song at play
Wisdom is truly gained from looking behind
Of the future we all are blind
"Nothing in this life comes for free."

We were wrong, but it felt right
Love and passion morning, noon, and night
Sparks flew as you looked my way
But that was then, this is today
Neither were happy so we walked away
"Nothing in this life comes for free."

Building a future from many broken strings
Made up of people, places, and things
Choices often both confine and also define
Prisons are made both yours and mine
"Nothing in this life comes for free."

"Glory to God, I'm in Love"

I want to be with you
To hold your hand
Your husband showered in love
I want to make you smile
Go that extra mile
You're my gift from God above
Glory to God, I'm in love
So you see, I've been trying to say
Who you are in my heart
Using pictures filled with love
I know you understand

No need to pretend
I can be who I am
Simply your loving man
To let loose and free
Who you are to me
A man simply in love
So you see, I wanted the world to know
Just who you were to me
I believed in you
Why don't they see
You're perfect. . . everything to me
So I reached on out
Gave you my hand
With the strength from God above
Pulled you up. . .
Dried your eyes. . .
All based out of true love
So you see I've made a simple design
Many gifts to make your own
To set you free
Encased within love
Knowing you felt the same
You've humbled me
More than I can say
So I'm using your rhythm today
To make you feel
What I truly feel
Encased within simple words
So you see, I'm in love with you
Just broke down and cried
I've never known true love before
But I know you understand

I'm unable to hide
Who you are inside
My gift from God above
I'm out of control
True love takes its toll
This I now know and understand
Wisdom comes to all in time
I want to be with you
To hold your hand
Your husband showered in love
I want to make you smile
Go that extra mile
You're my gift from God above
Glory to God I'm in love
Forgive me for falling in love
My angel from God above
Glory to God, I'm in love
Glory to God, I'm in love

"Pick up the Phone"

When will you be
Coming back to me?
I often sit alone, at home.
Waiting for your call.
Waiting I don't know for how long.
Some say to me,
"What do you love passionately?"
I know not why
Things are as they are.
Sometimes I try to understand too much.

I've given away too much!
You have me, that much is so.
So I say to you,
Can you not see me?
I've been waiting so patiently;
But you don't see.
I've given to you, always freely.
Gifts of prose, thoughts and of work.
But still, I don't hear from you!
So I say to you,
Pick up your phone!
I've reached across the great divide!
And given, freely of myself.
I know you are in need,
So I've freely given from the heart.
So I ask you very simply,
Pick up the phone, and let's start.
So when will you be?
Calling unto me?
My heart is already yours, waiting!
Patiently is not something easy.
So I ask you, when will you phone?
So I ask you,
Pick up the phone!

"Medicine"

Medicine. . .
What's it doing for me?
I said, medicine. . .

Oh, oh, oh. . .
Medicine, medicine. . .

Back in the day my father
Took what he was given.
Trying to hold back the reaper,
Trying to avoid the light.
In the end they took him,
He left us all behind.

Medicine. . .
What's it doing for me?
I said, medicine. . .
Oh, oh, oh. . .
Medicine, medicine. . .

Back in the day my mother
Took what she was given.
The doctor forgot she was allergic,
Thankfully she avoided the light.
In the end she took them,
He's the doctor, it's alright.

Medicine. . .
What's it doing for me?
I said, medicine. . .
Oh, oh, oh. . .
Medicine, medicine. . .

A new day's now upon me,
Taking what I am given.
Trying to hold back my depression,
Trying to be just right.

In the end I take them,
Trying to avoid the light.

Medicine. . .
What's it doing for me?
I said, medicine. . .
Oh, oh, oh. . .
Medicine, medicine. . .

"Sanity's Kiss"

You did us a favor by leaving
Even though it left me reeling

I ran away with a circus
In order to create my purpose

My sanity is built upon reflection
On top of all the rejection

Looking for love that will last
I have embraced my empty past

Sanity's kiss was in kindness
It cured me of my blindness

Saved me from my own destruction
Now the foundation in my construction

My mind and heart filled with purpose
My face is like stone on the surface

Looking for my life's true direction
Embracing my needs for your perfection

Event production is now my past
Age is slowly creeping on fast

I now embrace my art each day
Rather than simply giving it away

You have no idea what I have done
But I really can't tell anyone

Some believe in nothing but hate
I will leave them to their fate

The world's built upon perception
Some use the art of deception.

"Guess What?!"

Have you ever. . . kissed someone to say goodbye?
Tasted the tears of bitterness as love died?
Have you ever. . . walled away all your pain?
Embraced all your fears of loneliness as a game?
Have you ever. . . given away some priceless art?
Just so that someone else could have their start?
Have you ever. . . forgotten someone loved and lost?
Been driven by sadness but paid the emotional cost?

Guess what?! You don't care. . . You weren't there.
Guess what?! I don't need you! You're a fool!
You're going to love me now that I am gone.

Have you ever. . . sacrificed and chased your dream?
Closed your eyes so tight that you screamed?
Have you ever. . . thrown caution to the wind?

Only to have the fates seemingly hem you in?
Have you ever. . . reinvented yourself in every way?
Trying to please someone else each and every day?
Have you ever. . . lived life on the street?
Going hungry just so that someone else could eat?

Guess what? You don't care. . . You weren't there.
Guess what?! I don't need you! You're a fool!
You're going to love now that I am gone.

"United as One"

"Cracks surely appear upon my skin
But don't reveal me from within.
My mind's acted upon many things
'I don't exist' the usual ring."

"I have tried to embrace my dreams
She has escaped me so it seems.
I fill the silence with my art
It escapes from my broken down heart."

"I have encased my dream within art.
Many times have I truly fallen apart?
I have been diagnosed as mentally ill.
Here's the cure please take another pill."

"My blond hair has seen winter arrive.
My slender frame has expanded in size.
My skin now shows spots of age.
My heart refuses to turn the page."

"I am manic because of my love.
It truly fits me like a glove.
Married to the rose of my dreams.
Can you hear me? A phantom scream!?"

"To be a jester of a king
A silent mime sadly without a ring.
Because I have given away my prose
I have truly framed my heart's rose."

"Hate and love are united as one.
Both undo what the other has done. . . "

"Right and wrong are united as one.
Both undo what the other has done. . . "

"I Do"

How did we get so real?
Where did we go wrong?
How did we move on?
We both couldn't get enough!
Tears fall in my frustration.
We both said, "I Do"!

Stop. . . Stop! Please don't stop!
Those were the good old days?
We all leave others behind!
Doesn't matter whose wrong, right?
Life is a perpetual door!
Living in my personal Hell.

Standing in front of my mirror.
My reflection is framed therein.
A saint I have been called.
In this world filled with sin.
This has not altered my view.
A trapped twelve-year-old within.

"I'm Just a Schmuck"

I'm just a schmuck
Down on his luck
Let us just say
I'm under a rock

I'm trying to keep
My depression at bay
Hiding in plain sight
Giving my prose away

A man without love
And barely a home
Waiting for true love
Of my very own

I am a phantom
Trapped in a play
Dreaming of the rose
To come my way

Someone to have
Someone to hold
This door is closing
For I'm getting old

I wear my silence
I wear my mask
By working for free
I overcame my past.

"Hockey Heroes"

[E G D A E (Acoustic)]

Hockey was born of the mind but has its own soul.
A sport that brings joy to all! Whether they be young or old.
Each person, a story they hold, waiting for a time 'til it be told.
Special moments with family and friends, a moment in time, yet
with no end.
To bear witness as history's told, in awe and wonder, our heroes
we hold.

[Chorus]

Heroes who strive to be among the best! Each game, a gift. But
also, a test.
Although their time has come and gone, their game's now at
an end.
We have dreamt and lived through them all, of this, we do defend.
Although their jerseys are now all hung and sticks are on display,
They still find time to stop and play, our game, for charity.

[Chorus]

Individually, we shall always cherish our heroes; they stand out
above the rest.
To have lived life to the fullest and to be acknowledged as great,
the very best of the best.

They have embraced and lived, to become their dreams!
Not just individually, but as players, groups of individuals, for
their teams.
Now they hope to instill in the young, "Be the best they can be."
This is done through time spent, with us, for all to see.

[Chorus]

On blades they stride upon the ice with passion for the game.
A life of discipline, truth be told, in pursuit of a cup and ring.
Our heroes, our minds do hold. Memories flash, stories now told.
From the shadows, history past, our heroes are now in the hall, at
long last.
As Stanley's held on high for all to see, they won our hearts
through our game.

[Chorus]

[A G D F G A]
[A G D F G E]

Not all make the grade, it's a hard game to grab hold of.
But for those few who do, an Induction is held for you.
Within the Hall, your memories enshrined for us all to behold.
A simple gift for those who follow.

[F G A]

Who strive to be our hockey heroes. . .
[Repeat one last time final line for finale]
Who strive to be our hockey heroes. . .

"Pandora's Box"

You're the key to my Pandora
With you shall I open and become
Turn. . . you're the key; Turn. . . you're the key

I have gone through so many things
I have seen more than you can believe
I fear that without you, I shall remain closed
I need you, baby, please believe

Believe that you're the one
Destined to save me
In pursuit of my destiny
Please, baby, please, set me free

I have given away freely
What I can say with prose
In order to heal myself
But I realized I must have you

Some might say I'm crazy
Perhaps they are blind to see
What and who you are to me
You're my ecstasy, the better part of me

Oh, please, baby, set me free
Become one with me
I'm down upon my knees
I'll eat you up, baby

Did I mention. . . Please?!
Please, baby, please

I'm down on my knees
Set me free, baby, set me free

Baby, I have accomplished. . .
Many things
Beautiful you already. . .
Have my he(art)
I realize that I am nothing. . .
Without you
Baby, what must I do. . .
What must I do?

What can I offer?
Not material things
I can pledge my he(art)
I can pledge my soul
I can pledge my talents
Baby, without you,
I shall never be whole
You're the music
The only symphony
I am already yours
Think of me
Every time you play
A melody

Set me free; find me
That's right, baby
I am yours already
Open your he(art). . . It's me
Nothing means more
Love and art must be shared

The formulae to life
Music and performance
Expressing for others to behold
You're everything I need
Baby, it's you, only you
I have been waiting for a long time

I see you, the real you
I have too many walls within me
I am blind; through you I see
Baby, I need you. . .
Baby, I want you. . .

Baby, you're my dream. . .
Baby, you're my dream. . .
I am your Pandor . . .
You're the only key. . .
Turn, baby, turn. . .
Set my love. . .
He(art) and soul. . .
Free; believe, baby. . .
This isn't a dream. . .
I exist; turn, baby. . .
You're the only key

"Happy Valentine's Day!"

As I pray to God above
Please send to you all my love
On this very special day
It reminds me of you in every way
some make cards filled with prose

To celebrate romance and love
I dream of you every day
You've taken truly my breath away
As you sing from afar
Know I love you for who you are
My gift from God up above
Please accept this token of my love
It matters not where you go
My heart is with you, just so you know
So in this very special way
I wish to you happy Valentine's Day
Relationships come, many go
But true love comes only once you know
So I've prayed in every way
Send you my love on this special day
Now I confess to you, my love
To pull you close and express my love
All I'm really trying to say
Please marry me soon, to God I pray
I love you more than I can say
Tried in so many different ways
With the strength from God above
I submit to you my true love
Nothing greater upon this earth
Defend true love for all your worth
So now as I go down upon my knee
I'm simply asking: marry me
How does one show their love is true?
Don't be afraid to give yourself away
Always help others find their way
The essence of love is found today
Happy Valentine's Day

"Dreams vs. Reality"

[Refrain]
My words are swimmin'
On a river that's run dry
Oh, my words are swimmin'
To help the time pass by

[Main]
Time slips on by slowly
Yet it's always another day
Never knowin' where you're goin'
Come whatever that may
Tryin' hard to exist now
Livin' off my EIA
Another day older
But wiser, who's to say?

[Refrain]

You've seen the light
But you're in the dark
You've found your destination
But have nowhere to go
They say opportunity's knockin'
As they slam the door
Ya lookin' for a job now
I have nothin' but I spend more

[Refrain]

They say I am disabled
As I swallow pills galore
To keep my sanity

I'm the same as before
Lookin' for a prison
Of my own design
Spending other people's money
Because I don't have a dime

[Refrain]

Doctor says I'm bipolar
That's the real score
When you live in reality
Dreams don't exist no more
Tryin' to stay even
As life spins you round
I am rich with imagination
But material wealth I've not found

[Refrain]

Walkin' on the pavement
Echoes try to keep pace
Your shadow is followin'
Slightly out of place
The path keeps on turnin'
Your future is what you face
It doesn't matter how you're dressed
You're just another human in the race

[Refrain]

"I Do"

Take me into your arms
Wrap me within your embrace
Together we are now one
Walking at our own pace
In other words,
We said, "I do"
Yes, in other words,
Our love. . . has come true. . . true. . . true!

Most of us enter this world
Wrapped within their loving embrace
Four hands working in unison
Keeping time, tempo, and pace
In another words,
They said, "I do"
Yes, in other words
Their love. . . has come true. . . true. . . true!

As we start to develop
Wrapped within the "bonds of love"
All of our hands working in unison
Keeping time, tempo and pace
In another words,
Time flows on. . .
Yes, in other words
Love is the main part within you. . . you. . . you!

Soon the tables are turned
We're old enough to "fly away"
Leaving the nest of love
Come the unknown whatever that may

In other words,
I'm now me. . .
Yes, in other words. . .
I've been looking for you. . . you. . . you!

"The Crew"

As we arrive
Our vehicles in a row
TZ starts to holler
Telling us where to go
Just as we park
Within our assigned space
We race against time
Putting the tent
Within its place

No rest when we are done
The show must go on
Time to sell our trinkets
Time to sell our fare
As our patrons leave
The next line forms
As we close down the tent at ten
We realize at eight its call again

As we depart
Our vehicles in a row
TZ starts to holler
Over the CB with where to go
One road turns into another
One place onto the next

Everyone in their place
No time to rest
We start all over again.

"Monster's Masquerade"

All my monsters lurking
Behind their beautiful masks
Watch as our parade people
Unfolds at first glance
Let's have a ball, baby... yeah
I'm in charge of this dance
Our time is now... yeah
So let's get up off our butts
Yeah... Our time is now.
Monsters' masquerade!

Hahahaha [Soft laugh or chuckle]

Colorful artistic pageantry
A flow of patterns and life
Art and design combined
Living through participation
Or life will pass us by
To take your place, baby... yeah
Upon this floor of mine
Yeah... Before our time is over...
And we've gone out this door...

Hahahaha [Soft laugh and chuckle]

Eye catching costumes
High-fashion brands abound

Armani, Dior, Haus of Gaga
Come on, baby. . . ya
So let's get up off our butts
Cheer each other on
Let's make our time together baby. . .
Ya. . . One that will forever last. . .
Hold onto these memories. . .
As if this is our last dance. . .

Hahahaha [Soft laugh and chuckle]

Free-flowing structure
Claws up everyone
Let's see them raised up high
Get your bodies moving. . . ya
Let us make this song take flight
I'll make this song continue
Throughout the entire night. . .
Yeah. [Pause] Live life in the moment. . .
Take a bite out of this night. . .
Pop culture is here to stay. . .
Yeah. [Pause] Naysayers take flight. . .

Hahahaha [Soft laugh and chuckle]

"Unrealized Dream"

[Soft, sad voice speaking part]
Far too often in life
One seeks another
Their souls touch
Working as one

But circumstances
Prevent interaction
And the creation
Of unrealized dreams
No one ever truly believed in me

[Main]
Beauty in the acts of giving
Are meaningless without love
Love gives one inspiration
Without it, nothing gets done
The embers within my heart
Will never wither and die
My love for you has me consumed
Your memory, my dream lives on
Utterly and complete is my loss
Upon reflection within my soul
You will forever be the only one
My unrealized dream. . .

No one ever truly believed in me. [Soft, sad voice speaking part]

May you walk in the light of happiness
May you truly be happy is my wish
May you always remember
One man made a difference
And acted selflessly
A slave out of love
To make a difference in constructive ways
In the hopes of your heart and hand
My love for you shall always linger
My dreams of you shall never let me go

For me there is never going to be another
My unrealized dream. . .

No one ever truly believed in me. [Soft, sad voice speaking part]

May you truly be happy
I realize I'm forced to let you go. . .
Perhaps in time you will believe and see
That I'm your man and destiny
Perhaps in this life or the next
I will await my first chance
So for now I will simply back away. . .
My unrealized dream. . .

No one ever truly believed in me. [Soft, sad voice speaking part]

Silence again shall be my shield
Darkness will wrap me in its embrace
My love, I shall honor and pray for you daily
You're in control of our destinies
Perhaps in time you'll truly see me. . .
Until you allow for my touch again
Perhaps you'll need me is my hope
I shall persevere, awaiting your return
My unrealized dream. . .

No one ever truly believed in me. [Soft, sad voice speaking part]

Your phantom shall simply carry on
For you the river still flows. . .
My word given can never be broken
It's all I truly possess and own
My love for you shall guide me
As it has done many times before

You're the only one in my heart
My unrealized dream. . .

No one ever truly believed in me. [Soft, sad voice speaking part]

You're the one woman that I need
I hope in time, my love will be of worth
My challenge from the very start
Was simply that no one believes
Please don't settle for someone less
My unrealized dream. . .

No one ever truly believed in me. [Soft, sad voice speaking part]

[Video]
This is a sad, haunting melody. (Meatloaf style.)

[Wardrobe]
Costume of the Phantom with mask.

[Set]
Rolling fog on floor.
A single black rose with a piece of black lace tied to it laying upon
a small gothic-style table off to the right with a lit candle and a
picture of Lady Gaga in behind the rose.
One thick red velour stage curtain. Three large ornate gothic gold
frame mirrors (set in center of stage) with three banks of candles
(what you find in a Catholic church), and one bank in front of
each mirror (left angle, centered then right-angled mirror). Leave
room for me to face forward between mirrors (back drop) and
candle racks.

During the singing parts, I work at extinguishing the candles
until, at the end, I am covered in darkness. The table with the

single large candle, Lady Gaga's picture with the rose shall be the cameras last focus point.

Use Lady Gaga's lightning bolt dress photo with the teacup.

"You're My Gift from God Above"

I want to be with you
To hold your hand
Your husband showered in love
I want to make you smile
Go that extra mile
You're my gift from God above
Glory to God I'm in love
So you see I've been trying to say
Who you are in my heart
Using pictures filled with love
I know you understand
No need to pretend
I can be who I am
Simply your loving man
To let loose and free
Who you are to me
A man simply in love
So you see I wanted the world to know
Just who you were to me
I believed in you
Why don't they see
She's perfect everything to me
So I reached on out
Gave you my hand

With the strength from God above
Pulled you up, dried your eyes
All based out of true love
So you see I've made a simple design
Many gifts to make your own
To set you free encased within love
Knowing you felt the same
You've humbled me more than I can say
So I'm using your rhythm today
To make you feel what I truly feel
Encased within simple words
So you see I'm in love with you
Just broke down and cried
I've never known true love before
But I know you understand
I'm unable to hide who you are inside
My gift from God above
I'm out of control
True love takes its toll
This I now know and understand
Wisdom comes to all in time
I want to be with you
To hold your hand
Your husband showered in love
I want to make you smile
Go that extra mile
You're my gift from God above
Glory to God above
Forgive me for falling in love
My angel from God above
Glory to God I'm in love
Glory to God I'm in love

"Come Back to Me"

As I lie alone at night
I dream of your sweet love
I simply wish to hold you tight
So I pray to God above

As I go about my day
I think of your gentle touch
I simply wish you'd come my way
Dreaming doesn't give you much

Come back to me. . .
Come back to me. . .
I want my dream that's true
Oh, how I want you in my arms
Cause baby I need you

As I try to live my life
I think of your great smile
I've given you the best of me
So I'll wait for a while

As I listen to your songs
I realize that it's not enough
Sadly, fate has passed me by
The lack of you is tough

Come back to me. . .
Come back to me. . .
I want my dream, that's true
Oh, how I want you in my arms
'Cause, baby, I need you

"Pure Insanity"

[Refrain]
I dream of you constantly, baby
This is pure insanity
You don't really know me, baby
That's my simple reality
You're not in my circle, baby
Fates kept you from me

[Main]
And I. . .
Have done good deeds
I've worked for free
Through the Shrine and Masonry

When I. . .
Had given my art
You stole my heart
Right from the very start

But I. . .
Have torn my soul
Love takes a toll
Especially if you're never known.

"You May Be Hot"

You may be hot
You sure have style
But what you're lacking
Fills a country mile

You may have class
You may have fame
But without true love
It's just a game

You may have talent
You have my heart
But without my direction
Things start falling apart

I was truly into
Almost every single thing
And all I wanted
A prenup and ring

You've made a fortune
Off my heart
I worked for free
Gave you my art

So come on, baby
It's you I desire
It's up to you
To light my fire

I have my honor
I won't give in
I truly can't yield
To all that sin

[Refrain]
I want to be able to have ya!
How does that reach out and grab ya?

"Life Is a Masquerade"

Life is a masquerade
Monsters lurking behind their masks
Watch the parade unfold
But I'd rather run this dance
Let's have a ball, baby
Our time together is now
Monsters' masquerade

Colorful and artistic
A flow of patterns
Art and designs
Live through participation
Or life will pass you by
So take your place
Upon the floor
Before your time
Has flown out the door
Eye-catching costumes

High fashions abound
Armani and Dior
Come on, baby
Pick up your glass
Cheers to each other
Let's make this time last
Hold onto the memories
Live as if life's a dance

Free-flowing structure
Claws up on the floor
Get your bodies moving

Let this song take flight
I'll make our song continue
Throughout the entire night
Live in this moment
Take a bite out of this night
Pop culture's all right.

"Life's Crazy Dance"

As I lay dreaming
Thoughts of you were flowing
I had no way of knowing
Where this was going
Thoughts of you captured
My heart's pure rapture
It's you that I'm after
Forever after and forever more

I woke up restless
My soul filled with yearning
My mind was slowly learning
My passion was truly burning
Oh how I wanted to change my past
So I may have and hold her at long last

We've all had dreams
Unfulfilled it would seem
Due to strange circumstance
We've turned our backs upon chance
Life is one crazy dance
When fate smiles take a chance
For you never know the power of dreams

I woke up restless
My soul filled with yearning
My Mind was slowly turning
My passion was truly burning
Oh how I wanted to change my past
So I may have and hold her at long last

Years have now passed
I still lay dreaming
You know where this is going
My heart is still flowing
Thoughts of you still capture
My soul's true rapture
It's still you I'm after
Forever after and forever more.

"Show Me Your Ahas"

[Refrain]
Hey, there
Show me your ahas
I said, hey, there
Show me your ahas, ahas

[Main]
Let me get up on you
Let's go for a ride
Let me put it
Into your backside
Get up on my bone
Yeah, baby, that's right
Up and down

Day and night
You're my bank account
Let me force a withdrawal
I'm about to explode

[Refrain]

Get into the rhythm
Give me more grind
Let me slap you
Climb up your behind
Move with the flow
Let your feelings explode
Throw away inhibition
Out the window
Start moving faster
Excitement starts to build
Oh, how your body
Gives me such a thrill

[Refrain]

I'm gonna pull out
Suck up that spill
Give me a few moments
While I pop another blue pill
Our bodies pumping
As we do the grind
Attraction takes over
Nothing on our minds
Oh yeah, baby. . . Ride me again sometime

[Refrain]

"True Love Ain't No Game"

I am here
Never fear
Husband for life
Perhaps today
Is the day
We meet down the aisle

Sitting here
All alone
Killing time
Wanting more
Than anything
My place
By your side

Fashion, fame
In the game
As you walk
Talking stops
They all stare
Fresh new looks
From the air
When you have
A phantom's love
Gives it all away
For a chance
At your love
His true dream
Prices paid

Tried and true
Black and blue
Beatings on my soul
Nothing less
Do I want
In your arms
Hands to hold

It is sad
Makes me mad
Paper wins vs love
People kill
Makes me ill
So they can
Live a lie

It's a play
So I paid
Only asking for love
But the pain
In my heart
Twists my soul
Grows inside

Look at life
Then at love
Now at where we are
Look at greed
Then at money
Now at who we are
We've not come far

[Refrain]
I'm truly in pain for ya. . .
True love ain't no game,
Oh, no. . . oh, no. . . no, no
I want you so FN bad
Going stark raving mad
I'm giving away all that I am
For the chance. . . for the chance. . .
Oh yeah. . . for the chance. . .
For your love and hand

[Back to the main for one more run-through]

Your husband is who I am. . .
One that you can always depend.
Only your love will help me mend,
Oh yeah. . . oh yeah, baby. . .
This ain't no game of pretend. . .
Your husband is who I am. . .

"No Crying in the Chapels"

Happy birthday, Elvis Presley
Today you'd be eighty-seven years young [Update yearly]
Every time I hear your music
It brings to mind that you're not gone

Although you left us all too soon, I must say
Through each song, you live on
So I sing to you happy birthday
Best wishes and many more to come

In my mind and heart, you're not a day older
Through your gifts you've touched everyone
So, no crying in the chapels
Rejoice, sing. Give thanks and praise

For those gifts of joy you left us all
By sharing your life, creating fond memories
Rest assured that you're not forgotten
Through all your art, you live on

So, happy birthday, Elvis Presley
From a humble fan, that's all
I hope these simple words of thanks and praise
Return to you that which you freely shared

So sit back, relax, and carry on, my friends
The King lives on

The King lives on

"Kiss Me"

[Refrain]
Kiss me. . .
Please kiss me with passion
Let our feelings combine
And pledge that you're mine
For all time. . .

[Main]
My love [Pause] fills me with desire
Oh, how I want to pull you close all of the time
My love, [Pause] should your feelings ever fade away

Oh, how it would tear me apart. . . every day
My dreams of love would die in a horrible way
So kiss me [Pause]
And confess that you love me
Oh, how your lips send shivers. . . down my spine
My dreams of you are sweeter than wine
My love [Pause] sets me on fire
Oh, how I need to make you mine all of the time
My love, [Pause] should you ever simply walk away
Oh, how it would break my heart in every way
So kiss me. . .
And confess that you want me
Oh, how your body quickens the. . . beat of my heart
My passions lit for you right from the start

[Refrain]

"Skid Row"

Ill chill wind blows. Cold biting skin.
Down to the bone. Makeshift shelter.
No comfort. No home.
The storm is upon them. Sally Ann is full.
Living death. Way back when.
Each person's story. Is similar to a degree.
Some sort of trauma. Bad luck befallen.
Forced them to flee. Walking away.
Death of their will.

[Refrain]

Their spirit trapped. Within a vessel broken.
Shattered lives. Purgatory's kiss.
Hiding from the past. Wandering death.
Its embrace overpowers. The weak minded.
Broken hearted. Downtrodden, shredded.
Lying upon the ground. waiting for their end.

[Refrain]

Unable to cope. Begging for coins.
Broken vessels all. Ambassadors of society.
Unable to feel. Unable to see.
Unable to heal. Unable to conceal.
Left to fate. Lifeless reality.
They enter the void. All are equal on this path.

[Refrain]

Welcome to Skid Row.

[Refrain]
Welcome to Skid Row.
Nowhere to run.
Welcome to Skid Row.
Nowhere to go.
Welcome to Skid Row.
Nowhere to run.
Welcome to Skid Row.
Nowhere to go.

"Liberty's Call"

Soldiers lined up against the wall
Bullets fly then they fall
Someone's filming to send to all
Commercialized terror is their aim
All this death in his name

Liberty and freedom paid in blood
Lives the coins that are paid
No price too great and no life too small
Many answered their nation's call
May God see them safely home

Unmarked graves in the sand
Wives and husbands with empty hands
Children can never understand
Hearts so young now filled with hate
When they should only know love

Greed leads us to evil deeds
We then sow the devil's seeds
Intolerance, hatred then to war
Death knocking upon life's door
Love of life is worth so much more. . .

"Nothin'"

Oh why, oh why can't they not see. . .
That through their actions, they are murdering me
As hard as I try I might as well lie and die
They take what little is left of me

I attempt to build a house for my own
But the man says, "You owe me money"
And throws me out the door
Oh why can't they see. . .
Their actions are murdering me.
I go through life trying each door. . .
But in the end all you hear is the slamming, same as before
Oh why, oh why can't they all see?
That through their actions, their murdering me.

I am now forty plus years old
I have no home of my own, same as before
Nothin' I seem to do makes me happy that is true
Makes me happy but oh, how I try; I'll try as before.
You and I may tread separate paths
You may have wealth; mine didn't last
Oh I'm sure there are those more worse off than me
But as you can see, their actions have murdered me.

I go on day after day, trying to reflect upon what happened to me
So I can lend a hand to another and pull them up
I try to ensure those around me suffer. . . not.
Why, oh why, do others murder me?
Because they want what you got and they'll take it
They don't care. They go on through life
Talking the big talk that's true
But in the end you've got nothin'
They become nothin' to you!

Because you can't take nothin' with you
You have to leave it behind for others to go through
And in the end when those light beacons and you're called
Nothin' but silence will be left for all. . .

"Your Desire"

Love is a serious thing
Without it you have nothing
What is passion without fire?
Oh how it does inspire

Love is a precious thing
Without love there is no zing
We exist to create life
Through true love we overcome strife

Love is a mysterious thing
And it's created out of nothing
Brought upon you by desire
Only she can quench your fire

As your passions take flight
And your feelings begin to ignite
You pull each other to and fro
Neither wanting to let go

Desire grows, grows, grows. . .
Taking you higher
Heaven knows, knows, knows. . .
That you're on fire
And it finally explodes
Your desire, your desire, your desire

Soon you exchange your rings
The preacher exclaims, "Rejoice and sing!"
As you both cross the aisle
Both are wearing the brightest smiles

You found a partner to share your life
To have and to hold as your wife
United by God's love as one
Your life now truly just begun

Desire grows, grows, grows. . .
Taking you higher
Heaven knows, knows, knows. . .
That you're on fire
And it finally explodes
Your desire, your desire, your desire

Over the years you both have grown
A shared life you both now own
You create a child passing on what you know
The time will come when you'll have to let go

The time has come for you to go
Though out life you've put on a show
You lived each day as if it were your last
Leaving behind your treasured past

You leave behind most everything
The family decides who will get your things
You've lived your life through happiness and hurt
Your body is now encased within dirt

Darkness has fallen on your past
You've left behind memories you hope will last
As a ghost you wander the night
But in the end you must face the light

Judgement is upon you there is no flight
Heaven or Hell they'll place you yes that's right

Life is a test you've heard people say
In the end we all must pay.

"True Surrender"

Oh, how I cry in true surrender. . .
To the love inside my heart so tender. . .
I think back over many yesterdays. . .
To all the love I've given away. . .
I am really waiting expectantly. . .
For my love to come back to me. . .
I have given toward many through the Shrine. . .
For I love everyone for all time. . .

Oh, how I want to turn back time. . .
In order to make you mine. . .
Oh, how you are my true dream. . .
Waiting patiently is harder than it seems. . .
So I try not to give anymore away. . .
Until such time as you come my way. . .
My art is a part of my very soul. . .
Each piece I've given has taken its toll. . .
When you don't exist in people's lives. . .
You don't have the acquaintances that you deserve. . .
So I am waiting for that very day. . .
That you will finally come my way. . .

So you're finally coming my way. . .
When however I truly can't say. . .
In order to be whole you need someone. . .
To have and to hold becoming one. . .
Life not shared is truly no fun. . .

So I'm waiting for that very day. . .
Perhaps that day is actually today. . .
I am waiting to share our first embrace. . .
To share life at our own pace. . .
I look forward to being a part of your life. . .

"A Puppet with Many Strings"

I used to work real hard
A circus life no lie
One day then another
Simply flew on by
It's true what they say about working another man's dream
Your life fades. . . follow your own dreams

The future comes on hard
So put aside your past
Embrace all the wisdom learned
And have yourself a blast
It's true what they say about time not standing still
For times a. . . bitter fricken pill

I am just a puppet
With many different strings
When the master pulls
I get into the swing
It's true what they say about not controlling a thing
Doesn't this have. . . a bitter fricken ring

Age has taken its toll
Still a puppet with many strings
When the master pulls

Ya, it's hard to get into the swing
It's true what they say you still don't control a thing
Soon the time will come. . . you know what I mean. . .

Suddenly, your time has come
And you're placed upon a shelf
All of your strings are cut
You're replaced by someone else
It's true what they say about having an identity
Even though your strings are cut. . . you'll never be free. . .

As you're removed from the fricken shelf
You end up in a box
All by your fricken self
Oh, to be forgotten
Unwanted for anything
Oh, ya wouldn't you know. . . you still don't control a thing. . .

Suddenly the box is opened
By a new set of hands
They clean and polish you up
And put on some new strings
When the master pulls
You get into the swing
Oh, ya wouldn't you know. . . you still don't control a thing. . .

No matter the roll. . . no matter the goal. . . no matter the
place. . . no matter the time. . .
You're the same as before. . . a puppet with many strings . . .

CPSIA information can be obtained
at www.ICGtesting.com
Printed in the USA
BVHW010826260723
667776BV00003B/4